Human Nature in Politics

Human Nature in Politics

GRAHAM WALLAS

**With a New Introduction by
Sugwon Kang**

Transaction Books
New Brunswick (U.S.A.) and London (U.K.)

Transaction edition published 1981. Original edition copyright
© 1921 by F.S. Crofts & Co., Inc. Sugwon Kang's introduction,
originally entitled "Graham Wallas and Liberal Democracy," appeared in *The Review of Politics*, Vol. 41, No. 4 (October 1979)
and is reprinted with permission.

Library of Congress Catalog Number: 81-7566
ISBN: 0-87855-870-5 (paper)
Printed in the United States of America

Library of Congress Cataloging in Publication Data

Wallas, Graham, 1858-1932.
  Human nature in politics.

  (Social science classics series)
  Reprint. Originally published: New York: F.S. Crofts, 1921.
  Includes bibliographical references and index. 1. Politics,
Practical. 2. Political ethics. I. Title. II. Series.
JF2051.W33 1981   324.7   81-7566
ISBN 0-87855-870-5 (pbk.)   AACR2

Introduction to the Transaction Edition

Graham Wallas and Liberal Democracy

Sugwon Kang

During his lifetime (1858-1932) Graham Wallas's pioneering contributions to the study of politics were widely acknowledged. Thus, his *Human Nature in Politics* (1908) was rightly acclaimed as a turning point in British and American political science, away from the study of political institutions and toward the study of political behavior. With his later works, notably *The Great Society* (1914), *Our Social Heritage* (1921) and *The Art of Thought* (1926), Wallas's influence spilled over into other fields of social inquiry provoking a chain of serious debates among the pundits of various disciplines. And the term "Great Society," by which Wallas meant a complex, mechanized industrial society, the monster-child of the Industrial Revolution, became a household phrase in the 1930's among the New Deal liberals in the United States, where, according to Historian Samuel Eliot Morison, he had been the most influential English political philosopher since Herbert Spencer.[1]

But today, not yet fifty years after his death, Wallas is largely a forgotten name, even among the professional students of politics. He is occasionally mentioned in textbooks, usually in footnotes; otherwise, one will encounter his name in the history books in connection with the Fabian Society, which he helped to guide through its formative years in collaboration with Sidney and Beatrice Webb and George Bernard Shaw. As a living intellectual force Wallas's importance today is decidedly negligible. There is not even a small band of enthusiasts trying to restore the fame of this "great and inadequately honoured man," as George Catlin has described him.[2]

This is all the more regrettable because Wallas had a long and illustrious career as a university teacher. First, he was lecturer of political science at the newly created London School of Economics and Political Science, from its inception in 1895; and, then, between 1914 and his retirement in 1923, he was the first holder of

---

[1] Samuel Eliot Morison, *The Oxford History of the American People* (New York, 1965), p. 813.

[2] G.E.G. Catlin, *Systematic Politics: Elementa Politica et Sociologica* (Toronto, 1962), p. 8.

V

the chair of political science at the same institution.[3] We know from all available accounts that Wallas was a teacher of uncommon gifts,[4] who compares favorably with such legendary figures as John Ruskin of an earlier era, whom Wallas himself greatly admired as an undergraduate in Oxford. Indeed, Wallas was a living mine of suggestions and hints, and through his ability to arouse a sense of suspense and anticipation on the part of his readers and audiences he was able to elicit and sustain their enthusiasm as long as he kept teaching and writing. Yet, his genius lacked that power of construction upon which all thinkers must ultimately stake their claims to lasting fame. Wallas was not noted for the systematic thought for which Freud, Weber, Durkheim and Pareto are remembered, though in varying degrees.

After a careful study of his life and thought, however, one is made to realize that the generations following Wallas may have overlooked one very critical aspect of his work. Carried away as we are with the methodological concerns of political research, we tend to evaluate Wallas's contributions primarily as those of an advocate of a glamorous new science, thus glossing over the larger political lessons that are implicit in his search for methodological refinement. He is remembered as a critic of the "intellectualist fallacies" in political discussion, but seldom is he recalled as the first great diagnostician of the problems of liberal democracy. This neglect of course renders any analysis of Wallas's thought incomplete. But it may also exemplify the appalling lack of historical consciousness on the part of the partisans of liberal democracy today, living in a generation not noted for its thirst for historical knowledge.

Graham Wallas became as potent a critic of liberal democracy as he did, one suspects, partly because he was himself a liberal democrat with unimpeachable credentials. And he never doubted his historical mission: writing in 1908 he observed that the problems of liberal democracy had "in the past been mainly pointed out by the opponents of democracy," whereas, "if democracy is to succeed," these problems "must be frankly considered by the democrats themselves."[5]

---

[3] Wallas was succeeded to the Chair by Harold J. Laski, Michael Oakeshott and Maurice Cranston.

[4] See the eulogies of Graham Wallas published as "Graham Wallas" in *Economica,* vol. 12 (November, 1932), reprinted as *Graham Wallas: 1858-1932* (London, 1932).

[5] Graham Wallas, *Human Nature in Politics* (London, 1908; 4th ed. 1949), p. 253 (hereafter HNP).

The method which Wallas urged upon his fellow democrats to rescue liberal democracy from itself was political psychology; and in this effort he was clearly without equal, if not alone. Speaking of *Human Nature in Politics* Harold Laski commented:

> I am inclined to argue that no English thinker since Hobbes had seen more clearly the importance of the psychological foundations of politics; and since that book, few treatises on this theme have been usefully written that have not been coloured by its conclusions.[6]

Elsewhere Laski observed that the historical contribution of that book was nothing less than a "revolution in the methodology of political discussion, both in England and in America."[7] According to Horace Kallen, the "advent" of the "psychological political science" was "signalized with Graham Wallas's *Human Nature in Politics.*" Significantly, Kallen concluded his essay, "Political Science as Psychology," by asking rhetorically: "So, then, if political science is not psychology, what is it?"[8] Harold Lasswell once paid his teacher Charles Merriam the generous tribute that it was he who "first saw the importance of psychology for politics."[9] Merriam, however, passed the honor over to his English colleague Graham Wallas, saying that it was Wallas, not he, who first seriously attempted "to establish the significance of psychology in the domain of political inquiry"[10] and tried to "interpret political phenomena in terms of psychological forces rather than in terms of form and structure."[11]

Of the substantive contribution of *Human Nature in Politics* George H. Sabine has said that it was "the classical criticism of rationalism in political conduct."[12] "I tried in 1908 to make two main points clear," Wallas wrote in 1920: the first point had to do

---

[6] Harold J. Laski, "Lowes Dickinson and Graham Wallas," *Political Quarterly,* 3 (1932), 465.

[7] Laski's eulogy of Wallas in *Graham Wallas: 1858-1932,* p. 10.

[8] Horace Kallen, "Political Science as Psychology," *American Political Science Review,* 17 (1923), 194-195; 203.

[9] Quoted in Bernard Crick, *The American Science of Politics: Its Origins and Conditions* (Berkeley, 1959), pp. 137-138.

[10] Charles Merriam, "The Significance of Psychology for the Study of Politics," *American Political Science Review,* 18 (1924), 473.

[11] Charles Merriam and Harry Elmer Barnes, eds., *A History of Political Theories: Recent Times — Essays on Contemporary Developments in Political Theory* (New York, 1924), p. 19.

[12] George H. Sabine, "Political Science and Philosophy," *The Social Sciences and Their Interrelations,* eds. Ogburn and Goldenweiser (New York, 1927), p. 248.

with the "danger" of the "intellectualist" assumption "that every human action is the result of an intellectual process, by which a man first thinks of some end which he desires, and then calculates the means by which that end can be attained," and the second point concerned the "need of substituting for that assumption a conscious and systematic effort of thought."[13] Now, twelve years later, he was able to say, confidently:

> In 1920 insistence on my first point is not so necessary as it was in 1908. The assumption that men are automatically guided by "enlightened self-interest" has been discredited by the facts of the war and the peace, the success of an anti-parliamentary and anti-intellectualist revolution in Russia, the British election of 1918. . . . It is my second point which, in the world as the war has left it, is most important. There is no longer much danger that we shall assume that man always and automatically thinks of ends and calculates means. The danger is that we may be too tired or too hopeless to undertake the conscious effort by which alone we can think of ends and calculate means.[14]

It is difficult to determine to what extent Wallas's own efforts had contributed to such a change in the climate of opinion; we are certainly not justified in construing the above passage to imply any such causal connection. Surely, the anti-intellectualist forces which Wallas so penetratingly detected on the eve of the Great War in his *Great Society* must have been present in the Western mind when Wallas wrote his *Human Nature in Politics* only six years before. Nonetheless, Wallas's sense of relief, coupled with his irritation with the opposite form of reductionism, namely anti-intellectualism, was shared by some of his leading contemporaries. Writing in 1923, the Cambridge psychologist W. H. R. Rivers noted that the pendulum had already swung "too far in the opposite direction, so that there is now a tendency to underestimate the importance of the intellectual factors in the determination of human conduct."[15]

There was one notable exception to the public's judgment that Wallas had written a novel thesis in his refutation of the alleged "intellectualist fallacies" of the nineteenth-century British liberalism grounded in the Benthamite Utilitarian psychology.

---

[13] Wallas's preface to the third edition of HNP (1920).
[14] *Ibid.*
[15] W.H.R. Rivers, *Psychology and Politics and Other Essays,* with a prefatory note by G.E. Smith and an appreciation by C.S. Myers (London, 1923), p. 5.

One reviewer argued that Wallas's campaign against the "intellectualist" political psychology, for all its courage and eloquence, was
tantamount to knocking down a straw man, made, as it were,
with a language of politics largely restricted to public discussion,
which no one of average intelligence ever took very seriously in
the first place. The reviewer had no complaints about Wallas's
refutation of the alleged intellectualist assumption, according to
which "men always act on a reasoned opinion as to their interest";
he only doubted if such an improbable assumption could ever
have been "so closely interwoven with our habits of political and
economic thought," as Wallas would have us believe. Hardly. "It
is an assumption that falls down almost as soon as it is stated,"
said the critic, but Wallas "has a lively way of battering it."[16] This
reviewer went on to argue that there is a wide gap between public
talk of politics and private understanding of its realities and that
one who destroys public myths will not always surprise, much less
enlighten, very many private citizens, for they are seldom as easily fooled as their leaders would like them to be or as their
philosophers are inclined to believe.

Had Wallas fooled himself into thinking that people are more
foolish than they actually are? The critic thought he had. *Human
Nature in Politics,* he argued, was "an amusing attempt of a man in
political life to find his way back from the public simplicities we all
disbelieve to the complexities we are privately aware of. It would
be hard to find a public American who was half so frank or a
private American who was not more so."[17] The reviewer,
however, failed to take the next step by raising the question, If we
are, as private individuals, as illusion-free as he would have us
believe, what accounts for the practical utility of these public
myths? Ought we not to assume that there are enough people out
there who take these myths to be true?

At least, Henry Steele Commager did not seem to share this
critic's view that "in private life" most of us are hardheaded
realists. In discussing Walter Lippmann's essay on *Public Opinion*
Commager observed that "practicing politicians had doubtless
understood the true nature of public opinion, but scholars and

---

[16] F.M. Colby's review, *Bookman*, 30 (1909-1910), 396.
[17] *Ibid.,* p. 398.

publicists had assumed that it was rational and reliable."[18] That
was a distinction worth making. When chided by an old friend for
allegedly having written a book merely to explain the obvious,
Wallas replied:

> You say that the facts of human life and motive to which the
> psychology books give names are "perfectly well known to people
> who have not read them." They are, I believe, very largely well-
> known to experienced politicians by the time they reach fifty years
> of age, but I am convinced that they are not known to some of the
> best of the young men who enter politics each year.[19]

Wallas was not battering a straw man — not, at least, as far as
the scholars and publicists were concerned. For many among his
contemporaries who had come under the influence of book learning, the shallow rationalism of the Benthamite psychology was
worse than a nuisance; to borrow Wallas's own words, it presented
a "danger for all human activities, but especially for the working
of democracy."[20] In his 1938 reminiscence of the years preceding
the world war John Maynard Keynes, no fool by any stretch of
the imagination, described himself to be "amongst the first" of his
generation "to escape from the Benthamite tradition,"[21] and he
called that tradition "the worm which has been gnawing at the in-
sides of modern civilization and is responsible for its present
moral decay."[22] He then struck at the heart of the matter:

> As cause and consequence of our general state of mind we
> completely misunderstood human nature, including our own. The
> rationality which we attributed to it led to a superficiality, not only
> of judgment, but also of feeling. It was not only that intellectually
> we were pre-Freudian, but we had lost something which our pre-
> decessors had without replacing it. I still suffer incurably from
> attributing an unreal rationality to other people's feelings and
> behaviour (and doubtless to my own, too).[23]

Like Keynes, Bertrand Russell had a hard fight to free himself

---

[18] Henry Steele Commager, *The American Mind: An Interpretation of American Thought and Character Since the 1880's* (New Haven, 1950), p. 334. One obvious exception was Lipp-mann's own teacher, "the brilliant Graham Wallas . . ." (p. 332).
[19] Letter to Hastings Rashdall, 16 January 1909. Bodleian Library, Oxford.
[20] Preface to the third edition of HNP, 1920, p. 5.
[21] John Maynard Keynes, "My Early Beliefs," *Essays and Sketches in Biography* (New York, 1956), p. 251.
[22] *Ibid.*
[23] *Ibid.*, pp. 253-254.

from a faulty rationalism in which he had been reared, even though he did not associate it specifically with Bentham. But, more definitely than Keynes, Russell traced his intellectual awakening to his experiences during the war. In his autobiography Russell wrote:

> I had supposed until that time that it was quite common for parents to love their children, but the War persuaded me that it is a rare exception. I had supposed that most people liked money better than almost anything else, but I discovered that they liked destruction even better. I had supposed that intellectuals frequently loved truth, but I found here again that not ten per cent of them prefer truth to popularity.
>
> The War of 1914-1918 changed everything for me. I ceased to be academic and took to writing a new kind of books. I changed my whole conception of human nature.[24]

It is a supreme tribute to Wallas's intellectual acumen, then, that long before the outbreak of the world war he was able to see clearly, and also to define, the problems of social and political psychology which some of his most brilliant contemporaries were not able to see until after the war had brought them out in the open. Likewise, Wallas has been credited with having shown a "prophetic power"[25] in his analysis of the problems of the "Great Society" on the eve of the war, demonstrating how fragile was the fabric of modern industrial civilization and how bankrupt were liberal democracy's intellectual premises that had, in part, helped to bring about that civilization.

"To him more than to anyone else in the English tradition," wrote Max Lerner, "we owe our present knowledge that political behavior is irrational, that politics is the business of manipulating and exploiting the basic yet complex drives of men, and that all political progress must reckon with those drives."[26] Indeed, Wallas did view politics in terms of psychological manipulation, as an "empirical art" concerned with "the creation of opinion by the deliberate exploitation of subconscious non-rational inference."[27] And of all the brilliant arguments he presented in

---

[24] Bertrand Russell, *Autobiography* (Boston, 1968), vol. 2, 1914-44, pp. 6, 36.

[25] G.E.G. Catlin, *A Study of the Principles of Politics: Being an Essay Towards Political Rationalization* (New York, 1930), p. 220.

[26] Max Lerner, *Ideas Are Weapons: The History and Uses of Ideas* (New York, 1939), p. 316.

[27] HNP, p. 18.

Human Nature in Politics in his effort to discredit the rationalist assumptions of the Benthamite psychology, perhaps none was more so than his memorable characterization of politics as an art of advertisement. He wrote:

> The whole relation between party entities and political impulse can perhaps be best illustrated from the art of advertisement. In advertisement the intellectual process can be watched apart from its ethical implications, and advertisement and party politics are becoming more and more closely assimilated in method. The political poster is placed side by side with the trade or theatrical poster on the hoardings, it is drawn by the same artist, and follows the same empirical rules of art.[28]

Wallas left no doubt as to how he might first have acquired such a vulgar notion of politics, that is, through a politician: "I remember that before my first election my most experienced political friend said to me, 'Remember that you are undertaking a six weeks' advertising campaign.'"[29] "As long as he [the candidate] is so engaged," Wallas added, "the maxim that it is wrong to appeal to anything but the severest process of logical thought in his constituents will seem to him, if he has time to think of it, not so much untrue as irrelevant."[30]

In his use of advertisement as an analytical model Wallas was without doubt a pioneer, the first one ever to come to grips with the politics of mass society; no one of his generation saw as clearly as he did the relevance of salesmanship for statesmanship in an age of mass media and mass consumption. It was not until five years after the publication of *Human Nature in Politics* that the American political scientist A. Lawrence Lowell made the phrases "age of advertisement" and "age of brokers" famous, by presenting an extensive discussion of the politicians' manipulation of a mass electorate through the employment of the art of advertisement. Lowell called these politicians "brokers," who act as middlemen, or "go-betweens," among different social groups with conflicting interests.[31] The idea of brokerage politics, characteristic of a pluralistic society with countervailing powers, has been one of the

---

[28] *Ibid.,* p. 107.
[29] *Ibid.,* p. 190.
[30] *Ibid.,* p. 191.
[31] A. Lawrence Lowell, *Public Opinion and Popular Government* (New York, 1913), pp. 58-61.

more distinctly American contributions to political science, originating in James Madison's classical commentary on "factions" *(The Federalist,* No. 10) and more systematically treated in the twentieth century by a group of able political scientists beginning with Arthur Bentley.[32] This idea remained largely outside the purview of Wallas's own intellectual concern, but if anyone should be credited with first having detected the close similarity between political campaigns and commercial advertisement, it was clearly Wallas, and not Lowell.

It is of course something else to suggest, as I think may be said with justice, that Wallas failed to appreciate the fact that the commercialization and vulgarization of the democratic process are only a by-product of brokerage politics. But if Wallas may be criticized on that ground, that would not necessarily detract from the validity of his hypothesis that in his essential behavioral characteristics a politician is a salesman and that he relates himself to his constituents no differently than a manufacturer relates himself to the consumer. That assumption, I think, has been fully borne out in the decades that followed *Human Nature in Politics.* Some half-century after Wallas had spoken of advertisement and party politics "becoming more and more closely assimilated in method" and of political posters being "drawn by the same artist," following "the same empirical rules of art," as the trade or theatrical posters, both major parties in the United States — the Republican party in 1952 and the Democratic party four years later — turned over their campaign propaganda to the professional public relations firms on Madison Avenue. And today, true to Wallas's prophecy, political candidates are literally "sold" to the public by professional advertising agencies according to "the same empirical rules of art" as those employed, methodically, in the selling of toothpastes, breakfast cereals and ladies' hosiery.[33] These professional agencies endeavor to create in the minds of captive viewers, alternately, a false sense of insecurity and security, a false sense of need and satisfaction.

It may be said, in retrospect, that the single most enduring contribution Wallas made to the study of politics lay in his simple but eloquent plea that a discussion of human nature be made the foundation of all political inquiry — a plea which he himself put in-

[32] Arthur Bentley, *The Process of Government (1908).*

[33] See Joe McGinnis's insightful analysis of the management of the presidential campaign of Richard Nixon in his *The Selling of the President* (New York, 1968).

to practice with admirable success. "The deepest error of our political thinking," wrote the young Walter Lippmann, six years after the appearance of *Human Nature in Politics,* was "to talk of politics without reference to human beings." Lippmann believed that Wallas had succeeded in correcting that error by demonstrating how the behavior of concrete human beings could be made "the center of political investigation" and that, in so doing, he had turned the study of politics "back to the humane tradition of Plato to Machiavelli."[34] Harold Lasswell has since spoken of this "humanizing trend" in political science, which "has always been represented in the 'classics,' usually in the form of some theory of 'human nature,' " and has given Wallas and "his students" the credit for having revived that venerable tradition.[35]

The relevance of political psychology for the survival of liberal democracy was not left merely to the reader's imagination. Even though the "main controversy over the best form of government appears to have been finally settled in favor of representative democracy," Wallas noted in his introduction to *Human Nature in Politics,* "in the very nations which have most wholeheartedly accepted representative democracy, politicians and political students seem puzzled and disappointed by their experience of it." With the expansion of suffrage the Western societies appeared to have more and more democracy but, somehow, enjoying it less and less. Wallas was particularly disturbed by the fact that in the two most advanced representative democracies, the United States and England, it was "the growing, and not the decaying, forces of society" that seemed to "create the most disquieting problems."[36] Is liberal democracy inherently incompatible with modern society?

Within a few years of the publication of *Human Nature in Politics* England witnessed what Historian George Dangerfield was later to describe as "the Strange Death of Liberal England," as it plunged into what may have been the most serious domestic political crisis since the Chartist and anti-Corn Law agitations of the late 1830's, under the combined pressures of the suffragette and trade union agitations and the parliamentary dispute over the

---

[34] Walter Lippmann, *Preface to Politics* (New York, 1913), pp. 32 and 77.
[35] Harold D. Lasswell and Abraham Kaplan, *Power and Society: A Framework for Political Inquiry* (New Haven, 1950), p. 14.
[36] HNP, pp. 25-26 and 27.

Irish Home Rule.[37] Compromise, courtesy, good manners, and all the social amenities so closely identified with the British way of life suddenly seemed things of the past. Many were driven into a state of melancholy musing over the death of a tradition. Already in 1905 the Liberal politician C.F.G. Masterman could write that "expectancy and surprise" were the "notes of the age." He would describe himself, in the vein of Matthew Arnold ("Grande Chartreuse," St. 15), as poised in suspension between two worlds divided by a great void: "On the one hand is a past still showing faint survivals of vitality; on the other is the future but hardly coming to birth."[38] Four years later, now a Liberal M.P., Masterman was able to offer a diagnosis that was less prophetic but also less ambiguous: "It is rather in the region of the spirit that the doubts are still disturbing," he declared, noting how over the years "fulness of bread" had been "accompanied with leanness of soul."[39]

This sense of uncertainty, indeed foreboding, so characteristic of the closing years of a protracted garden party called the Edwardian age, was only to prove a signpost to things to come, and to stay, even though there were conflicting voices trying to explain the precise meaning of the malaise. For Graham Wallas, who was less given to prophetic fancy than Masterman and still less liable to fret over a few cracks in the citadel of social conventions, the challenge of the age was more immediately political: to scrutinize the reigning wisdom, that is, liberalism, which had rendered the political system incapable of coping with the unruly forces of modern society.

Wallas became conscious of the troubles of liberalism early in his life as he came under the twin spells of Darwinian biology and Aristotelian politics. In the same year he was born, 1858, the son of an evangelical minister of an orthodox persuasion, the world saw the publication of the joint thesis on "natural selection" by Charles Darwin and Alfred Russel Wallace, which was followed a year later by the historic appearance of Darwin's *Origin of Species*. Wallas first encountered the Darwinian theory when he was a student at Corpus Christi College, Oxford, and he was quickly con-

---

[37] George Dangerfield, *The Strange Death of Liberal England* (New York, 1935).

[38] C.F.G. Masterman, *In Peril of Change* (London, 1905), p. xii.

[39] C.F.G. Masterman, *The Condition of England* (London, 1909), p. 208.

verted. Once the young Wallas had the temerity to submit a tract in defense of Darwin's theory against what he deemed an unfounded attack made upon it by the resident professor of moral philosophy. Following his years in college Darwinism became something of a religion to Wallas, for during the rest of his life he was to sing the praises of Darwin for having first "demonstrated the blood-relationship of men with the other animals."[40] He argued that "the proved continuity of human and non-human life" demanded "a biological outlook which should study mankind, not in isolation but as one of a member of related species,"[41] and advocated, tirelessly, that political science incorporate the findings of the new biological science as it revises its conception of human nature.

Wallas was not slow to appreciate the social implications of the Darwinian biology but was harshly critical of the vulgar use that was then being made of it under the label of "Social Darwinism"; he condemned it as a thinly disguised apology for militarism, imperialism and racism, characterizing it as "thoroughly unscientific."[42] Rather, the lesson to be drawn from the Darwinian world view, so Wallace believed, was that we must come to terms with the incongruity between man and his environment before we can fully understand the crisis of the modern industrial society. The problem of the modern age, he said, was that "the coming of the Great Society has created an environment in which, for most of us, neither our instinctive nor our intelligent dispositions find it easy to discover their most useful stimuli."[43] Given the conflict between man's nature and his present social environment, leaving the situation where it was would do human nature gross violence. On the other hand, so Wallas argued in his postwar work, *Our Social Heritage,* given man's helpless dependence on his inherited habits and customs, any attempt at eliminating that social heritage would be suicidal. There is a way out of our predicament: progressive alteration of our social heritage to make that heritage more compatible with our biological nature, particularly to improve our existing modes of cooperation. This is what Wallas   meant   by   his   often-repeated   phrase   "social

---

[40] See *The Literary Guide and Rationalist Review,* July 1926, p.126.

[41] Graham Wallas, *The Great Society: A Psychological Analysis* (London, 1914), p. 118 (hereafter GS).

[42] HNP, p. 302.

[43] GS, p. 62.

reconstruction," a phrase very much in vogue in the postwar years.

"My earlier book dealt in the main with the problem of representative government," so wrote Wallas in introducing his *Great Society*. "This will deal with general social organization, considered with special reference to the difficulties created by the formation of what I have called the Great Society."[44] Wallas had written his new book in part in response to the suggestion of William James that there was a need for a book which would deal specifically with "the diseases of society and their prevention."[45] The continuity from *Human Nature in Politics* to *The Great Society* was not lost on the reading public, in spite of the author's own attempt to distinguish their aims. Thus, Ernest Barker described the new book as "a treatise on social therapeutics," adding that it was Wallas's intention "in the light of social psychology . . . to diagnose the diseases of our present system of representative government and to suggest their remedies."[46]

Wallas's consciousness of the importance of environment was further heightened by his exposure to the teachings of Aristotle, which came even earlier than his encounter with the Darwinian theory. As a young lad he was trained at Shrewsbury, which was then one of the most prestigious "public schools" in England, particularly distinguished for its curriculum in classics. At the age of nineteen Wallas was sent to Oxford on a classical scholarship, to graduate four years later with "Class II Honours" in *Literae Humaniores*, to embark upon what was to be a brief career as a classical schoolmaster. After all that training in classics, however, Wallas did not become a classicist as such. Rather, the training had the effect of impressing upon him the urgent need to reexamine the moral and intellectual foundations of the contemporary society in the light of the Greek conception of polity as a community of friends engaged in a common task, that is, the pursuit of the good life — which was in sharp contrast with the prevailing liberal conception of society essentially as a legal association. Wallas found the liberal conception hopelessly atomistic.

When Wallas went to Oxford in 1877, the philosophy of John Stuart Mill was the dominant voice there, even though he had been dead for four years. Wallas's tutor, Thomas Case, was him-

---

[44] GS, pp. 18-19.
[45] Letter to Wallas, 8 December 1908. Wallas Papers, L.S.E.
[46] Sir Ernest Barker, *Political Thought in England: 1848-1914* (London, 1959), pp. 204-205.

self a great admirer of Mill, the last of the Utilitarians, and under Case's tutelage Wallas devoured *The System of Logic* then considered the most important of Mill's works. In that book Mill complained of the backwardness of the "moral sciences" and urged that the methods of physical sciences be applied to the moral sciences to remedy their sorry state. Wallas could not have agreed with Mill more, and yet Mill's own political views seemed strangely formalistic and dry, seemingly out of touch with what Wallas later came to understand to be the realities of social life. Liberty as defined by Mill in his classic treatise under that title had a certain air of unreality: it seemed at once negative and static. Hobbes's formula of liberty as the "absence of external impediments" had been left intact in its essential components. Wallas viewed this conception of liberty as a serious obstacle to the forces of social change because of its inherent tendency to treat any political action as an infringement upon personal liberties. The problem was particularly serious because, in spite of his unimpressive record as a political inventor, Mill remained the "intellectual autocrat" of British liberalism.[47]

Mill's static conception of liberty was hardly improved upon by the Oxford idealists, Wallas believed. Despite their noble intentions to give liberty some positive and dynamic content, they were powerless to bring about the desired change because, like the German thinkers they were emulating, these idealists went about their business the wrong way, that is, as "metaphysicians" rather than as psychologists. When Wallas was a senior at Corpus Christi, T. H. Green was delivering his lectures on the "Principles of Political Obligation" just a block away at Balliol and was making many converts. Wallas went to hear Green one day and came away quite unimpressed because the eminent professor seemed singularly lacking in biological or psychological insight.[48]

In his own time Wallas found the lingering influence of Mill's negative concept of liberty in Sidney Webb's definition, according to which liberty is the "practical opportunity that we have of exercising our faculties and fulfilling our desires."[49] Wallas argued that this definition was "insufficient," because, as he put it, "it does not recognize that the unfreedom-reaction depends more on the

---

[47] Graham Wallas, *Our Social Heritage* (New Haven, 1921), p. 176 (hereafter OSH).
[48] See Wallas's review of *L. T. Hobhouse: His Life and Work* by J.A. Hobson and Morris Ginsberg in *The New Statesman and Nation,* 25 April 1931, p. 326.
[49] Quoted in OSH, p. 159.

cause of obstruction to impulse than on the mere fact of obstruction."[50] In short, the sense of deprivation of liberty comes not
from actually losing the ability to do this or that but, rather, from
one's resentment of the perceived causes of that deprivation. This
was Aristotle's profound insight,[51] and for Wallas it was but a
facet of the "many-sided positive conception"[52] of the ancient
Greeks, according to which liberty is closely linked with "the instinct of resentment."[53] Thus, Wallas praised Pericles for having
"understood the explosive mine of resentment which may lie
beneath the surface of a community that ignores" the sensibilities
of ordinary people and, above all, for having realized that "free
government means something more subtle and more difficult than
the mere avoidance" of what is but an external manifestation of
that resentment.[54]

In the final analysis, Wallas argued, again echoing Aristotle,
no cooperative effort on a national scale, under whatever label,
can satisfy the needs of a modern society unless it is grounded on a
firm basis of popular consent. But conscious consent, the secret of
political stability, is the child of economic and social equality, and
the only thing that will enable a large majority of the population
wilfully and consciously to play its part in any cooperative
endeavor is "a much nearer approximation to economic and social
equality than now exists in any industrial nation."[55] Thus,
Wallas's egalitarianism was deeply rooted in his conviction that
the social fabric of a complex modern industrial society cannot endure the psychological strains of gross economic and social inequality. "If our civilization is to survive, greater social equality
must indeed come," he wrote in 1908. "Men will not continue to
live peacefully together," he added, prophetically, "in huge cities
under conditions that are intolerable to any sensitive mind, both
among those who profit and those who suffer by them."[56]

When the young Wallas left Oxford in 1881, upon gradua-

---

[50] *Ibid.*, p. 168.
[51] See Aristotle's *Politics* bk. 5, where he drew the important distinction between actual
inequality and a perception, or consciousness, of inequality. The latter, not the former, so
Aristotle thought, leads to a "sense of injustice," which in turn leads to *stasis,* or a seditious
atmosphere.
[52] OSH, p. 166.
[53] *Ibid.*, p. 165.
[54] *Ibid.*, p. 167.
[55] *Ibid.*, p. 88.
[56] HNP, p. 245.

tion, he had become not only a devotee of Aristotle and Darwin but also a convert to the new religion of social conscience. The eighties were a decade of moral agitation spurred by the sight of an enormous and ever-widening gulf between wealth and poverty that appeared literally to tear the English society asunder into "two nations," in the memorable phrase of Disraeli. This aliena- tion of social classes was particularly glaring in London where the division between the wealthy "West End" and the poverty-stricken "East End" seemed complete, neither understanding the life-style of the other. It was the vision of bringing these "two nations" together that inspired the creation of the University Settlements throughout England, beginning with the foundation of Toynbee Hall in East London in 1884, and also the introduction, through Toynbee Hall, of the Ethical Society movement from the United States shortly thereafter. Wallas was drawn into the Settlement movement from the beginning and took an active part therein for most of his life, as he did in the Ethical Society movement.

But it was the Fabian Society, also founded in 1884, that was to claim the largest share of his energies and talents for many years, both because of the strategic place it was to occupy in British national politics and because of the leadership role he was to play in the society until he resigned his membership twenty years later. Wallas did not join the society until 1886, a year after he had been dismissed from a teaching post for refusing to take Holy Communion; but he had known three of the present members, George Bernard Shaw, Sidney Webb and Sydney Olivier, with whom he was to form the "Fabian Junta."

Within a year of his initiation into the Fabian Society Wallas chose historical research as his particular contribution to the cause of socialism. By 1888 he was delivering a series of lectures on the Chartist movement, which was received as a pioneering contribu- tion to historiography. These lectures "wrought a tremendous disillusion as to the novelty of our [Fabian] own ideas and methods of propaganda," so recalled Shaw afterwards, and "it was in this new frame of mind that the monumental series of works by the Webbs came into existence."[57] It was during his work on Chartism in the British Museum, in the early nineties, that Wallas stumbled upon a huge mass of papers of Francis Place, the English radical reformer and Chartist leader who helped draft the

---

[57] Quoted in Edward R. Pease, *History of the Fabian Society*, 2nd ed. (London, 1925), pp. 277-278.

"People's Charter." When *The Life of Francis Place* appeared later in the decade, it was widely acclaimed as a masterpiece of political biography. "There are perhaps five or six living men who can disentangle the social history of England in the nineteenth century with the same knowledge and wisdom as Mr. Wallas," wrote Harold Laski years later. "That has made him," Laski argued, "in a real sense the parent of what is rapidly becoming the most significant part of modern English historiography."[58] Even though Wallas's reputation as a political theorist was soon to outshine his reputation as a historian, many have continued to rate *The Life of Francis Place* as one of the author's finest efforts.[59]

Wallas once said of his work that he had emerged from his research a "different man."[60] Apart from gaining a rich insight into the history of the radical movement in England, Wallas made an important discovery that was to guide and shape his thinking for the rest of his life: the idea of "invention." Throughout his biography Place is portrayed not merely as a supreme political tactician, agitator and lobbyist but also as a "political inventor," in whom the life of thought and the life of action seemed to be joined in a happy blend. It is no coincidence that such a person should have been a friend and pupil of the greatest political inventor of them all, or "by far the most successful political inventor whom we have produced in England,"[61] as Wallas would say of Jeremy Bentham. If, indeed, it had not been for the many daring political inventions of Place and other progenies of Bentham, such as E. Chadwick, Gibbon Wakefield and Rowland Hill, that were brought to bear on the tasks of social reform of the day,[62] British liberalism might have become obsolete in the illustrious hands of John Stuart Mill.

When Wallas brought Bentham into the Fabian discussions Bentham was hardly obscure, but he was distinctly unpopular. He had long since been effectively replaced by the towering figure of Mill, and for a while, at least in Oxford, to be a "Benthamite"

---

[58] Harold J. Laski, "A Social Pioneer" (review of *The Life of Francis Place*), *The Dial*, 68 (May, 1920), 619.

[59] Lord Bertrand Russell believed that *Place* ranked with *Human Nature in Politics* as Wallas's two greatest works. Letter to me, 17 July 1968.

[60] *Men and Ideas: Essays by Graham Wallas,* ed. May Wallas, with a preface by Gilbert Murray (London, 1940), pp. 208-209 (hereafter MI).

[61] MI, p. 45.

[62] OSH, p. 176.

was an invitation to ostracism.[63] Wallas could recall that when he was an undergraduate students were "trained to despise Bentham," noting, further, that some of their tutors "made, indeed, a considerable proportion of their income by jeering at those quotations from Bentham's writings which they met with in the manuals of philosophy."[64] By the beginning of the nineties all the leading Fabians, most of whom were still in their early thirties, had contemporary social thinkers whom they would identify as their heroes, though in a rather vague sort of way. Webb was often thought of as a Millite, Shaw a Henry Georgeite, Olivier a Comtean, William Clarke a Mazzinian, and so forth. Wallas alone was without a master in modern social thought, having to make do with the incongruous pair of Aristotle and Darwin. So it was that when he discovered and began preaching Bentham's philosophy of invention — not to be confused with his Utilitarian psychology, which Wallas came to despise heartily — he had made a significant breakthrough not only for the popularization of Bentham's timely philosophy but also for his own sake as a member of the club. Bentham the inventor remained Wallas's hero to the end of his life; Bentham seemed to complete Wallas's trinity of idolatry, with the other sacred chairs already reserved for Aristotle and Darwin.

In 1888 Wallas was elected into the Fabian Society's executive with Shaw, Webb, Olivier, William Clarke, Annie Besant and Hubert Bland; these were the authors of the celebrated "Fabian Essays," which were published the following year to rousing public acclaim. But in 1895 Wallas resigned from the executive and became deeply involved in the politics of public education, having been elected the previous year to the London School Board, and also, shortly thereafter, in the politics of the London County Council. Nine years later he resigned from the Fabian Society itself when he could not prevail upon the majority to reject Joseph Chamberlain's protective tariff and to reaffirm free trade. Like a good Liberal, though he never was a member of the Liberal party, Wallas had also protested against the expansionist foreign policy of Lord Salisbury's Conservative government; at the outbreak of the Boer War in 1899, he was part of that group which demanded that the Fabian Society "dissociates itself from

---

[63] See Robert Louis Stevenson's *The Story of a Lie* and Emery Neff's *Carlyle and Mill: An Introduction to Victorian Thought.*

[64] MI, p. 34.

the imperialism of capitalism and vainglorious nationalism." [65]
But nothing could have offended the liberal sensibilities of an
agnostic educator more than the reintroduction of religion into
public education. [66]

No one in the Fabian Society championed the cause of
secularism more passionately than did Wallas. In an article written in 1888 he described his mood as "savagely Anti-Christian" in
matters relating to religious indoctrination "as if I were a
Secularist, pure and simple" and expressed his conviction that the
country would be better off "if only we disestablished the Church"
and "induced a sufficient number of persons to 'make game of the
patriarchs.' "[67] It did not take him long, however, to discover that
the patriarchs had powerful allies not only in the government but
also within the Fabian Society itself.

Sidney Webb, who shared Wallas's distaste for religious interference in education, had his new education act on the drawing
board and courted the support of the Conservatives to ensure its
adoption. The Conservatives, on the other hand, could not ignore
the sentiment of the clergy, their traditional allies, who wanted
the school boards abolished, because the school boards were then
widely, and correctly, perceived as the bastions of secularism.
Furthermore, the clergy insisted that the new law should make a
provision whereby the beleaguered sectarian schools would be
supported out of the local rates, that is, property tax. Wallas opposed these efforts strenuously and was able to rally the Liberals
and the Nonconformists behind the school boards as the last line
of defense for freedom in the realm of public education. But, in

---

[65] A.M. McBriar, *Fabian Socialism and English Politics: 1884-1918* (London, 1962), p. 121.

[66] In the last quarter of the nineteenth century there were two different systems of elementary education, one, "denominational schools" run by churches, mostly Anglican, and the other, those run by elected "school boards" of which the London School Board was by far the largest, the most efficient and the most prestigious. As a general rule, the board-supported schools were much superior to the "denominational" ones both in facilities and in the quality of teachers, and even though they were required to provide some type of "undenominational" religious teaching under the Cowper-Temple clause of the Education Act of 1870, they could nevertheless boast of themselves as the bastions of secularism in the realm of education. Orginally elected to the London School Board in 1894, Wallas served on the board for 10 years, including the seven years from 1897 to 1904 as chairman of its powerful School Management Committee.

[67] Graham Wallas, "Socialists and the School Boards," *Today*, 10, no. 60 (November,1888), 130.

the end, Webb and the Fabian majority gave in to the Conservative demands. The Education Act of 1902 was a major victory for the Anglican and Catholic clergy, who had been apprehensive lest their schools should go bankrupt, and a major setback for the secularists, who had hoped that they would do so, in order that the elected school boards might take over the entire system of elementary education. Needless to add, it was also a personal defeat for Wallas, who had staked his reputation on the belief that a free society cannot allow its educational process to be dominated by the forces of religious obscurantism.[68]

To be sure, Wallas did not resign from the Fabian Society over the education issue. However, as Edward Pease, the Fabian secretary and historian, later pointed out, Wallas eventually left the society "because in the long controversy over education policy he had found himself constantly in the position of a hostile critic."[69] Shortly after his resignation, in January 1904, Wallas wrote Pease reflecting on his own politics: "On the questions which divide the Liberal and Conservative parties, I am a Liberal."[70] Indeed, in all three disputes Wallas fought on the losing side, the Liberal side, or the anti-Conservative side, invariably crossing swords with his old friends Webb and Shaw, who took turns to lead the majority within the society. Wallas decided to leave, wrote Historian Élie Halévy, because "he felt himself compromised by the deliberately anti-Liberal attitude the heads of the Fabian Society had adopted." Halévy also recorded, again correctly, that Wallas's retirement from the society was "perfectly amicable," adding that he "continued to be the friend and admirer of those with whom he had worked throughout his youth."[71] But one can see, in retrospect, that as their friendships lasted unbroken and undiminished so did their fundamental differences of temperament and outlook.

During the early days of the Fabian Society Beatrice Webb

---

[68] Shortly after the passage of the education act, Beatrice Webb made the following entry in her diary: [Wallas] has a deeply-rooted suspicion that Sidney is playing false with regard to religious education. He wants all religious teaching abolished. As Sidney is not himself a 'religionist,' Graham thinks that he too should wish it swept away. Politically, this seems to Sidney impossible, whilst I do not desire it even if it were possible." (Beatrice Webb, *Our Partnership* [New York, 1948], pp. 256-257).

[69] Pease, *Fabian Society*, p. 156.

[70] Letter to Pease, quoted in May Wallas's letter to me dated 17 February 1972.

[71] Élie Havlévy, *A History of the English People in the Nineteenth Century*, vol. 5 ("Imperialism and the Rise of Labour: 1895-1905"), trans. E.I. Watkin (London, 1929), p. 366.

observed that her husband, Sidney, was the "organizer" and giver of "most of the practical initiative," whereas Wallas represented "morality and scrupulousness," which appealed "to those of the upper and educated class who have good intentions." As for Shaw, he "gives the sparkle and flavour" and "leads off the men of straw, men with light heads — the would-be revolutionaries, who are attracted by his wit, his daring onslaughts and amusing paradoxes."[72] The years following the Great War seemed to bring to relief, relentlessly, the political consequences of these temperamental differences among old friends who had been brought together by a common devotion to the cause of social equality. Just as he had found himself outnumbered in the Fabian Society by those willing to abandon liberal principles for reasons of political expediency, so in the postwar years Wallas found himself swimming in a pool full of unfriendly creatures calling themselves "realists."

These were the years that witnessed the rise of communism and fascism, ideologies of violence so different and yet so alike, clamoring at the gate of liberal democracy, trying to lure the uncommitted with promises of equality and efficiency, and testing the souls of liberal democrats who were growing increasingly suspicious that their agreeable form of government might at last have outlived its usefulness. In a state of exhaustion owing to four years of killing and destruction, some people were doubtful whether liberal democracy could ever be repaired; exasperated by the slowness and inefficiency of its ways, some believed that it was time to jump ship.

In 1932 the Webbs paid their visit to the Soviet Union, returning home convinced that communism was the answer to much of what the democratic systems had failed to solve. Three years later they presented their conclusions to a stunned British public in the *Soviet Communism,* in which the doctrine of gradualism, the essence of Fabian Socialism, appeared completely abandoned. Death spared Wallas the embarrassment of reading it. But there was no way Wallas could have avoided getting involved in the debate over fascism in the mid-twenties as Shaw carried on his open love affair with *Il Duce,* agitating a vulnerable British public which was already displaying a penchant for political ruffianism in its toleration of the likes of Winston Churchill.

---

[72] B. Webb, *Our Partnership,* pp.38-39.

"Credere, obbedire, combattere" ("have faith, obey, fight") and "Mussolini ha sempre ragione" ("Mussolini is always right"), so the slogans read. But the Abyssinian war was still several years away, and until after Mussolini's defeat in the Second World War not many people could have imagined the true scope of the Fascist inefficiency, which he managed to conceal behind the facade of military discipline. From its inception in 1922 fascism had billed itself as the antithesis of all the governing principles of liberal democracy; yet, to the "realists," fascism appeared to promise the kind of social equality and economic recovery democratic systems could not deliver. Admittedly, Shaw was something of a showman, given to clowning and hyperbole, unafraid to lavish a sense of humor at the expense of the public. But his praises of Mussolini were the confessions of a sober social critic, who was merely echoing a widely held sentiment of his time.

Among those who shared Shaw's pro-Fascist sympathies was Churchill. He had undergone one of his political conversions, departing from his previous Liberal radicalism and now behaving more and more like a regular Tory diehard. During the General Strike of 1926 Churchill was by far the stoutest on Stanley Baldwin's cabinet to oppose a negotiated settlement with labor; to him the strike was communist-inspired blackmail, to which the only workable response was a militant one. It was in this frame of mind that Churchill, while vacationing in Italy, saw fit to declare that Mussolini had "rendered a service to the whole world."

In February of 1927, following a round of public flirtations with fascism, Shaw received a letter from Wallas, which read in part:

> In Vienna last year I watched a body of "Nationalist" (Fascist) ex-officers marching through the streets, and they were a formidable body of men, and I watched Winston Churchill's armoured cars marching last May through London streets, and realised that he and the young members of his defence bodies were probably thinking of the ease with which they could bring about a Fascist coup de main in London. [73]

Shaw had urged that if one could not support fascism one ought at least to hold his tongue and refrain from minding other people's

---

[73] Wallas to Shaw, 13 February 1927, G.B.S. Collection, British Museum.

business. Wallas was not impressed by Shaw's sudden plea for international good manners and expressed his sense of dismay: "And your influence all over the world is very great."[74] Even T. S. Eliot, who was then acquiring a reputation as a reactionary, largely through his editorship of the literary quarterly *The Criterion*, echoed this concern two years later when he offered his editorial observation that the "aging Fabians," like Shaw and H.G. Wells, seemed to prefer "some kind of fascism" and "autocracy." He feared that this fascination with dictatorship on the part of the eminent men of letters could "become the instinctive attitude of thousands of unthinking people a few years hence."[75]

Amid all this frenzy over the Fascist movement in Italy Wallas greeted the public with his fifth book, *The Art of Thought,* a masterpiece in introspective psychology. In it he demonstrated how the nonrational and involuntary forces within the human mind could be rationally guided and coordinated to produce fruitful thought. Having previously written three books diagnosing various aspects of the problems of modern society, Wallas had now shifted his attention to the practical question of how best to make use of our mental faculties in coping with those problems. Max Lerner, who greatly admired the book, described it as "a sort of handbook for political inventors."[76] But, more than that, *The Art of Thought* was further testimony to Wallas's enduring attachment to the liberal tradition; the book was, in effect, a reaffirmation of the psychological individualism that is implict in the entire British liberal tradition, from Hobbes to Mill. Not surprisingly, Wallas has always been an unyielding foe of the "group mind" school of social psychology. He took particular disliking to the doctrine of "imitation," calling Gabriel Tarde's classic *Lois de l'Imitation* "one of the most baffling and unsatisfactory books that I have ever read,"[77] because it tended to legitimate the "group mind" hypothesis. Even the venerable authority of William James seemed powerless to persuade Wallas to modify his dogged stance.[78]

---

[74] *Ibid.*
[75] Editorial "Commentary," *The Criterion,* 8, no. 32 (April, 1929), 378-379.
[76] Max Lerner, *Ideas,* p. 317.
[77] GS, pp. 120-121.
[78] James wrote: "I myself see things à la Tarde, perhaps too exclusively." Letter to Wallas, quoted in GS, p. 121.

In an age when the leading students of human affairs were prone to seek intellectual respectability by debunking reason's false claims, Wallas sought patiently to maximize the chances for realizing her true possibilities. In an age when self-styled political realism and totalitarian élitism seemed to go hand in hand, both drawing their intellectual sustenance from antirationalism of some kind, Wallas remained unalterably opposed to any easy solution that was incompatible with the ideals of liberty and self-government, because he knew only too well that trading off one type of tyranny for another was hardly a solution. He held firm to his liberal conviction that, for all its failings, liberal democracy must find its own cures for its peculiar problems. When he died in the summer of 1932, at the age of 74, the fateful movements just north of the Alps had begun making Mussolini's experiment seem relatively harmless. Events were soon to turn the fashionable realism of the day on its head.

Today, once again, liberal democracy is on the defensive. Its existence is tenuous in those very nations in which it has survived over the past hundred years or more, though with intermittent success — those countries where it must prove its viability if it is to have a future at all. Under the deceptive veneer of self-confidence born of the industrial growth and technological advancement of the postworld war years, the Western nations are gripped with a mood of uncertainty. Rape of the environment, nuclear proliferation, racial tensions, the energy crisis, terrorism, and a host of other problems have suddenly shaken the liberal democrat's confidence in the continuing validity of his inherited creed: liberty, equality and representative government. Most recently we have been forced to ask the question, What must be the organic deficiency of representative democracy that such large numbers of voters throughout Western Europe should feel the need to embrace communism at the polls, while, admittedly, making it clear that they are in no mood to abandon the basic tenets of parliamentary system?

Shall liberal democracy prove equal to the challenges of the day, or has it become truly obsolete, waiting to be dumped into the ideological graveyard of history? What are the chances of rescuing it from the perplexity of its own divided soul? Should we sing with the poet,

Vex not his ghost: O, Let him pass! He hates him

That would upon the rack of this tough world
Stretch him out longer.
                    King Lear, Act 5, Scene 3

Or should we grant liberal democracy a second medical opinion before rushing to its funeral?

Such questions have been raised before in the troubled career of liberal democracy; they are worth raising again only because they have never been answered satisfactorily. Warnings have been posted and counsels given; the state of perplexity in which we live today may be a measure of our failure to give heed to these past warnings and to profit from the lessons. Graham Wallas was a political philosopher who at another critical juncture in the evolution of liberal democracy sought to stave off the decline of the political system he held dear. He argued that the traditional liberal hostility toward the state and the disbelief in the power of political action to make society more just and more livable had stood in the way of much-needed social change. Later in his life, following the Great War, Wallas was forced to confront a political challenge of an altogether different stripe: the learned infatuation with the cult of "direct action." Both these tendencies, perversions of democratic thought, seemed symptomatic of a deeper malaise: liberal democracy's unconscionable neglect of the human foundation of political and social order.

Wallas did not reject the intellectual tradition of liberal democracy in toto; rather, he sought to repair its troubled foundations by scrutinizing its assumptions that had been taken for granted. Nor did he have answers to all the practical problems he had detected in liberal democracy; as a partial remedy for its impending obsolescence, he merely sought to implant in the minds of the committed an awareness of its mortal ambiguities.

PREFACE TO THE THIRD EDITION (1920)

THIS edition is, like the second edition (1910), a reprint, with a few verbal corrections, of the first edition (1908).

I tried in 1908 to make two main points clear. My first point was the danger, for all human activities, but especially for the working of democracy, of the "intellectualist" assumption, "that every human action is the result of an intellectual process, by which a man first thinks of some end which he desires, and then calculates the means by which that end can be attained" (p. 21). My second point was the need of substituting for that assumption a conscious and systematic effort of thought. "The whole progress," I argued, "of human civilization beyond its earliest stages, has been made possible by the invention of methods of thought which enable us to interpret and forecast the working of nature more successfully than we could, if we merely followed the line of least resistance in the use of our minds" (p. 114).

In 1920 insistence on my first point is not so necessary as it was in 1908. The assumption that men are auto-

matically guided by "enlightened self-interest" has been
discredited by the facts of the war and the peace, the
success of an anti-parliamentary and anti-intellectualist
revolution in Russia, the British election of 1918, the
French election of 1919, the confusion of politics in
America, the breakdown of political machinery in
Central Europe, and the general unhappiness which has
resulted from four years of the most intense and heroic
effort that the human race has ever made.   One only
needs to compare the disillusioned realism of our present
war and post-war pictures and poems with the nineteenth-
century war pictures at Versailles and Berlin, and the
war poems of Campbell, and Berenger, and Tennyson,
to realize how far we now are from exaggerating human
rationality.

It is my second point, which, in the world as the war
has left it, is most important.   There is no longer much
danger that we shall assume that man always and automatically thinks of ends and calculates means.   The
danger is that we may be too tired or too hopeless to
undertake the conscious effort by which alone we can
think of ends and calculate means.

The great mechanical inventions of the nineteenth
century have given us an opportunity of choosing for
ourselves our way of living such as men have never

had before. Up to our own time the vast majority of mankind have had enough to do to keep themselves alive, and to satisfy the blind instinct which impels them to hand on life to another generation. An effective choice has only been given to a tiny class of hereditary property owners or a few organizers of other men's labours. Even when, as in ancient Egypt or Mesopotamia, nature offered whole populations three hundred free days in the year if they would devote two months to ploughing and harvest, all but a fraction still spent themselves in unwilling toil, building tombs or palaces, or equipping armies, for a native monarch or a foreign conqueror. The monarch could choose his life, but his choice was poor enough. "There is," says Aristotle, "a way of living so brutish that it is only worth notice because many of those who can live any life they like make no better choice than did Sardanapalus."

The Greek thinkers started modern civilization, because they insisted that the trading populations of their walled cities should force themselves to think out an answer to the question, what kind of life is good. "The origin of the city-state," says Aristotle, "is that it enables us to live; its justification is that it enables us to live well."

Before the war, there were in London and New York,

and Berlin, thousands of rich men and women as free to choose their way of life as was Sardanapalus, and as dissatisfied with their own choice.   Many of the sons and daughters of the owners of railways and coal mines and rubber plantations were "fed up" with motoring or bridge, or even with the hunting and fishing which meant a frank resumption of palaeolithic life without the spur of palaeolithic hunger.   But my own work brought me into contact with an unprivileged class, whose degree of freedom was the special product of modern industrial civilization, and on whose use of their freedom the future of civilization may depend.   A clever young mechanic, at the age when the Wanderjahre of the mediaeval craftsman used to begin, would come home after tending a "speeded up" machine from 8 A. M., with an hour's interval, till 5 P. M.   At 6 P. M. he had finished his tea in the crowded living-room of his mother's house, and was "free" to do what he liked. That evening, perhaps, his whole being tingled with half-conscious desires for love and adventure and knowledge, and achievement.   On another day he might have gone to a billiard match at his club or have hung round the corner for a girl who smiled at him as he left the factory, or might have sat on his bed and ground at a chapter of Marx or Hobson.   But this evening he saw

his life as a whole. The way of living that had been im-
plied in the religious lessons at school seemed strangely
irrelevant; but still he felt humble, and kind, and
anxious for guidance. Should he aim at marriage, and
if so should he have children at once or at all? If he
did not marry, could he avoid self-contempt and disease? Should he face the life of a socialist organizer,
with its strain and uncertainty, and the continual possibility of disillusionment? Should he fill up every evening with technical classes and postpone his ideals until
he had become rich? And if he became rich what
should he do with his money? Meanwhile, there was
the urgent impulse to walk and think; but where should
he walk to, and with whom?

The young schoolmistress, in her bed-sitting-room a
few streets off, was in no better case. She and a friend
sat late last night, agreeing that the life they were living
was no real life at all; but what was the alternative?
Had the "home duties" to which her High Church sister
devoted herself with devastating self-sacrifice any more
meaning. Ought she, with her eyes open, and without
much hope of spontaneous love, to enter into the child-
less "modern" marriage which alone seemed possible
for her? Ought she to spend herself in a reckless
campaign for the suffrage? Meanwhile, she had had

her tea, her eyes were too tired to read, and what on earth should she do till bedtime?

Such moments of clear self-questioning were of course rare, but the nerve-fretting problems always existed. Industrial civilization had given the growing and working generation a certain amount of leisure, and education enough to conceive of a choice in the use of that leisure; but had offered them no guidance in making their choice.

We are faced, as I write, with the hideous danger that fighting may blaze up again throughout the whole Eurasian continent, and that the young men and girls of Europe may have no more choice in the way they spend their time than they had from 1914 to 1918 or the serfs of Pharaoh had in ancient Egypt. But if that immediate danger is avoided, I dream that in Europe and in America a conscious and systematic discussion by the young thinkers of our time of the conditions of a good life for an unprivileged population may be one of the results of the new vision of human nature and human possibilities which modern science and modern industry have forced upon us.

Within each nation, industrial organization may cease to be a confused and wasteful struggle of interests, if it is consciously related to a chosen way of life for which it offers to every worker the material means. International relations may cease to consist of a constant plotting of evil by each nation for its neighbours, if ever the youth of all nations know that French, and British, and Germans, and Russians, and Chinese, and Americans, are taking a conscious part in the great adventure of discovering ways of living open to all, and which all can believe to be good.

GRAHAM WALLAS.

August 1920.

CONTENTS

SYNOPSIS OF CONTENTS

(Introduction page 25)

The study of politics is now in an unsatisfactory position. Throughout Europe and America, representative democracy is generally accepted as the best form of government; but those who have had most experience of its actual working are often disappointed and apprehensive. Democracy has not been extended to non-European races, and during the last few years many democratic movements have failed.

This dissatisfaction has led to much study of political institutions; but little attention has been recently given in works on politics to the facts of human nature. Poltical science in the past was mainly based on conceptions of human nature, but the discredit of the dogmatic political writers of the early nineteeth century has made modern students of politics overanxious to avoid anything which recalls their methods. That advance therefore of psychology which has transformed pedagogy and criminology has left politics largely unchanged.

The neglect of the study of human nature is likely, however, to prove only a temporary phase of political thought, and there are already signs that it is coming to an end.

(PART I.—Chapter I.—Impulse and Instinct in Politics,
page 45

Any examination of human nature in politics must begin with an attempt to overcome that "intellectualism" which re-

15

sults both from the traditions of political science and from the mental habits of ordinary men.

Political impulses are not mere intellectual inferences from calculations of means and ends; but tendencies prior to, though modified by, the thought and experience of individual human beings. This may be seen if we watch the action in politics of such impulses as personal affection, fear, ridicule, the desire of property, etc.

All our impulses and instincts are greatly increased in their immediate effectiveness if they are "pure," and in their more permanent results if they are "first hand" and are connected with the earlier stages of our evolution. In modern politics the emotional stimulus which reaches us through the news-papers is generally "pure," but "second hand," and therefore is both facile and transient.

The frequent repetition of an emotion or impulse is often distressing. Politicians, like advertisers, must allow for this fact, which again is connected with that combination of the need of privacy with intolerance of solitude to which we have to adjust our social arrangements.

Political emotions are sometimes pathologically intensified when experienced simultaneously by large numbers of human beings in physical association, but the conditions of political life in England do not often produce this phenomenon.

The future of international politics largely depends on the question whether we have a specific instinct of hatred for human beings of a different racial type from ourselves. The point is not yet settled, but many facts which are often ex-plained as the result of such an instinct seem to be due to other and more general instincts modified by association.

(Chapter II.—Political Entities, page 81)

Political acts and impulses are the result of the contact between human nature and its environment. During the period studied by the politician, human nature has changed very little, but political environment has changed with ever-increasing rapidity.

Those facts of our environment which stimulate impulse and action reach us through our senses, and are selected from the mass of our sensations and memories by our instinctive or acquired knowledge of their significance. In politics the things recognized are, for the most part, made by man himself, and our knowledge of their significance is not instinctive but acquired.

Recognition tends to attach itself to symbols, which take the place of more complex sensations and memories. Some of the most difficult problems in politics result from the relation between the conscious use in reasoning of the symbols called words, and their more or less automatic and unconscious effect in stimulating emotion and action. A political symbol whose significance has once been established by association, may go through a psychological development of its own, apart from the history of the facts which were originally symbolized by it. This may be seen in the case of the names and emblems of nations and parties; and still more clearly in the history of those commercial entities—"teas" or "soaps"—which may be already made current by advertisement before any objects to be symbolized by them have been made or chosen. Ethical difficulties are often created by the relation between the quickly changing opinions of any individual politician and such slowly changing entities as his reputation, his party name, or the traditional personality of a newspaper which he may control.

(Chapter III.—Non-Rational Inference in Politics, page 118)

Intellectualist political thinkers often assume, not only that political action is necessarily the result of inferences as to means and ends, but that all inferences are of the same "rational" type.

It is difficult to distinguish sharply between rational and non-rational inferences in the stream of mental experience, but it is clear that many of the half-conscious processes by which men form their political opinions are non-rational. We can generally trust non-rational inferences in ordinary life, because they do not give rise to conscious opinions until they have been strengthened by a large number of undesigned coincidences. But conjurers and others who study our non-rational mental processes can so play upon them as to make us form absurd beliefs. The empirical art of politics consists largely in the creation of opinion by the deliberate exploitation of subconscious non-rational inference. The process of inference may go on beyond the point desired by the politician who started it, and is as likely to take place in the mind of a passive newspaper-reader as among the members of the most excited crowd.

(Chapter IV.—The Material of Political Reasoning, page 133)

But men can and do reason, though reasoning is only one of their mental processes. The rules for valid reasoning laid down by the Greeks were intended primarily for use in politics, but in politics reasoning has in fact proved to be more difficult and less successful than in the physical sciences. The chief cause of this is to be found in the character of its material. We have to select or create entities to reason about, just as we select or create entities to stimulate our impulses and non-rational inferences. In the physical sciences these selected entities are of two types, either concrete things made exactly alike, or abstract qualities in respect of which things otherwise unlike can be exactly compared. In politics, entities of the first type cannot be created, and political philosophers have constantly sought for some simple entity of the second type, some fact or quality, which may serve as an exact "standard" for political calculation. This search has hitherto been unsuccessful, and the analogy of the biological sciences suggests that politicians are most likely to acquire the power of valid reasoning when they, like doctors, avoid the oversimplification of their material and aim at using in their reasoning as many facts as possible about the human type, its individual variations, and its environment. Biologists have shown that large numbers of facts as to individual variations within any type can be remembered if they are arranged as continuous curves rather than as uniform rules or arbitrary exceptions. On the other hand, any attempt to arrange the facts of environment with the same approach to continuity as is possible with the facts of human nature is likely to result in error; the study of history cannot be assimilated to that of biology.

(*Chapter V.—The Method of Political Reasoning, page* 156)

The method of political reasoning has shared the traditional over-simplification of its subject-matter.

In Economics, where both method and subject-matter were originally still more completely simplified, "quantitative" methods have since Jevons's time tended to take the place of "qualitative." How far is a similar change possible in politics?

Some political questions can obviously be argued quantitatively. Others are less obviously quantitative. But even on the most complex political issues experienced and responsible statesmen do in fact think quantitatively, although the methods by which they reach their results are often unconscious.

When, however, politicians start with intellectualist assumptions, though some half-consciously acquire quantitative habits of thought, many desert politics altogether from disillusionment and disgust. What is wanted in the training of a statesman is the fully conscious formulation and acceptance of methods which will not have to be unlearned.

Such a conscious change is already taking place in the work of Royal Commissions, International Congresses, and other bodies and persons who have to arrange and draw conclusions from large masses of specially collected evidence. Their methods and vocabulary, even when not numerical, are nowadays in large part quantitative.

In parliamentary oratory, however, the old tradition of oversimplification is apt to persist.

(PART II.—Chapter I.—Political Morality, page 185)

But in what ways can such changes in political science affect the actual trend of political forces?

In the first place, the abandonment by political thinkers and writers of the intellectualist conception of politics will sooner or later influence the moral judgments of the working politician. A young candidate will begin with a new conception of his moral relation to those whose will and opinions he is attempting to influence. He will start, in that respect, from a position hitherto confined to statesmen who have been made cynical by experience.

If that were the only result of our new knowledge, political morality might be changed for the worse. But the change will go deeper. When men become conscious of psychological processes of which they have been unconscious or half-conscious, not only are they put on their guard against the exploitation of those processes in themselves by others, but they become better able to control them from within.

If, however, a conscious moral purpose is to be strong enough to overcome, as a political force, the advancing art of political exploitation, the conception of control from within must be formed into an ideal entity which, like "Science," can appeal to popular imagination, and be spread by an organized system of education. The difficulties in this are great (owing in part to our ignorance of the varied reactions of self-consciousness on instinct), but a wide extension of the idea of causation is not inconsistent with an increased intensity of moral passion.

(Chapter II.—Representative Government, page 215)

The changes now going on in our conception of the psychological basis of politics will also re-open the discussion of representative democracy.

Some of the old arguments in that discussion will no longer be accepted as valid, and it is probable that many political thinkers (especially among those who have been educated in the natural sciences) will return to Plato's proposal of a despotic government carried on by a selected and trained class, who live apart from the "ostensible world"; though English experience in India indicates that even the most carefully selected official must still live in the "ostensible world," and that the argument that good government requires the consent of the governed does not depend for its validity upon its original intellectualist associations.

Our new way of thinking about politics will, however, certainly change the form, not only of the argument for consent, but also of the institutions by which consent is expressed. An election (like a jury-trial) will be, and is already beginning to be, looked upon rather as a process by which right decisions are formed under right conditions, than as a mechanical expedient by which decisions already formed are ascertained.

Proposals for electoral reform which seem to continue the old intellectualist tradition are still brought forward, and new difficulties in the working of representative government will arise from the wider extension of political power. But that conception of representation may spread which desires both to increase the knowledge and public spirit of the voter and to provide that no strain is put upon him greater than he can bear.

(Chapter III.—Official Thought, page 255)

A quantitative examination of the political force created by popular election shows the importance of the work of non-elected officials in any effective scheme of democracy.

What should be the relation between these officials and the elected representatives? On this point English opinion already shows a marked reaction from the intellectualist conception of representative government. We accept the fact that most state officials are appointed by a system uncontrolled either by individual members of parliament or by parliament as a whole, that they hold office during good behaviour, and that they are our main source of information as to some of the most difficult points on which we form political judgments. It is largely an accident that the same system has not been introduced into our local government.

But such a half-conscious acceptance of a partially independent Civil Service as an existing fact is not enough. We must set ourselves to realize clearly what we intend our officials to do, and to consider how far our present modes of appointment, and especially our present methods of organizing official work, provide the most effective means for carrying out that intention.

(Chapter IV.—Nationality and Humanity, page 282)

What influence will the new tendencies in political thought have on the emotional and intellectual conditions of political solidarity?

In the old city-states, where the area of government corresponded to the actual range of human vision and memory, a kind of local emotion could be developed which is now impossible in a "delocalized" population. The solidarity of a modern state must therefore depend on facts not of observation but of imagination.

The makers of the existing European national states, Mazzini and Bismarck, held that the possible extent of a state depended on national homogeneity, *i.e.* on the possibility that every individual member of a state should believe that all the others were like himself. Bismarck thought that the degree of actual homogeneity which was a necessary basis for this belief could be made by "blood and iron"; Mazzini thought that mankind was already divided into homogeneous groups, whose limits should be followed in the reconstruction of Europe. Both were convinced that the emotion of political solidarity was impossible between individuals of consciously different national types.

During the last quarter of a century this conception of the

world as composed of a mosaic of homogeneous nations has been made more difficult (a) by the continued existence and even growth of separate national feelings within modern states, and (b) by the fact that the European and non-European races have entered into closer political relationships. The attempt, therefore, to transfer the traditions of national homogeneity and solidarity either to the inhabitants of a modern world-empire as a whole, or to the members of the dominant race in it, disguises the real facts and adds to the danger of war.

Can we, however, acquire a political emotion based, not upon a belief in the likeness of individual human beings, but upon the recognition of their unlikeness? Darwin's proof of the relation between individual and racial variation might have produced such an emotion, if it had not been accompanied by the conception of the "struggle for life" as a moral duty. As it is, interracial and even interimperial wars can be represented as necessary stages in the progress of the species. But present-day biologists tell us that the improvement of any one race will come most effectively from the conscious co-operation, and not from the blind conflict of individuals; and it may be found that the improvement of the whole species will also come rather from a conscious world-purpose based upon a recognition of the value of racial as well as individual variety, than from mere fighting.

INTRODUCTION

THE study of politics is just now (1908) in a curiously unsatisfactory position.

At first sight the main controversy as to the best form of government appears to have been finally settled in favour of representative democracy. Forty years ago it could still be argued that to base the sovereignty of a great modern nation upon a widely extended popular vote was, in Europe at least, an experiment which had never been successfully tried. England, indeed, by the "leap in the dark" of 1867, became for the moment the only large European State whose government was democratic and representative. But to-day a parliamentary republic based upon universal suffrage exists in France without serious opposition or protest. Italy enjoys an apparently stable constitutional monarchy. Universal suffrage has just been enacted in Austria. Even the German Emperor for an instant after the election of 1907 spoke of himself rather as the successful leader of a popular electoral campaign than as the inheritor of a divine right. The vast majority of the Russian nation passionately desires a sovereign parliament, and a reactionary Duma finds itself steadily pushed by circumstances towards that position. The most ultramontane Roman Catholics demand temporal power for the Pope, no longer as an ideal system of world government, but as an expedient for securing in a few square miles of Italian territory liberty of action for the directors of a church almost all of whose members will remain voting citizens of constitutional States.   None of the proposals for a non-representative democracy which were associated with the communist and anarchist movements of the nineteenth century have been at all widely accepted, or have presented themselves as a definite constructive scheme; and almost all those who now hope for a social change by which the results of modern scientific industry shall be more evenly distributed put their trust in the electoral activity of the working classes.

And yet, in the very nations which have most wholeheartedly accepted representative democracy, politicians and political students seem puzzled and disappointed by their experience of it.   The United States of America have made in this respect by far the longest and most continuous experiment.   Their constitution has lasted for a century and a quarter, and, in spite of controversy and even war arising from opposing interpretations of its details, its principles have been, and still are, practically unchallenged.   But as far as an English visitor can judge, no American thinks with satisfaction of the electoral "machine," whose power alike in Federal, State, and Municipal politics is still increasing.

In England not only has our experience of representative democracy been much shorter than that of America, but our political traditions have tended to delay the full acceptance of the democratic idea even in the working of democratic institutions. Yet, allowing for differences of degree and circumstance, one finds in England among the most loyal democrats, if they have been brought into close contact with the details of electoral organization, something of the same disappointment which has become more articulate in America. I have helped to fight a good many parliamentary contests, and have myself been a candidate in a series of five London municipal elections. In my last election I noticed that two of my canvassers, when talking over the day's work, used independently the phrase, "It is a queer business." I have heard much the same words used in England by those professional political agents whose efficiency depends on their seeing electoral facts without illusion. I have no first-hand knowledge of German or Italian electioneering, but when a year ago I talked with my hosts of the Paris Municipal Council, I seemed to detect in some of them indications of good-humoured disillusionment with regard to the working of a democratic electoral system.

In England and America one has, further, the feeling that it is the growing, and not the decaying, forces of society which create the most disquieting problems. In America the "machine" takes its worst form in those great new cities whose population and wealth and energy represent the goal towards which the rest of American civilization is apparently tending. In England, to any one who looks forward, the rampant bribery of the old fishing-ports, or the traditional and respectable corruption of the cathedral cities, seem comparatively small and manageable evils. The more serious grounds for apprehension come from the newest inventions of wealth and enterprise, the up-to-date newspapers, the power and skill of the men who direct huge aggregations of industrial capital, the organised political passions of working men who have passed through the standards of the elementary schools, and who live in hundreds of square miles of new, healthy, indistinguishable suburban streets. Every few years some invention in political method is made, and if it succeeds both parties adopt it. In politics, as in football, the tactics which prevail are not those which the makers of the rules intended, but those by which the players find that they can win; and men feel vaguely that the expedients by which their party is most likely to win may turn out not to be those by which a State is best governed.

More significant still is the fear, often expressed as new questions force themselves into politics, that the existing electoral system will not bear the strain of an intensified social conflict. Many of the arguments used in the discussion of the tariff question in England, or of the concentration of capital in America, or of social-democracy in Germany, imply this. Popular election, it is said, may work fairly well as long as those questions are not raised which cause the holders of wealth and industrial power to make full use of their opportunities. But if the rich people in any modern state thought it

worth their while, in order to secure a tariff, or legalise a
trust, or oppose a confiscatory tax, to subscribe a third of
their income to a political fund, no Corrupt Practices Act
yet invented would prevent them from spending it.   If
they did so, there is so much skill to be bought, and the
art of using skill for the production of emotion and
opinion has so advanced, that the whole condition of
political contests would be changed for the future.   No
existing party, unless it enormously increased its own
fund, or discovered some new source of political
strength, would have any chance of permanent success.

The appeal, however, in the name of electoral purity,
to protectionists, trust-promoters, and socialists, that they
should drop their various movements and so confine
politics to less exciting questions, falls, naturally enough,
on deaf ears.

The proposal, again, to extend the franchise to women *gndr*
is met by that sort of hesitation and evasion which is
characteristic of politicians who are not sure of their intellectual ground.   A candidate who has just been
speaking on the principles of democracy finds it, when
he is heckled, very difficult to frame an answer which
would justify the continued exclusion of women from the
franchise.   Accordingly a large majority of the successful candidates from both the main parties at the general
election of 1906 pledged themselves to support female
suffrage.   But, as I write, many, perhaps the majority,
of those who gave that pledge seem to be trying to avoid
the necessity of carrying it out.   There is no reason to

suppose that they are men of exceptionally dishonest character, and their fear of the possible effect of a final decision is apparently genuine. They are aware that certain differences exist between men and women, though they do not know what those differences are, nor in what way they are relevant to the question of the franchise. But they are even less steadfast in their doubts than in their pledges, and the question will, in the comparatively near future, probably be settled by importunity on the one side and mere drifting on the other.

race

This half conscious feeling of unsettlement on matters which in our explicit political arguments we treat as settled, is increased by the growing urgency of the problem of race. The fight for democracy in Europe and America during the eighteenth and early nineteenth centuries was carried on by men who were thinking only of the European races. But, during the extension of democracy after 1870, almost all the Great Powers were engaged in acquiring tropical dependencies, and improvements in the means of communication were bringing all the races of the world into close contact. The ordinary man now finds that the sovereign vote has (with exceptions numerically insignificant) been in fact confined to nations of European origin. But there is nothing in the form or history of the representative principle which seems to justify this, or to suggest any alternative for the vote as a basis of government. Nor can he draw any intelligible and consistent conclusion from the practice of democratic States in giving or refusing the vote to their non-European subjects. The United States, for instance, have silently and almost unanimously dropped the experiment of negro suffrage. In that case, owing to the wide intellectual gulf between the West African negro and the white man from North-West Europe, the problem was comparatively simple; but no serious attempt has yet been made at a new solution of it, and the Americans have been obviously puzzled in dealing with the more subtle racial questions created by the immigration of Chinese and Japanese and Slavs, or by the government of the mixed populations in the Philippines.

England and her colonies show a like uncertainty in the presence of the political questions raised both by the migration of non-white races and by the acquisition of tropical dependencies. Even when we discuss the political future of independent Asiatic States we are not clear whether the principle, for instance, of "no taxation without representation" should be treated as applicable to them. Our own position as an Asiatic power depends very largely on the development of China and Persia, which are inhabited by races who may claim, in some respects, to be our intellectual superiors. When they adopt our systems of engineering, mechanics, armament we have no doubt that they are doing a good thing for themselves, even though we may fear their commercial or military rivalry. But no follower of Bentham is now eager to export for general Asiatic use our latest inventions in political machinery. We hear that the Persians have established a parliament, and watch the development of their experiment with a complete suspension of judgment as to its probable result. We have helped the Japanese to preserve their independence as a constitutional nation, and most Englishmen vaguely sympathize with the desire of the Chinese progressives both for national independence and internal reform. Few of us, however, would be willing to give any definite advice to an individual Chinaman who asked whether he ought to throw himself into a movement for a representative parliament on European lines.

Africa

Within our own Empire this uncertainty as to the limitations of our political principles may at any moment produce actual disaster. In Africa, for instance, the political relationship between the European inhabitants of our territories and the non-European majority of Kaffirs, Negroes, Hindoos, Copts, or Arabs is regulated on entirely different lines in Natal, Basutoland, Egypt, or East Africa. In each case the constitutional difference is due not so much to the character of the local problem as to historical accident, and trouble may break out anywhere and at any time, either from the aggression of the Europeans upon the rights reserved by the Home Government to the non-Europeans, or from a revolt of the non-Europeans themselves. Blacks and Whites are equally irritated by the knowledge that there is one law in Nairobi and another in Durban.

India

This position is, of course, most dangerous in the case of India. For two or three generations the ordinary

English Liberal postponed any decision on Indian political problems because he believed that we were educating the inhabitants for self-government, and that in due time they would all have a vote for an Indian parliament. Now he is becoming aware that there are many races in India, and that some of the most important differences between those races among themselves, and between any of them and ourselves, are not such as can be obliterated by education. He is told by men whom he respects that this fact makes it certain that the representative system which is suitable for England will never be suitable for India, and therefore he remains uneasily responsible for the permanent autocratic government of three hundred million people, remembering from time to time that some of these people or their neighbours may have much more definite political ideas than his own, and that he ultimately may have to fight for a power which he hardly desires to retain.

Meanwhile, the existence of the Indian problem loosens half-consciously his grip upon democratic principle in matters nearer home. Newspapers and magazines and steamships are constantly making India more real to him, and the conviction of a Liberal that Polish immigrants or London "latch-key" lodgers ought to have a vote is less decided than it would have been if he had not acquiesced in the decision that Rajputs, and Bengalis, and Parsees should be refused it.

Practical politicians cannot, it is true, be expected to stop in the middle of a campaign merely because they have an uncomfortable feeling that the rules of the game require re-stating and possibly re-casting. But the winning or losing of elections does not exhaust the whole political duty of a nation, and perhaps there never has been a time in which the disinterested examination of political principles has been more urgently required. Hitherto the main stimulus to political speculation has been provided by wars and revolutions, by the fight of the Greek States against the Persians, and their disastrous struggle for supremacy among themselves, or by the wars of religion in the sixteenth and seventeenth centuries, and the American and French revolutions in the eighteenth century. The outstanding social events in Europe in our own time have, however, been so far the failures rather than the successes of great movements; the apparent wasting of devotion and courage in Russia, owing to the deep-seated intellectual divisions among the reformers and the military advantage which modern weapons and means of communication give to any government however tyrannous and corrupt; the baffling of the German social-democrats by the forces of religion and patriotism and by the infertility of their own creed; the weakness of the successive waves of American democracy when faced by the political power of capital.

But failure and bewilderment may present as stern a demand for thought as the most successful revolution, and, in many respects, that demand is now being well answered. Political experience is recorded and examined with a thoroughness hitherto unknown. The history of political action in the past, instead of being left to isolated scholars, has become the subject of organized and minutely subdivided labour. The new political developments of the present, Australian Federation, the Referendum in Switzerland, German Public Finance, the Party system in England and America, and innumerable others, are constantly recorded, discussed and compared in the monographs and technical magazines which circulate through all the universities of the globe.

The only form of study which a political thinker of one or two hundred years ago would now note as missing is any attempt to deal with politics in its relation to the nature of man. The thinkers of the past, from Plato to Bentham and Mill, had each his own view of human nature, and they made those views the basis of their speculations on government. But no modern treatise on political science, whether dealing with institutions or finance, now begins with anything corresponding to the opening words of Bentham's "Principles of Morals and Legislation"—"Nature has placed mankind under the governance of two sovereign masters, pain and pleasure"; or to the "first general proposition" of Nassau Senior's "Political Economy," "Every man desires to obtain additional wealth with as little sacrifice as possible." [1] In most cases one cannot even discover whether the writer is conscious of possessing any conception of human nature at all.

[1] *Political Economy* (in the *Encyclopedia Metropolitana*), 2nd edition (1850), p. 26.

It is easy to understand how this has come about. Political science is just beginning to regain some measure of authority after the acknowledged failure of its confident professions during the first half of the nineteenth century. Bentham's Utilitarianism, after superseding both Natural Right and the blind tradition of the lawyers, and serving as the basis of innumerable legal and constitutional reforms throughout Europe, was killed by the unanswerable refusal of the plain man to believe that ideas of pleasure and pain are the only sources of human motive. The "classical" political economy of the universities and the newspapers, the political economy of MacCulloch and Senior and Archbishop Whately, was even more unfortunate in its attempts to deduce a whole industrial polity from a "few simple principles" of human nature. It became identified with the shallow dogmatism by which well-to-do people in the first half of Queen Victoria's reign tried to convince working men that any change in the distribution of the good things of life was "scientifically impossible." Marx and Ruskin and Carlyle were masters of sarcasm, and the process is not yet forgotten by which they slowly compelled even the newspapers to abandon the "laws of political economy," which from 1815 to 1870 stood, like gigantic stuffed policemen, on guard over rent and profits.

When the struggle against "Political Economy" was at its height, Darwin's "Origin of Species" revealed a universe in which the "few simple principles" seemed a little absurd, and nothing has hitherto taken their place. Mr. Herbert Spencer, indeed, attempted to turn a single hasty generalization from the history of biological evolution into a complete social philosophy. He preached what he called "the beneficent working of the survival of the fittest" ("Man versus the State" p. 50), and Sir Henry Maine called "beneficent private war," [1] a process which they conceived of as no more dangerous than that degree of trade competition which prevailed among English provincial shopkeepers about the year 1884. Mr. Spencer failed to secure even the whole-hearted support of the newspapers; but in so far as his system gained currency it helped further to discredit any attempt to connect political science with the study of human nature.

For the moment, therefore, nearly all students of politics analyse institutions and avoid the analysis of man. The study of human nature by the psychologists has, it is true, advanced enormously since the discovery of human evolution, but it has advanced without affecting or being affected by the study of politics. Modern text-books of psychology are illustrated with innumerable facts from the home, the school, the hospital, and the psychological laboratory; but in them politics are hardly ever mentioned. The professors of the new science of sociology are beginning, it is true, to deal with human nature in its relation not only to the family and to

---

[1] "The beneficent private war which makes one man strive to climb over the shoulders of another man." (Maine, *Popular Government*, p. 50). See D. G. Ritchie, *Darwinism and Politics*, p. 4.

religion and industry, but also to certain political institutions.   Sociology, however, has had, as yet, little influence on political science.

I believe myself that this tendency to separate the study of politics from that of human nature will prove to be only a momentary phase of thought; that while it lasts its effects, both on the science and on the conduct of politics, are likely to be harmful; and that there are already signs that it is coming to an end.

It is sometimes pleaded that, if thorough work is to be done, there must, in the moral as in the physical sciences, be division of labour.   But this particular division cannot, in fact, be kept up.   The student of politics must, consciously or unconsciously, form a conception of human nature, and the less conscious he is of his conception the more likely he is to be dominated by it.   If he has had wide personal experience of political life his unconscious assumptions may be helpful; if he has not they are certain to be misleading.   Mr. Roosevelt's little book on "American Ideals" is, for instance, useful, because when he thinks about mankind in politics, he thinks about the politicians whom he has known.   After reading it one feels that many of the more systematic books on politics by American university professors are useless, just because the writers dealt with abstract men, formed on assumptions of which they were unaware and which they had never tested either by experience or by study.

In the other sciences which deal with human actions, this division between the study of the thing done and the study of the being who does it is not found. In criminology Beccaria and Bentham long ago showed how dangerous that jurisprudence was which separated the classification of crimes from the study of the criminal. The conceptions of human nature which they held have been superseded by evolutionary psychology, but modern thinkers like Lombroso have brought the new psychology into the service of a new and fruitful criminology.

In pedagogy also, Locke, and Rousseau, and Herbart, and the many-sided Bentham, based their theories of education upon their conceptions of human nature. Those conceptions were the same as those which underlay their political theories, and have been affected in the same way by modern knowledge. For a short time it even looked as if the lecturers in the English training colleges would make the same separation between the study of human institutions and human nature as has been made in politics. Lectures on School Method were distinguished during this period from those on the Theory of Education. The first became mere descriptions and comparisons of the organization and teaching in the best schools. The second consisted of expositions, with occasional comment and criticism, of such classical writers as Comenius, or Locke, or Rousseau, and were curiously like those informal talks on Aristotle, Hobbes, Locke, and Rousseau, which, under the name of the Theory of Politics, formed in my time such a pleasant interlude in the Oxford course of Humaner

Letters. But while the Oxford lecture-courses still, I believe, survive almost unchanged, the training college lectures on the Theory of Education are beginning to show signs of a change as great as that which took place in the training of medical students, when the lecturers on anatomy, instead of expounding the classical authorities, began to give, on their own responsibility, the best account of the facts of human structure of which they were capable.

The reason for this difference is, apparently, the fact that while Oxford lecturers on the Theory of Politics are not often politicians, the training college lecturers on the Theory of Teaching have always been teachers, to whom the question whether any new knowledge could be made useful in their art was one of living and urgent importance. One finds accordingly that under the leadership of men like Professors William James, Lloyd Morgan, and Stanley Hall, a progressive science of teaching is being developed, which combines the study of types of school organization and method with a determined attempt to learn from special experiments, from introspection, and from other sciences, what manner of thing a child is.

Modern pedagogy, based on modern psychology, is already influencing the schools whose teachers are trained for their profession. Its body of facts is being yearly added to; it has already caused the abandonment of much dreary waste of time; has given many thousands of teachers a new outlook on their work; and has increased the knowledge and happiness of many tens of thousands of children.

This essay of mine is offered as a plea that a corresponding change in the conditions of political science is possible. In the great university whose constituent colleges are the universities of the world, there is a steadily growing body of professors and students of politics who give the whole day to their work. I cannot but think that as years go on, more of them will call to their aid that study of mankind which is the ancient ally of the moral sciences. Within every great city there are groups of men and women who are brought together in the evenings by the desire to find something more satisfying than current political controversy. They have their own unofficial leaders and teachers, and among these one can already detect an impatience with the alternative offered, either of working by the bare comparison of existing institutions, or of discussing the fitness of socialism or individualism, of democracy or aristocracy for human beings whose nature is taken for granted.

If my book is read by any of these official or unofficial thinkers, I would urge that the study of human nature in politics, if ever it comes to be undertaken by the united and organized efforts of hundreds of learned men, may not only deepen and widen our knowledge of political institutions, but open an unworked mine of political invention.

PART I
THE CONDITIONS OF THE PROBLEM

CHAPTER I

IMPULSE AND INSTINCT
IN POLITICS

WHOEVER sets himself to base his political thinking on a re-examination of the working of human nature, must begin by trying to overcome his own tendency to exaggerate the intellectuality of mankind.

We are apt to assume that every human action is the result of an intellectual process, by which a man first thinks of some end which he desires, and then calculates the means by which that end can be attained. An investor, for instance, desires good security combined with five per cent. interest. He spends an hour in studying with an open mind the price-list of stocks, and finally infers that the purchase of Brewery Debentures will enable him most completely to realize his desire. Given the original desire for good security, his act in purchasing the Debentures appears to be the inevitable result of his inference. The desire for good security itself may further appear to be merely an intellectual inference as to the means of satisfying some more general desire, shared by all mankind, for "happiness," our own "interest," or the like. The satisfaction of this general desire can then be treated as the supreme "end" of life, from which all our acts and impulses, great and small, are derived by the same intellectual process as that by

45

which the conclusion is derived from the premises of an argument.

This way of thinking is sometimes called "common sense." A good example of its application to politics may be found in a sentence from Macaulay's celebrated attack on the Utilitarian followers of Bentham in the *Edinburgh Review* of March 1829. This extreme instance of the foundation of politics upon dogmatic psychology is, curiously enough, part of an argument intended to show that "it is utterly impossible to deduce the science of government from the principles of human nature." "What proposition," Macaulay asks, "is there respecting human nature which is absolutely and universally true? We know of only one: and that is not only true, but identical; that men always act from self-interest. . . . *When we see the actions of a man, we know with certainty what he thinks his interest to be."* [1] Macaulay believes himself to be opposing Benthamism root and branch, but is unconsciously adopting and exaggerating the assumption which Bentham shared with most of the other eighteenth and early nineteenth century philosophers—that all motives result from the idea of some preconceived end.

If he had been pressed, Macaulay would probably have admitted that there are cases in which human acts and impulses to act occur independently of any idea of an end to be gained by them. If I have a piece of grit in my eye, and ask some one to take it out with the

[1] *Edinburgh Review*, March 1829, p 185. (The italics are mine.)

corner of his handkerchief, I generally close the eye as soon as the handkerchief comes near, and always feel a strong impulse to do so.   Nobody supposes that I close my eye because, after due consideration, I think it my interest to do so.   Nor do most men choose to run away in battle, to fall in love, or to talk about the weather in order to satisfy their desire for a preconceived end.   If, indeed, a man were followed through one ordinary day, without his knowing it, by a cinematographic camera and a phonograph, and if all his acts and sayings were reproduced before him next day, he would be astonished to find how few of them were the result of a deliberate search for the means of attaining ends.   He would, of course, see that much of his activities consisted in the half-conscious repetition, under the influence of habit, of movements which were originally more fully conscious.   But even if all cases of habit were excluded he would find that only a small proportion of the residue could be explained as being directly produced by an intellectual calculation.   If a record were also kept of those of his impulses and emotions which did not result in action, it would be seen that they were of the same kind as those which did, and and that very few of them were preceded by that process which Macaulay takes for granted.

If Macaulay had been pressed still further, he would probably have admitted that even when an act is preceded by a calculation of ends and means, it is not the inevitable result of that calculation.   Even when we know what a man thinks it his interest to do, we do

not know for certain that he will do it.   The man who
studies the Stock Exchange list does not buy his Debentures, unless, apart from his intellectual inference on the
subject, he has an impulse to write to his stockbroker
sufficiently strong to overcome another impulse to put
the whole thing off till the next day.

Macaulay might even further have admitted that the
mental act of calculation itself results from, or is accompanied by, an impulse to calculate, which impulse
may have nothing to do with any anterior consideration
of means and ends, and may vary from the half-conscious yielding to a train of reverie up to the obstinate
driving of a tired brain into the difficult task of exact
thought.

The text-books of psychology now warn every student
against the "intellectualist" fallacy which is illustrated
by my quotation from Macaulay.   Impulse, it is now
agreed, has an evolutionary history of its own earlier
than the history of those intellectual processes by which
it is often directed and modified.   Our inherited organization inclines us to re-act in certain ways to certain
stimuli because such reactions have been useful in the
past in preserving our species.   Some of the reactions
are what we call specifically "instincts," that is to say,
impulses towards definite acts or series of acts, independent of any conscious anticipation of their probable effects. [1]   Those instincts are sometimes unconscious and

[1] "Instinct is usually defined as the faculty of acting in such a way as to
produce certain ends without foresight of the ends and without previous

involuntary; and sometimes, in the case of ourselves and
apparently of other higher animals, they are conscious
and voluntary. But the connection between means and
ends which they exhibit is the result not of any contrivance by the actor, but of the survival, in the past, of the
"fittest" of many varying tendencies to act. Indeed the
instinct persists when it is obviously useless, as in the
case of a dog who turns round to flatten the grass before lying down on a carpet; and even when it is known
to be dangerous, as when a man recovering from ty-
phoid hungers for solid food.

The fact that impulse is not always the result of
conscious foresight is most clearly seen in the case of
children. The first impulses of a baby to suck, or to
grasp, are obviously "instinctive." But even when the
unconscious or unremembered condition of infancy
has been succeeded by the connected consciousness of
childhood, the child will fly to his mother and hide
his face in her skirts when he sees a harmless stranger.
Later on he will torture small beasts and run away from
big beasts, or steal fruit, or climb trees, though no one
has suggested such actions to him, and though he may
expect disagreeable results from them.

We generally think of "instinct" as consisting of a
number of such separate tendencies, each towards some
distinct act or series of acts. But there is no reason to
suppose that the whole body of inherited impulse even

education in the performance"—W. James, *Principles of Psychology*,
vol. ii. p. 383.

among non-human animals has ever been divisible in that way. The evolutionary history of impulse must have been very complicated. An impulse which survived because it produced one result may have persisted with modifications because it produced another result; and side by side with impulses towards specific acts we can detect in all animals vague and generalized tendencies, often overlapping and contradictory, like curiosity and shyness, sympathy and cruelty, imitation and restless activity. It is possible, therefore, to avoid the ingenious dilemma by which Mr. Balfour argues that we must either demonstrate that the desire, e.g., for scientific truth, is lineally descended from some one of the specific instincts which teach us "to fight, to eat, and to bring up children," or must admit the supernatural authority of the Shorter Catechism.[1]

instincts modified

The prerational character of many of our impulses is, however, disguised by the fact that during the lifetime of each individual they are increasingly modified by memory and habit and thought. Even the non-human animals are able to adapt and modify their inherited impulses either by imitation or by habits founded on individual experience. When telegraph wires, for instance, were first put up many birds flew against them and were killed. But although the number of those that

---

[1] *Reflections suggested by the New Theory of Matter*, 1904, p. 21. "So far as natural science can tell us, every quality of sense or intellect which does *not* help us to fight, to eat, and to bring up children, is but a by-product of the qualities which do."

were killed was obviously insufficient to produce a change in the biological inheritance of the species, very few birds fly against the wires now. The young birds must have imitated their elders, who had learnt to avoid the wires; just as the young of many hunting animals are said to learn devices and precautions which are the result of their parents' experience, and later to make and hand down by imitation inventions of their own.

Many of the directly inherited impulses, again, appear, both in man and other animals, at a certain point in the growth of the individual, and then, if they are checked, die away, or, if they are unchecked, form habits; and impulses, which were originally strong and useful, may no longer help in preserving life, and may, like the whale's legs or our teeth and hair, be weakened by biological degeneration. Such temporary or weakened impulses are especially liable to be transferred to new objects, or to be modified by experience and thought.

With all these complicated facts the schoolmaster has to deal. In Macaulay's time he used to be guided by his "common-sense," and to intellectualize the whole process. The unfortunate boys who acted upon an ancient impulse to fidget, to play truant, to chase cats, or to mimic their teacher, were asked, with repeated threats of punishment, "why" they had done so. They, being ignorant of their own evolutionary history, were forced to invent some far-fetched lie, and were punished for that as well. The trained schoolmaster of today takes the existence of such impulses as a normal fact; and decides how far, in each case, he shall check them by relying on that half-conscious imitation which makes the greater part of class-room discipline, and how far by stimulating a conscious recognition of the connection, ethical or penal, between acts and their consequences. In any case his power of controlling instinctive impulse is due to his recognition of its non-intellectual origin. He may even be able to extends this recognition to his own impulses, and to overcome the conviction that his irritability during afternoon school in July is the result of an intellectual conclusion as to the need of special severity in dealing with a set of unprecedentedly wicked boys.

The politician, however, is still apt to intellectualize impulse as completely as the schoolmaster did fifty years ago. He has two excuses, that he deals entirely with adults, whose impulses are more deeply modified by experience and thought than those of children, and that it is very difficult for any one who thinks about politics not to confine his consideration to those political actions and impulses which are accompanied by the greatest amount of conscious thought, and which therefore come first into his mind. But the politician thinks about men in large communities, and it is in the forecasting of the action of large communities that the intellectualist fallacy is most misleading. The results of experience and thought are often confined to individuals or small groups, and when they differ may

cancel each other as political forces. The original
human impulses are, with personal variations, common
to the whole race, and increase in their importance with
an increase in the number of those influenced by them.

It may be worth while, therefore, to attempt a description of some of the more obvious or more important
political impulses, remembering always that in politics
we are dealing not with such clear-cut separate instincts
as we may find in children and animals, but with
tendencies often weakened by the course of human evolution, still more often transferred to new uses, and acting
not simply but in combination or counteraction.

Aristotle, for instance, says that it is "affection" (or
"friendship," for the meaning of φιλία stands halfway
between the two words) which "makes political union
possible," and "which law-givers consider more important than justice." It is, he says, a hereditary instinct
among animals of the same race, and particularly
among men.[1] If we look for this political affection in
its simplest form, we see it in our impulse to feel
"kindly" towards any other human being of whose
existence and personality we become vividly aware.
This impulse can be checked and overlaid by others, but
any one can test its existence and its prerationality in his
own case by going, for instance, to the British Museum

[1] *Ethics*, Bk. viii. chap. 1. Φύσει τ' ἐνυπάρχειν ἔοικε · · · οὐ μόνον
ἐν ἀνθρώποις ἀλλὰ καὶ ἐν ὄρνισι καὶ τοῖς πλείστοις τῶν ζῴων, καὶ τοῖς
ὁμοεθνέσι πρὸς ἄλληλα, καὶ μάλιστα τοῖς ἀνθρώποις . . . ἔοικε δὲ καὶ τὰς
πόλεις συνέχειν ἡ φιλία, καὶ οἱ νομοθέται μᾶλλον περὶ αὐτὴν σπουδάζειν
ἢ τὴν δικαιοσύνην

and watching the effect on his feelings of the discovery that a little Egyptian girl baby who died four thousand years ago rubbed the toes of her shoes by crawling upon the floor.

The tactics of an election consist largely of contrivances by which this immediate emotion of personal affection may be set up. The candidate is advised to "show himself" continually, to give away prizes, to "say a few words" at the end of other people's speeches—all under circumstances which offer little or no opportunity for the formation of a reasoned opinion of his merits, but many opportunities for the rise of a purely instinctive affection among those present. His portrait is periodically distributed, and is more effective if it is a good, that is to say, a distinctive, than if it is a flattering likeness. Best of all is a photograph which brings his ordinary existence sharply forward by representing him in his garden smoking a pipe or reading a newspaper.

A simple-minded supporter whose affection has been so worked up will probably try to give an intellectual explanation of it. He will say that the man, of whom he may know really nothing except that he was photographed in a Panama hat with a fox-terrier, is "the kind of man we want," and that therefore he has decided to support him; just as a child will say that he loves his mother because she is the best mother in the world,[1] or a man in love will give an elaborate explanation of his

[1] A rather unusually reflective little girl of my acquaintance, felt, one

perfectly normal feelings, which he describes as an intellectual inference from alleged abnormal excellences in his beloved. The candidate naturally intellectualizes in the same way. One of the most perfectly modest men I know once told me that he was "going round" a good deal among his future constituents "to let them see what a good fellow I am." Unless, indeed, the process can be intellectualized, it is for many men unintelligible.

A monarch is a life-long candidate, and there exists a singularly elaborate traditional art of producing personal affection for him. It is more important that he should be seen than that he should speak or act. His portrait appears on every coin and stamp, and apart from any question of personal beauty, produces most effect when it is a good likeness. Any one, for instance, who can clearly recall his own emotions during the later years of Queen Victoria's reign, will remember a measurable increase of his affection for her, when, in 1897, a thoroughly life-like portrait took the place on the coins of the conventional head of 1837-1887, and the awkward compromise of the first Jubilee year. In the case of monarchy one can also watch the intellectualization of the whole process by the newspapers, the official biographers, the courtiers, and possibly the

day, while looking at her mother, a strong impulse of affection. She first gave the usual intellectual explanation of her feeling, "Mummy, I do think you are the most beautiful Mummy in the whole world," and then, after a moment's thought, corrected herself by saying, "But there, they do say love is blind."

monarch himself.   The daily bulletion of details as to his walks and drives is, in reality, the more likely to create a vivid impression of his personality, and therefore to produce this particular kind of emotion, the more ordinary the events described are in themselves. But since an emotion arising out of ordinary events is difficult to explain on a purely intellectual basis, these events are written about as revealing a life of extraordinary regularity and industry.   When the affection is formed it is even sometimes described as an inevitable reasoned conclusion arising from reflection upon a reign during which there have been an unusual number of good harvests or great inventions.

Sometimes the impulse of affection is excited to a point at which its non-rational character becomes obvious.   George the Third was beloved by the English people because they realized intensely that, like themselves, he had been born in England, and because the published facts of his daily life came home to them. Fanny Burney describes, therefore, how when, during an attack of madness, he was to be taken in a coach to Kew, the doctors who were to accompany him were seriously afraid that the inhabitants of any village who saw that the King was under restraint would attack them.[1]   The kindred emotion of personal and dynastic loyalty (whose origin is possibly to be found in the fact

[1] *Diary of Madame D'Arblay*, ed. 1905, vol. iv, p. 184, "If they even attempted force, they had not a doubt but his smallest resistance would call up the whole country to his fancied rescue."

that the loosely organized companies of our pre-
human ancestors could not defend themselves from their
carnivorous enemies until the general instinct of
affection was specialized into a vehement impulse to
follow and protect their leader), has again and again
produced destructive and utterly useless civil wars.

Fear often accompanies and, in politics, is confused
with affection.   A man, whose life's dream it has been
to get sight and speech of his King, is accidentally
brought face to face with him.   He is "rooted to the
spot," becomes pale, and is unable to speak, because a
movement might have betrayed his ancestors to a lion
or a bear, or earlier still, to a hungry cuttlefish.   It
would be an interesting experiment if some professor of
experimental psychology would arrange his class in the
laboratory with sphygmographs on their wrists ready to
record those pulse movements which accompany the
sensation of "thrill," and would then introduce into the
room without notice, and in chance order, a bishop, a
well-known general, the greatest living man of letters,
and a minor member of the royal family.   The resulting
records of immediate pulse disturbances would be of
real scientific importance, and it might even be possible
to continue the record in each case say, for a quarter of
a minute, and to trace the secondary effects of
variations in political opinions, education, or the sense
of humour among the students.   At present almost the
only really scientific observation on the subject from
its political side is contained in Lord Palmerston's

protest against a purely intellectual account of aristocracy: "there is no damned nonsense about merit," he
said, "in the case of the Garter." Makers of new
aristocracies are still, however, apt to intellectualize.
The French government, for instance, have created an
order, "Pour le Mérite Agricole," which ought, on the
basis of mere logic, to be very successful; but one is told
that the green ribbon of that order produces in France no
thrill whatever.

laughter

The impulse to laugh is comparatively unimportant
in politics, but it affords a good instance of the way
in which a practical politician has to allow for prerational impulse. It is apparently an immediate
effect of the recognition of the incongruous, just as
trembling is of the recognition of danger. It may have
been evolved because an animal which suffered a slight
spasm in the presence of the unexpected was more likely
to be on its guard against enemies, or it may have
been the merely accidental result of some fact in our
nervous organization which was otherwise useful.
Incongruity is, however, so much a matter of habit and
association and individual variation, that it is extraordinarily difficult to forecast whether any particular act
will seem ridiculous to any particular class, or how
long the sense of incongruity will in any case
persist. Acts, for instance, which aim at producing
exalted emotional effect among ordinary slow-witted
people—Burke's dagger, Louis Napoleon's tame eagle,
the German Kaiser's telegrams about Huns and mailed

fists—may do so, and therefore be in the end politically successful, although they produce spontaneous laughter in men whose conception of good political manners is based upon the idea of self-restraint.

Again, almost the whole of the economic question between socialism and individualism turns on the nature and limitatons of the desire for property. There seem to be good grounds for supposing that this is a true specific instinct, and not merely the result of habit or of the intellectual choice of means for satisfying the desire of power. Children, for instance, quarrel furiously at a very early age over apparently worthless things, and collect and hide them long before they can have any clear notion of the advantages to be derived from individual possession. Those children who in certain charity schools are brought up entirely without personal property, even in their clothes or pocket-handkerchiefs, show every sign of the bad effect on health and character which results from complete inability to satisfy a strong inherited instinct. The evolutionary origin of the desire for property is indicated also by many of the habits of dogs or squirrels or magpies. Some economist ought therefore to give us a treatise in which this property instinct is carefully and quantitatively examined. Is it, like the hunting instinct, an impulse which dies away if it is not indulged? How far can it be eliminated or modified by education? Is it satisfied by a leasehold or a life-interest, or by such an arrangement of corporate property as is offered by a collegiate foundation or by the provision of a public park? Does it require for its satisfaction material and visible things such as land or houses, or is the holding, say, of colonial railway shares sufficient? Is the absence of unlimited proprietary rights felt more strongly in the case of personal chattels (such as furniture and ornaments) than in the case of land or machinery? Does the degree and direction of the instinct markedly differ among different individuals or races, or between the two sexes?

Pending such an inquiry my own provisional opinion is that, like a good many instincts of very early evolutionary origin, it can be satisfied by an avowed pretence; just as a kitten which is fed regularly on milk can be kept in good health if it is allowed to indulge its hunting instinct by playing with a bobbin, and a peaceful civil servant satisfies his instinct of combat and adventure at golf. If this is so, and if it is considered for other reasons undesirable to satisfy the property instinct by the possession, say, of slaves or of freehold land, one supposes that a good deal of the feeling of property may in the future be enjoyed, even by persons in whom the instinct is abnormally strong, through the collection of shells or of picture postcards.

The property instinct is, it happens, one of two instances in which the classical economists deserted their usual habit of treating all desires as the result of a calculation of the means of obtaining "utility" or "wealth." The satisfaction of the instinct of absolute property by peasant proprietorship turned, they said, "sand to gold," although it required a larger expenditure of labour for every unit of income than was the case in salaried employment. The other instance was the instinct of family affection. This also still needs a special treatise on its stimulus, variation, and limitations. But the classical economists treated it as absolute and unvarying. The "economic man," who had no more concern than a lone wolf with the rest of the human species, was treated as possessing a perfect and permanent solidarity of feeling with his "family." The family was apparently assumed as consisting of those persons for whose support a man in Western Europe is legally responsible, and no attempt was made to estimate whether the instinct extended in any degree to cousins or great-uncles.

A treatise on political impulses which aimed at completeness would further include at least the fighting instinct (with the part which it plays, together with affection and loyalty, in the formation of parties), and the instincts of suspicion, curiosity, and the desire to excel.

All these primary impulses are greatly increased in immediate effectiveness when they are "pure," that is to say, unaccompanied by competing or opposing impulses; and this is the main reason why art, which aims at producing one emotion at a time, acts on most men so much more easily than does the more varied appeal of real life. I once sat in a suburban theatre

among a number of colonial troopers who had come
over from South Africa for the King's Coronation.
The play was "Our Boys," and between the acts my
next neighbour gave me, without any sign of emotion,
a hideous account of the scene at Tweefontein after De
Wet had rushed the British camp on the Christmas
morning of 1901—the militiamen slaughtered while
drunk, and the Kaffir drivers tied to the blazing waggons.
The curtain rose again, and, five minutes later, I saw
that he was weeping in sympathy with the stage
misfortunes of two able-bodied young men who had to
eat "inferior Dorset" butter. My sympathy with the
militiamen and the Kaffirs was "pure," whereas his was
overlaid with remembered race-hatred, battle-fury, and
contempt for British incompetence. His sympathy, on
the other hand, with the stage characters was not
accompanied, as mine was, by critical feelings about
theatrical conventions, indifferent acting, and middle-
Victorian sentiment.

It is this greater immediate effect of pure and
artificial as compared with mixed and concrete emotion
which explains the traditional maxim of political
agents that it is better that a candidate should not live
in his constituency. It is an advantage that he should
be able to represent himself as a "local candidate," but
his local character should be *ad hoc*, and should consist
in the hiring of a large house each year in which he
lives a life of carefully dramatized hospitality. Things
in no way blameworthy in themselves—his choice of

tradesmen, his childrens' hats and measles, his difficulties with his relations—will be, if he is a permanent resident, "out of the picture," and may confuse the impression which he produces. If one could, by the help of a time-machine, see for a moment in the flesh the little Egyptian girl who wore out her shoes, one might find her behaving so charmingly that one's pity for her death would be increased. But it is more probable that, even if she was, in fact, a very nice little girl, one would not.

This greater immediate facility of the emotions set up by artistic presentment, as compared with those resulting from concrete observation, has, however, to be studied in its relation to another fact—that impulses vary, in their driving force and in the depth of the nervous disturbance which they cause, in proportion, not to their importance in our present life, but to the point at which they appeared in our evolutionary past. We are quite unable to resist the impulse of mere vascular and nervous reaction, the watering of the mouth, the jerk of the limb, the closing of the eye, which we share with some of the simplest vertebrates. We can only with difficulty resist the instincts of sex and food, of anger and fear, which we share with the higher animals. It is, on the other hand, difficult for us to obey consistently the impulses which attend on the mental images formed by inference and association. A man may be convinced by a long train of cogent reasoning that he will go to hell if he visits a certain house; and yet he will do so in satisfaction of a half conscious craving whose existence he is ashamed to recognize. It may be that when a preacher makes hell real to him by physical images of fire and torment his conviction will acquire coercive force. But that force may soon die away as his memory fades, and even the most vivid description has little effect as compared with a touch of actual pain. At the theatre, because pure emotion is facile, three-quarters of the audience may cry, but because second-hand emotion is shallow, very few of them will be unable to sleep when they get home, or will even lose their appetite for a late supper. My South African trooper probably recovered from his tears over "Our Boys" as soon as they were shed. The transient and pleasurable quality of the tragic emotions produced by novel reading is well known. A man may weep over a novel which he will forget in two or three hours, although the same man may be made insane, or may have his character changed for life, by actual experiences which are far less terrible than those of which he reads, experiences which at the moment may produce neither tears nor any other obvious nervous effect.

Both these facts are of first-rate political importance in those great modern communities in which all the events which stimulate political action reach the voters through newspapers. The emotional appeal of journalism, even more than that of the stage, is facile because it is pure, and transitory because it is second-hand. Battles and famines, murders and the evidence of inquiries into destitution, all are presented by the journalist in literary form, with a careful selection of 'telling' detail. Their effect is therefore produced at once, in the half-hour that follows the middle-class breakfast, or in the longer interval on the Sunday morning when the workman reads his weekly paper. But when the paper has been read the emotional effect fades rapidly away.

Any candidate at an election feels for this reason the strangeness of the conditions under which what Professor James calls the "pungent sense of effective reality," [1] reaches or fails to reach, mankind, in a civilization based upon newspapers. I was walking along the street during my last election, thinking of the actual issues involved, and comparing them with the vague fog of journalistic phrases, and the half-conscious impulses of old habit and new suspicion which make up the atmosphere of electioneering. I came round a street corner upon a boy of about fifteen returning from work, whose whole face lit up with genuine and lively interest as soon as he saw me. I stopped, and he said: "I know you, Mr. Wallas, you put the medals on me." All that day political principles and arguments had refused to become real to my constituents, but the emotion excited by the bodily fact that I had at a school ceremony pinned a medal for good

[1] "The moral tragedy of human life comes almost wholly from the fact that the link is ruptured which normally should hold between vision of the truth and action, and that this pungent sense of effective reality will not attach to certain ideas." W. James, *Principles of Psychology*, vol. ii. p. 547.

attendance on a boy's coat, had all the pungency of a first-hand experience.

Throughout the contest the candidate is made aware, at every point, of the enormously greater solidity for most men of the work-a-day world which they see for themselves, as compared with the world of inference and secondary ideas which they see through the newspapers. A London County Councillor, for instance, as his election comes near, and he begins to withdraw from the daily business of administrative committees into the cloud of the electoral campaign, finds that the officials whom he leaves behind, with their daily stint of work, and their hopes and fears about their salaries, seem to him much more real than himself.   The old woman at her door in a mean street who refuses to believe that he is not being paid for canvassing, the prosperous and good-natured tradesman who says quite simply, "I expect you find politics rather an expensive amusement," all seem to stand with their feet upon the ground.   However often he assures himself that the great realities are on his side, and that the busy people round him are concerned only with fleeting appearances, yet the feeling constantly recurs to him that it is he himself who is living in a world of shadows.

This feeling is increased by the fact that a candidate has constantly to repeat the same arguments, and to stimulate in himself the same emotions, and that mere repetition produces a distressing sense of unreality. The preachers who have to repeat every Sunday the same

gospel, find also that "dry times" alternate with times of
exaltation. Even among the voters the repetition of the
same political thoughts is apt to produce weariness. The
main cause of the recurring swing of the electoral pendulum seems to be that opinions which have been held with
enthusiasm become after a year or two stale and flat, and
that the new opinions seem fresh and vivid.

swing of electoral pendulum

A treatise is indeed required from some trained
psychologist on the conditions under which our nervous
system shows itself intolerant of repeated sensations
and emotions. The fact is obviously connected with
the purely physiological causes which produce giddiness,
tickling, sea-sickness, etc. But many things that are
"natural," that is to say, which we have constantly
experienced during any considerable part of the ages
during which our nervous organization was being
developed, apparently do not so affect us. Our heart-
beats, the taste of water, the rising and setting of the
sun, or, in the case of a child, milk, or the presence of
its mother, or of its brothers, do not seem to become, in
sound health, distressingly monotonous. But "artificial"
things, however pleasant at first—a tune on the piano,
the pattern of a garment, the greeting of an acquaintance
—are likely to become unbearable if often exactly
repeated. A newspaper is an artificial thing in this
sense, and one of the arts of the newspaper-writer
consists in presenting his views with that kind of
repetition which, like the phrases of a fugue, constantly
approaches, but never oversteps the limit of monotony.

artificiality + repetition

Advertisers again are now discovering that it pays to vary the monotony with which a poster appeals to the eye by printing in different colours those copies which are to hang near each other, or still better, by representing varied incidents in the career of "Sunny Jim" or "Sunlight Sue."

A candidate is also an artificial thing. If he lives and works in his constituency, the daily vision of an otherwise admirable business man seated in a first-class carriage on the 8.47 A. M. train in the same attitude and reading the same newspaper may produce a slight and unrecognized feeling of discomfort among his constituents, although it would cause no such feeling in the wife whose relation to him is "natural." For the same reason when his election comes on, although he may declare himself to be the "old member standing on the old platform," he should be careful to avoid monotony by slightly varying his portrait, the form of his address, and the details of his declaration of political faith.

Another fact, closely connected with our intolerance of repeated emotional adjustment, is the desire for privacy, sufficiently marked to approach the character of a specific instinct, and balanced by a corresponding and opposing dread of loneliness. Our ancestors in the ages during which our present nervous system became fixed, lived, apparently, in loosely organized family groups, associated for certain occasional purposes into larger, but still more loosely organized, tribal groups.

No one slept alone, for the more or less monogamic family assembled nightly in a cave or "lean to" shelter. The hunt for food which filled the day was carried on, one supposes, neither in complete solitude nor in constant intercourse. Even if the female were left at home with the young, the male exchanged some dozen times a day rough greetings with acquaintances, or joined in a common task. Occasionally, even before the full development of language, excited palavers attended by some hundreds would take place, or opposing tribes would gather for a fight.

It is still extremely difficult for the normal man to endure either much less or much more than this amount of intercourse with his fellows. However safe they may know themselves to be, most men find it difficult to sleep in an empty house, and would be distressed by anything beyond three days of absolute solitude. Even habit cannot do much in this respect. A man required to submit to gradually increasing periods of solitary confinement would probably go mad as soon as he had been kept for a year without a break. A settler, though he may be the son of a settler, and may have known no other way of living, can hardly endure existence unless his daily intercourse with his family is supplemented by a weekly chat with a neighbour or a stranger; and he will go long and dangerous journeys in order once a year to enjoy the noise and bustle of a crowd.

But, on the other hand, the nervous system of most men will not tolerate the frequent repetition of that

adjustment of the mind and sympathies to new acquaint-
anceship, a certain amount of which is so refreshing
and so necessary. One can therefore watch in great
modern cities men half consciously striving to preserve
the same proportion between privacy and intercourse
which prevailed among their ancestors in the woods, and
one can watch also the constant appearance of proposals
or experiments which altogether ignore the primary facts
of human nature in this respect. The habitual intellectualism of the writers of political Utopias prevents
them from seeing any "reason" why men should not find
happiness as well as economy in a sort of huge
extension of family life. The writer himself at his
moments of greatest imaginative exaltation does not
perhaps realize the need of privacy at all. His affections
are in a state of expansion which, without fancifulness,
one may refer back to the emotional atmosphere
prevalent in the screaming assemblies of his pre-human
ancestors; and he is ready, so long as this condition lasts,
to take the whole world almost literally to his bosom.
What he does not realize is that neither he nor any
one else can keep himself permanently at this level.
In William Morris's "News from Nowhere" the customs
of family life extend to the streets, and the tired student
from the British Museum talks with easy intimacy to the
thirsty dustman. I remember reading an article written
about 1850 by one of the early Christian Socialists. He
said that he had just been riding down Oxford Street in

an omnibus, and that he had noticed that when the omnibus passed over a section of the street in which macadam had been substituted for paving, all the passengers turned and spoke to each other. "Some day," he said, "all Oxford street will be macadamized, and then, because men will be able to hear each other's voices, the omnibus will become a delightful informal club." Now nearly all London is paved with wood, and people as they sit in chairs on the top of omnibuses can hear each other whispering: but no event short of a fatal accident is held to justify a passenger who speaks to his neighbour.

Clubs were established in London, not so much for the sake of the cheapness and convenience of common sitting-rooms and kitchens, as to bring together bodies of men, each of whom should meet all the rest on terms of unrestrained social intercourse. One can see in Thackeray's "Book of Snobs," and in the stories of Thackeray's own club quarrels, the difficulties produced by this plan. Nowadays clubs are successful exactly because it is an unwritten law in almost every one of them that no member must speak to any other who is not one of his own personal acquaintances. The innumerable communistic experiments of Fournier, Robert Owen, and others, all broke up essentially because of the want of privacy. The associates got on each other's nerves. In those confused pages of the "Politics," in which Aristotle criticizes from the point of view of experience the communism of Plato, the same point stands out: "It is difficult to live together in community," communistic colonists have always "disputed with each other about the most ordinary matters"; we most often disagree with those slaves who are brought into daily contact with us." [1]

The Charity Schools of 1700 to 1850 were experiments in the result of a complete refusal of scope, not only for the instinct of property, but for the entirely distinct instinct of privacy, and part of their disastrous nervous and moral effect must be put down to that. The boys in the contemporary public boarding-schools secured a little privacy by the adoption of strange and sometimes cruel social customs, and more has been done since then by systems of "studies" and "houses." Experience seems, however, to show that during childhood a day school with its alternation of home, class-room, and playing field, is better suited than a boarding-school to the facts of normal human nature.

This instinctive need of privacy is again a subject which would repay special and detailed study. It varies very greatly among different races, and one supposes that the much greater desire for privacy which is found among Northern, as compared to Southern Europeans, may be due to the fact that races who had to spend much or little of the year under cover, adjusted themselves biologically to a different standard in this respect. It is clear, also, that it is our emotional nature,

[1] *Politics*, Book II. ch. v.

and not the intellectual or muscular organs of talking, which is most easily fatigued. Light chatter, even among strangers, in which neither party "gives himself away," is very much less fatiguing than an intimacy which makes some call upon the emotions. An actor who accepts the second alternative of Diderot's paradox, and *feels* his part, is much more likely to break down from overstrain, than one who only simulates feeling and keeps his own emotional life to himself.

It is in democratic politics, however, that privacy is most neglected, most difficult, and most necessary. In America all observers are agreed as to the danger which results from looking on a politician as an abstract personification of the will of the people, to whom all citizens have an equal and inalienable right of access, and from whom every one ought to receive an equally warm and sincere welcome. In England our compara-tively aristocratic tradition as to the relation between a representative and his constituents has done something to preserve customs corresponding more closely to the actual nature of man. A tired English statesman at a big reception is still allowed to spend his time rather in chaffing with a few friends in a distant corner of the room than in shaking hands and exchanging effusive commonplaces with innumerable unknown guests. But there is a real danger lest this tradition of privacy may be abolished in English democracy, simply because of its connection with aristocratic manners. A young labour politician is expected to live in more than

American conditions of intimate publicity. Having, perhaps, just left the working bench, and having to adjust his nerves and his bodily health to the difficult requirements of mental work, he is expected to receive every caller at any hour of the day or night with the same hearty good will, and to be always ready to share or excite the enthusiasm of his followers. After a year or two, in the case of a man of sensitive organization, the task is found to be impossible. The signs of nervous fatigue are at first accepted by him and his friends as proofs of his sincerity. He begins to suffer from the curate's disease, the bright-eyed, hysterical condition in which a man talks all day long to a succession of sympathetic hearers about his own overwork, and drifts into actual ill-health, though he is not making an hour's continuous exertion in the day. I knew a young agitator in that state who thought that he could not make a propagandist speech unless the deeply admiring pitman, in whose cottage he was staying, played the Marseillaise on a harmonium before he started. Often such a man takes to drink. In any case he is liable, as the East End clergymen who try to live the same life are liable, to the most pitiable forms of moral collapse.

Such men, however, are those who being unfit for a life without privacy, do not survive. Greater political danger comes perhaps from those who are comparatively fit. Anyone who has been in America, who has stood among the crowd in a Philadelphia law-court during the trial of a political case, or has seen the thousands of cartoons in a contest in which Tammany is concerned, will find that he has a picture in his mind of one type at least of those who do survive. Powerfully built, with the big jaw and loose mouth of the dominant talker, practised by years of sitting behind saloon bars, they have learnt the way of "selling cheap that which should be most dear." But even they generally look as if they drank, and as if they would not live to old age.

Other and less dreadful types of politicians without privacy come into one's mind, the orator who night after night repeats the theatrical success of his own personality, and, like the actor, keeps his recurring fits of weary disgust to himself; the busy organizing talkative man to whom it is a mere delight to take the chair at four smoking concerts a week. But there is no one of them who would not be the better, both in health and working power, if he were compelled to retire for six months from the public view, and to produce something with his own hand and brain, or even to sit alone in his own house and think.

These facts, in so far as they represent the nervous disturbance produced by certain conditions of life in political communities, are again closely connected with the one point in the special psychology of politics which has as yet received any extensive consideration—the so-called "Psychology of the Crowd," on which the late M. Tarde, M. Le Bon, and others have written. In the case of human beings, as in the case of many other social and semi-social animals, the simpler impulses—especially those of fear and anger—when they are consciously shared by many physically associated individuals, may become enormously exalted, and may give rise to violent nervous disturbances. One may suppose that this fact, like the existence of laughter, was originally an accidental and undesirable result of the mechanism of nervous reaction, and that it persisted because when a common danger was realized (a forest fire, for instance, or an attack by beasts of prey), a general stampede, although it might be fatal to the weaker members of the herd, was the best chance of safety for the majority.

My own observation of English politics suggests that in a modern national state, this panic effect of the combination of nervous excitement with physical contact is not of great importance. London in the twentieth century is very unlike Paris in the eighteenth century, or Florence in the fourteenth, if only because it is very difficult for any considerable proportion of the citizens to be gathered under circumstances likely to produce the special "Psychology of the Crowd." I have watched two hundred thousand men assembled in Hyde Park for a Labour Demonstration. The scattered platforms, the fresh air, the wide grassy space, seemed to be an unsuitable environment for the production of purely instinctive excitement, and the attitude of such an assembly in London is good-tempered and lethargic. A crowd in a narrow street is more likely to get "out of hand," and one may see a few thousand men in a large hall reach a state approaching genuine pathological exaltation on an exciting occasion, and when they are in the hands of a practised speaker. But as they go out of the hall they drop into the cool ocean of London, and their mood is dissipated in a moment. The mob that took the Bastille would not seem or feel an overwhelming force in one of the business streets of Manchester. Yet such facts vary greatly among different races, and the exaggeration which one seems to notice when reading the French sociologists on this point may be due to their observations having been made among a Latin and not a Northern race.

So far I have dealt with the impulses illustrated by the internal politics of a modern state. But perhaps the most important section in the whole psychology of political impulse is that which is concerned not with the emotional effect of the citizens of any state upon each other, but with those racial feelings which reveal themselves in international politics. The future peace of the world largely turns on the question whether we have, as is sometimes said and often assumed, an instinctive affection for those human beings whose features and colour are like our own, combined with an instinctive hatred for those who are unlike us. On this point, pending a careful examination of the evidence by the psychologists, it is difficult to dogmatize. But I am inclined to think that those strong and apparently simple cases of racial hatred and affection which can

racial hatred as weak instincts combined

certainly be found, are not instances of a specific and universal instinct, but the result of several distinct and comparatively weak instincts combined and heightened by habit and association. I have already argued that the instinct of political affection is stimulated by the vivid realization of its object. Since therefore it is easier, at least for uneducated men, to realize the existence of beings like than of beings unlike themselves, affection for one's like would appear to have a natural basis, but one likely to be modified as our powers of realization are stimulated by education.

education

Again, since most men live, especially in childhood, among persons belonging to the same race as themselves, any markedly unusual face or dress may excite the instinct of fear of that which is unknown. A child's fear, however, of a strangely shaped or coloured face is more easily obliterated by familiarity than it would be if it were the result of a specific instinct of race-hatred. White or Chinese children show, one is told, no permanent aversion for Chinese or white or Hindoo or negro nurses and attendants. Sex love, again, even when opposed by social tradition, springs up freely between very different human types; and widely separated races have been thereby amalgamated. Between some of the non-human species (horses and camels, for instance) instinctive mutual hatred, as distinguished from fear, does seem to exist, but nowhere, as far as I know, is it found between varieties so nearly related to each other and so readily interbreeding as the various human races.

Anglo-Indian officials sometimes explain, as a case of specific instinct, the fact that a man who goes out with an enthusiastic interest in the native races often finds himself, after a few years, unwillingly yielding to a hatred of the Hindoo racial type. But the account which they give of their sensations seems to me more like the nervous disgust which I described as arising from a constantly repeated mental and emotional adjustment to inharmonious surroundings. At the age when an English official reaches India most of his emotional habits are already set, and he makes, as a rule, no systematic attempt to modify them. Therefore, just as the unfamiliarity of French cookery or German beds, which at the beginning of a continental visit is a delightful change, may become after a month or two an intolerable *gêne,* so the servility and untruthfulness, and even the patience and cleverness of those natives with whom he is brought into official contact, get after a few years on the nerves of an Anglo-Indian. Intimate and uninterrupted contact during a long period, after his social habits have been formed, with people of his own race but of a different social tradition would produce the same effect.

Perhaps, however, intellectual association is a larger factor than instinct in the causation of racial affection and hatred. An American working man associates, for instance, the Far Eastern physical type with that lowering of the standard wage which overshadows as a dreadful possibility every trade in the industrial world.

Fifty years ago the middle class readers to whom *Punch* appeals associated the same type with stories of tortured missionaries and envoys.   After the battle of the Sea of Japan they associated it with that kind of heroism which, owing to our geographical positiion, we most admire; and drawings of the unmistakably Asiatic features of Admiral Togo, which would have excited genuine and apparently instinctive disgust in 1859, produced a thrill of affection in 1906.

But at this point we approach that discussion of the objects, sensible or imaginary, of political impulse (as distinguished from the impulses themselves), which must be reserved for my next chapter.

CHAPTER II

POLITICAL ENTITIES

MAN's impulses and thoughts and acts result from the *nature meets environment* relation between his nature and the environment into which he is born. The last chapter approached that relation (in so far as it affects politics) from the side of man's nature. This chapter will approach the same relation from the side of man's political environment.

The two lines of approach have this important difference, that the nature with which man is born is looked on by the politician as fixed, while the environ- *politician's view of nature + environ.* ment into which man is born is rapidly and indefinitely changing. It is not to changes in our nature, but to changes in our environment only—using the word to include the traditions and expedients which we acquire after birth as well as our material surroundings—that all our political development from the tribal organization of the Stone Ages to the modern nation has apparently been due.

The biologist looks on human nature itself as chang- *biologist's view of nature + environ.* ing, but to him the period of a few thousands or tens of thousands of years which constitute the past of politics is quite insignificant. Important changes in biological types may perhaps have occurred in the his-

81

tory of the world during comparatively short periods, but they must have resulted either from a sudden biological "sport" or from a process of selection fiercer and more discriminating than we believe to have taken place in the immediate past of our own species. The present descendants of those races which are pictured in early Egyptian tombs show no perceptible change in their bodily appearance, and there is no reason to believe that the mental faculties and tendencies with which they are born have changed to any greater degree.

The numerical proportions of different races in the world have, indeed, altered during that period, as one race proved weaker in war or less able to resist disease than another; and races have been mingled by marriage following upon conquest. But if a baby could now be exchanged at birth with one born of the same breeding-stock even a hundred thousand years ago, one may suppose that neither the ancient nor the modern mother would notice any startling difference. The child from the Stone Age would perhaps suffer more seriously than our children if he caught measles, or might show somewhat keener instincts in quarrelling and hunting, or as he grew up be rather more conscious than his fellows of the "will to live" and "the joy of life." Conversely, a transplanted twentieth-century child would resist infectious disease better than the other children in the Stone Age, and might, as he grew up, be found to have a rather exceptionally colourless and adaptable character. But there apparently the difference would end.

In essentials the type of each human stock may be supposed to have remained unchanged throughout the
the whole period.   In the politics of the distant future
that science of eugenics which aims at rapidly improving our type by consciously directed selective breeding
may become a dominant factor, but it has had little
influence on the politics of the present or the past.

Those new facts in our environment which have produced the enormous political changes which separate
us from our ancestors have been partly new habits of
thought and feeling, and partly new entities about which
we can think and feel.

It is of these new political entities that this chapter
will treat.   They must have first reached us through
our senses, and in this case almost entirely through
the senses of seeing and hearing.   But man, like other
animals, lives in an unending stream of sense impressions, of innumerable sights and sounds and feelings,
and is only stirred to deed or thought by those which
he recognizes as significant to him.   How then did the
new impressions separate themselves from the rest and
become sufficiently significant to produce political
results?

The first requisite in anything which is to stimulate
us toward impulse or action is that it should be recognizable—that it should be like itself when we met it
before, or like something else which we have met before.
If the world consisted of things which constantly and
arbitrarily varied their appearance, if nothing was ever

like anything else, or like itself for more than a moment at a time, living beings as at present constituted would not act at all. They would drift like seaweed among the waves.

The new-born chicken cowers beneath the shadow of the hawk, because one hawk is like another. Animals wake at sunrise, because one sunrise is like another; and find nuts or grass for food, because each nut and blade of grass is like the rest.

But the recognition of likeness is not in itself a sufficient stimulus to action. The thing recognized must also be *significant,* must be felt in some way to matter to us. The stars re-appear nightly in the heavens, but, as far as we can tell, no animals but men are stimulated to action by recognizing them. The moth is not stimulated by recognizing a tortoise, nor the cow by a cobweb.

Sometimes this significance is automatically indicated to us by nature. The growl of a wild beast, the sight of blood, the cry of a child in distress, stand out, without need of experience or teaching, from the stream of human sensations, just as, to a hungry fox-club, the movement or glimpse of a rabbit among the undergrowth separates itself at once from the sounds of the wind and the colours of the leaves and flowers. Sometimes the significance of a sensation has to be learned by the individual animal during its own life, as when a dog, who recognizes the significance of a rat by instinct, learns to recognize that of a whip (provided

it looks like the whip which he saw and felt before)
by experience and association.

In politics man has to make like things as well as
to learn their significance. Political tactics would
indeed be a much simpler matter if ballot-papers were
a natural product, and if on beholding a ballot-paper
at about the age of twenty-one a youth who had never
heard of one before were invariably seized with a desire
to vote.

The whole ritual of social and political organization
among savages, therefore, illustrates the process of
creating artificial and easily recognizable political like-
nesses. If the chief is to be recognized as a chief he
must, like the ghost of Patroclus, "be exceedingly like
unto himself." He must live in the same house, wear
the same clothes, and do the same things year by year;
and his successor must imitate him. If a marriage or
an act of sale is to be recognized as a contract, it must
be carried out in the customary place and with the customary gestures. In some few cases the things thus artificially brought into existence and made recognizable
still produces its impulsive effect by acting on those biologically inherited associations which enable man and
other animals to interpret sensations without experience.
The scarlet paint and wolfskin headdress of a warrior,
or the dragon-mask of a medicine man, appeal, like the
smile of a modern candidate, directly to our instinctive
nature. But even in very early societies the recognition
of artificial political entities must generally have owed

its power of stimulating impulse to associations acquired during life. A child who had been beaten by the herald's rod, or had seen his father bow down before the king or a sacred stone, learned to fear the rod, or the king, or the stone by association.

Recognition often attaches itself to certain special points (whether naturally developed or artificially made) in the thing recognized. Such points then become symbols of the thing as a whole. The evolutionary facts of mimicry in the lower animals show that to some flesh-eating insects a putrid smell is a sufficiently convincing symbol of carrion to induce them to lay their eggs in a flower, and that the black and yellow bands of the wasp if imitated by a fly are a sufficient symbol to keep off birds.[1] In early political society most recognition is guided by such symbols. One cannot make a new king, who may be a boy, in all respects like his predecessor, who may have been an old man. But one can tattoo both of them with the same pattern. It is even more easy and less painful to attach a symbol to a king which is not a part of the man himself, a royal staff for instance, which may be decorated and enlarged until it is useless as a staff, but unmistakable as a symbol. The king is then recognized as king because he is the "staff-bearer" (σκηπτοῦχος βασιλεύς). Such a staff is very like a name, and there may, perhaps, have been

Symbols

[1] _Cf._ William James, _Principles of Psychology_, vol. ii. p. 392:--"The whole story of our dealings with the lower wild animals is the history of our taking advantage of the ways in which they judge of everything by its mere label, as it were, so as to ensnare or kill them."

an early Mexican system of sign-writing in which a
model of a staff stood for a king.

At this point it is already difficult not to intellectualize the whole process. Our "common-sense"
and the systematized common-sense of the eighteenth-
century philosophers would alike explain the fear of tribal man for a royal staff by saying that he was reminded
thereby of the original social contact between ruler
and ruled, or of the pleasure and pain which experience
had shown to be derived from royal leadership and royal
punishment, and that he therefore decided by a process
of reasoning on seeing the staff to fear the king.

When the symbol by which our impulse is stimulated is actual language, it is still more difficult not
to confuse acquired emotional association with the full
process of logical inference.   Because one of the effects
of those sounds and signs which we call language is
to stimulate in us a process of deliberate logical thought
we tend to ignore all their other effects.   Nothing is
easier than to make a description of the logical use of
language, the breaking up by abstraction of a bundle
of sensations—one's memory, for instance, of a royal
person; the selection of a single quality—kingship, for
instance—shared by other such bundles of sensations,
the giving to that quality the name king, and the use of
the name to enable us to repeat the process of abstraction.   When we are consciously trying to reason correctly by the use of language all this does occur, just
as it would occur if we had not evolved the use of voice-

language at all, and were attempting to construct a valid logic of colours and models and pictures. But any text-book of psychology will explain why it errs, both by excess and defect, if taken as a description of that which actually happens when language is used for the purpose of stimulating us to action.

Indeed the "brass-instrument psychologists," who do such admirable work in their laboratories, have invented an experiment on the effect of significant words which every one may try for himself. Let him get a friend to write in large letters on cards a series of common political terms, nations, parties, principles, and so on. Let him then sit before a watch recording tenths of seconds, turn up the cards, and practise observation of the associations which successively enter his consciousness. The first associations revealed will be automatic and obviously "illogical." If the word be "England" the white and black marks on the paper will, if the experimenter is a "visualizer," produce at once a picture of some kind accompanied by a vague and half conscious emotional reaction of affection, perhaps, or anxiety, or the remembrance of puzzled thought. If the experimenter is "audile," the marks will first call up a vivid sound image with which a like emotional reaction may be associated. I am a "visualizer," and the picture in my case was a blurred triangular outline. Other "visualizers" have described to me the picture of a red flag, or of a green field (seen from a railway carriage), as automatically called up by the word Eng-

land. After the automatic picture or sound image and
its purely automatic emotional accompaniment comes
the "meaning" of the word, the things one knows about
England, which are presented to the memory by a process semi-automatic at first, but requiring before it is
exhausted a severe effort. The question as to what
images and feelings shall appear at each stage is, of
course, settled by all the thoughts and events of our
past life, but they appear, in the earlier moments at
least of the experiment, before we have time consciously to reflect or choose.

A corresponding process may be set up by other
symbols besides language. If in the experiment the
hats belonging to members of a family be substituted
for the written cards, the rest of the process will go
on—the automatic "image," automatically accompanied
by emotional association, being succeeded in the course
of a second or so by the voluntary realization of "meaning," and finally by a deliberate effort of recollection
and thought. Tennyson, partly because he was a born
poet, and partly perhaps because his excessive use of
tobacco put his brain occasionally a little out of focus,
was extraordinarily accurate in his account of those
separate mental states which for most men are merged
into one by memory. A song, for instance, in the "Prin-
cess," describes the succession which I have been discussing:—

> 'Thy voice is heard through rolling drums,
>   That beat to battle where he stands.

Thy face across his fancy comes,
　　And gives the battle to his hands:
A moment, while the trumpets blow,
　　He sees his brood about thy knee;
The next, like fire he meets the foe,
　　And strikes him dead for thine and thee.'

"Thine and thee" at the end seem to me to express precisely the change from the automatic images of "voice" and "face" to the reflective mood in which the full meaning of that for which he fights is realized.

But it is the "face" that "gives the battle to his hands." Here again, as we saw when comparing impulses themselves, it is the evolutionarily earlier, more automatic, fact that has the greater, and the later intellectual fact which has the less impulsive power. Even as one sits in one's chair one can feel that that is so.

Still more clearly can one feel it if one thinks of the phenomena of religion. The only religion of any importance which has ever been consciously constructed by a psychologist is the Positivism of Auguste Comte. In order to produce a sufficiently powerful stimulus to ensure moral action among the distractions and temptations of daily life, he required each of his disciples to make for himself a visual image of Humanity. The disciple was to practise mental contemplation, for a definite period each morning, of the remembered figure of some known and loved woman—his mother, or wife, or sister. He was to keep the figure always in the same attitude and dress, so that it should always present itself automatically as a definite mental image in immediate association with the word Humanité.[1] With that would be automatically associated the original impulse of affection for the person imaged. As soon as possible after that would come the meaning of the word, and the fuller but less cogent emotional associations connected with that meaning. This invention was partly borrowed from certain forms of mental discipline in the Roman Catholic Church, and partly suggested by Comte's own experiences of the effect on him of the image of Madame de Vaux. One of the reasons that it has not come into greater use may have been that men in general are not quite such good "visualizers" as Comte found himself to be.

Cardinal Newman, in an illuminating passage of his *Apologia*, explains how he made for himself images of personified nations, and hints that behind his belief in the real existence of such images was his sense of the convenience of creating them. He says that he identified the "character and the instinct" of "states and governments" and of those "religious communities," from which he suffered so much, with spirits "partially fallen, capricious, wayward; noble or crafty, benevolent or malicious, as the case might be. . . . My preference of the Personal to the Abstract would naturally lead me to this view. I thought it countenanced by the men-

[1] *The Catechism of Positive Religion* (Tr. by Congreve), First Part, "Explanation of the Worship," *e.g.* p. 65: "The Positivist shuts his eyes during his private prayers, the better to see the internal image."

tion of the 'Prince of Persia' in the prophet Daniel:
and I think I considered that it was of such intermediate
beings that the Apocalypse spoke, when it introduced
'the angels of the seven churches.'

"In 1837 . . . I said . . . 'Take England with many
high virtues and yet a low Catholicism.   It seems to me
that John Bull is a spirit neither of Heaven nor Hell.' " [1]

Harnack, in the same way, when describing the causes
of the expansion of Christianity, lays stress on the use
of the word "church" and the "possibilities of personification which it offered. [2]   This use may have owed its
origin to a deliberate intellectual effort of abstraction
applied by some Christian philosopher to the common
qualities of all Christian congregations, though it more
likely resulted from a half conscious process of adaptation in the employment of a current term.   But when it
was established the word owed its tremendous power
over most men to the emotions automatically stimulated
by the personification, and not to those which would
follow on a full analysis of the meaning.   Religious
history affords innumerable such instances.   The "truth
embodied in a tale" has more emotional power than the
unembodied truth, and the visual realization of the central figure of the tale more power than the tale itself.
The sound-image of a sacred name at which "every knee
shall bow," or even of one which may be formed in the
mind but may not be uttered by the lips, has more

[1] Newman, *Apologia* (1864), pp. 91, 92.
[2] Harnack, *Expansion of Christianity* (Tr.), vol. ii. p. 11.

power at the moment of intensest feeling than the realization of its meaning.   Things of the sense—the sacred food which one can taste, the Virgin of Kevlaar
whom one can see and touch, are apt to be more real than
their heavenly anti-types.

If we turn to politics for instances of the same fact,
we again discover how much harder it is there than in
religion, or morals, or education, to resist the habit of
giving intellectual explanations of emotional experiences.   For most men the central political entity is their
country.   When a man dies for his country, what does
he die for?   The reader in his chair thinks of the size
and climate, the history and population, of some region
in the atlas, and explains the action of the patriot by
his relation to all these things.   But what seems to happen in the crisis of battle is not the logical building up
or analyzing of the idea of one's country, but that automatic selection by the mind of some thing of sense
accompanied by an equally automatic emotion of affection which I have already described.   Throughout his
life the conscript has lived in a stream of sensations, the
printed pages of the geography book, the sight of streets
and fields and faces, the sound of voices or of birds or
rivers, all of which go to make up the infinity of facts
from which he might abstract an idea of his country.
What comes to him in the final charge?   Perhaps the
row of pollard elms behind his birth-place.   More likely
some personification of his country, some expedient of
custom or imagination for enabling an entity which one

can love to stand out from the unrealized welter of experience. If he is an Italian it may be the name, the musical syllables, of Italia. If he is a Frenchman, it may be the marble figure of France with her broken sword, as he saw it in the market-square of his native town, or the maddening pulse of the "Marseillaise." Romans have died for a bronze eagle on a wreathed staff, Englishmen for a flag, Scotchmen for the sound of the pipes.

Once in a thousand years a man may stand in a funeral crowd after the fighting is over, and his heart may stir within him as he hears Pericles abstract from the million qualities of individual Athenians in the present and the past just those that make the meaning of Athens to the world. But afterwards all that he will remember may be the cadence of Pericles' voice, the movement of his hand, or the sobbing of some mother of the dead.

In the evolution of politics, among the most important events have been the successive creations of new moral entities—of such ideals as justice, freedom, right. In their origin that process of conscious logical abstraction, which we are tempted to accept as the explanation of all mental phenomena, must have corresponded in great part to the historical fact. We have, for instance, contemporary accounts of the conversations in which Socrates compared and analysed the unwilling answers of jurymen and statesmen, and we know that the word Justice was made by his work an infinitely more effec-

tive political term. It is certain too that for many
centuries before Socrates the slow adaptation of the same
word by common use was from time to time quickened
by some forgotten wise man who brought to bear upon
it the intolerable effort of conscious thought. But as
soon as, at each stage, the work was done, and Justice,
like a rock statue on which successive generations of
artists have toiled, stood out in compelling beauty, she
was seen not as an abstraction but as a direct revelation.
It is true that this revelation made the older symbols
mean and dead, but that which overcame them seemed
a real and visible thing, not a difficult process of comparison and analysis. Antigone in the play defied in
the name of Justice the command which the sceptre-bear-
ing king had sent through the sacred person of his herald. But Justice to her was a goddess, "housemate of
the nether gods"—and the sons of those Athenian citizens who applauded the Antigone condemned Socrates
to death because his dialectic turned the gods back into
abstractions.

The great Jewish prophets owed much of their spirit-
ual supremacy to the fact that they were able to present
a moral idea with intense emotional force without stif-
fening it into a personification; but that was because
they saw it always in relation to the most personal of all
gods. Amos wrote, "I hate, I despise your feasts, and I
will not smell the savour of your assemblies. . . . Take
thou away from me the noise of thy songs; for I will
not hear the melody of thy viols. But let judgment roll

down as waters, and righteousness as an ever-flowing stream." [1]   Here "judgment" and "righteousness" are not goddesses; but the voice which Amos heard was not the voice of an abstraction.

Sometimes a new moral or political entity is created rather by immediate insight than by the slow process of deliberate analysis.   Some seer of genius perceives in a flash the essential likeness of things hitherto kept apart in men's mind—the impulse which leads to anger with one's brother, and that which leads to murder, the charity of the widow's mite and of the rich man's gold, the intemperance of the debauchee and of the party leader.   But when the master dies the vision too often dies with him.   Plato's "ideas" became the formulæ of a system of magic, and the command of Jesus that one should give all that one had to the poor handed over one-third of the land of Europe to be the untaxed property of wealthy ecclesiastics.

It is this last relation between words and things which makes the central difficulty of thought about politics.   The words are so rigid, so easily personified, so associated with affection and prejudice; the things symbolized by the words are so unstable.   The moralist or the teacher deals, as a Greek would say, for the most part, with "natural," the politician always with "conventional" species.   If one forgets the meaning of motherhood or childhood, Nature has yet made for us unmistakable mothers and children who reappear, true

[1] Amos, ch. v., vs. 21, 23, 24 (R. V. M.) .

to type, in each generation. The chemist can make
sure whether he is using a word in precisely the same
sense as his predecessor by a few minutes' work in his
laboratory. But in politics the thing named is always
changing, may indeed disappear and may require hundreds of years to restore. Aristotle defined the word
"polity" to mean a state where "the citizens as a body
govern in accordance with the general good." [1]   As he
wrote, self-government in those States from which he
abstracted the idea was already withering beneath the
power of Macedonia.   Soon there were no such States at
all, and, now that we are struggling back to Aristotle's
conception, the name which he defined is borne by the
"police" of Odessa.   It is no mere accident of philology
that makes "Justices' Justice" a paradox.   From the
time that the Roman jurisconsults resumed the work of
the Greek philosophers, and by laborious question and
answer built up the conception of "natural justice," it,
like all other political conceptions, was exposed to the
two dangers.   On the one hand, since the original effort
of abstraction was in its completeness incommunicable,
each generation of users of the word subtly changed its
use.   On the other hand, the actions and institutions
of mankind, from which the conception was abstracted,
were as subtly changing.   Even although the manu-
scripts of the Roman lawyers survived, Roman law and
Roman institutions had both ceased to be.   When the
phrases of Justinian were used by a Merovingian king or

[1] *Politics*, Bk. III. ch. vii.

a Spanish Inquisitor, not only was the meaning of the words changed, but the facts to which the words could have applied in their old sense were gone.   Yet the emotional power of the bare words remained.   The civil law and canon law of the Middle Ages were able to enforce all kinds of abuses because the tradition of reverence still attached itself to the sound of "Rome."   For hundreds of years, one among the German princes was made somewhat more powerful than his neighbours by the fact that he was "Roman Emperor," and was called by the name of Caesar.

The same difficulties and uncertainties as those which influence the history of a political entity when once formed confront the statesman who is engaged in making a new one.   The great men, Stein, Bismarck, Cavour, or Metternich, who throughout the nineteenth century worked at the reconstruction of the Europe which Napoleon's conquests shattered, had to build up new States which men should respect and love, whose governments they should willingly obey, and for whose continued existence they should be prepared to die in battle.   Races and languages and religions were intermingled throughout central Europe, and the historical memories of the kingdoms and dukedoms and bishoprics into which the map was divided were confused and unexciting.   Nothing was easier than to produce and distribute new flags and coins and national names. But the emotional effect of such things depends upon associations which require time to produce, and which may have to contend against associations already existing. The boy in Lombardy or Galicia saw the soldiers and the schoolmaster salute the Austrian flag, but the real thrill came when he heard his father or mother whisper the name of Italy or Poland. Perhaps, as in the case of Hanover, the old associations and the new are for many years almost equally balanced.

In such times men fall back from the immediate emotional association of the national name and search for its meaning. They ask what *is* the Austrian or the German Empire. As long as there was only one Pope men handed on unexamined the old reverence from father to son. When for forty years there had been two Popes, at Rome and at Avignon, men began to ask what constituted a Pope. And in such times some men go further still. They may ask not only what is the meaning of the word Austrian Empire, or Pope, but what in the nature of things is the ultimate reason why the Austrian Empire or the Papacy should exist.

The work therefore of nation-building must be carried forward on each plane. The national name and flag and anthem and coinage all have their entirely non-logical effect based on habitual association. Meanwhile the statesmen strive to create as much meaning as possible for such symbols. If all the subjects of a State serve in one army and speak, or understand, one language, or even use a black-letter alphabet which has been abandoned elsewhere, the national name will mean more to them. The Saxon or the Savoyard will have a fuller answer to give himself when he asks "What does it mean, that I am a German or a Frenchman?" A single successful war waged in common will create not only a common history, but a common inheritance of passionate feeling. "Nationalists," meanwhile, may be striving, by songs and pictures and appeals to the past, to revive and intensify the emotional associations connected with older national areas—and behind all this will go on the deliberate philosophical discussion of the advantages to be derived from large or small, racial or regional States, which will reach the statesman at second-hand and the citizen at third-hand. As a result, Italy, Belgium, and the German Empire succeed in establishing themselves as States resting upon a sufficient basis of patriotism, and Austria-Hungary may, when the time of stress comes, be found to have failed.

But if the task of State building in Europe during the nineteenth century was difficult, still more difficult is the task before the English statesman of the twentieth century of creating an imperial patriotism. We have not even a name, with any emotional associations, for the United Kingdom itself. No Englishman is stirred by the name "British," the name "English" irritates all Scotchmen, and the Irish are irritated by both alike. Our national anthem is a peculiarly flat and uninspiring specimen of eighteenth-century opera libretto and opera music. The little naked St. George on the gold coins, or the armorial pattern on the silver coins never inspired any one. The new copper coinage bears, it is true, a graceful figure of Miss Hicks Beach. But we have made it so small and ladylike that it has none of the emotional force of the glorious portrait heads of France or Switzerland.

The only personification of his nation which the artisan of Oldham or Middlesbrough can recognize is the picture of John Bull as a fat, brutal, early nineteenth-century Midland farmer. One of our national symbols alone, the "Union Jack," though it is as destitute of beauty as a patchwork quilt, is fairly satisfactory. But all its associations so far are with naval warfare.

When we go outside the United Kingdom we are in still worse case. "The United Kingdom of Great Britain and Ireland together with its Colonies and Dependencies" has no shorter or more inspiring name. Throughout the Colonial Conference of 1907 statesman and leader writers tried every expedient of periphrasis and allusion to avoid hurting any one's feelings even by using such a term as "British Empire." To the *Sydney Bulletin*, and to the caricaturists of Europe, the fact that any territory on the map of the world is coloured red still recalls nothing but the little greedy eyes, huge mouth, and gorilla hands of "John Bull."

If, again, the young Boer or Hindoo or ex-American Canadian asks himself what is the meaning of membership ("citizenship," as applied to five-sixths of the inhabitants of the Empire, would be misleading) of the Empire, he finds it extraordinarily difficult to give an answer. When he goes deeper and asks for what purpose the Empire exists, he is apt to be told that the inhabitants of Great Britain conquered half the world in a fit of absence of mind and have not yet had time to think out an *ex post facto* justification for so doing. The only product of memory or reflection that can stir in him the emotion of patriotism is the statement that so far the tradition of the Empire has been to encourage and trust to political freedom. But political freedom, even in its noblest form, is a negative quality, and the word is apt to bear different meanings in Bengal and Rhodesia and Australia.

States, however, constitute only one among many types of political entities. As soon as any body of men have been grouped under a common political name, that name may acquire emotional associations as well as an intellectually analysable meaning. For the convenience, for instance, of local government the suburbs of Birmingham are divided into separate boroughs. Partly because these boroughs occupy the site of ancient villages, partly because football teams of Scotch professionals are named after them, partly because human emotions must have something to attach themselves to, they are said to be developing a fierce local patriotism, and West Bromwich is said to hate Aston as the Blues hated the Greens in the Byzantine theatre. In London, largely under the influence of the Birmingham instance, twenty-nine new boroughs were created in 1899, with names—at least in the case of the City of Westminster—deliberately selected in order to revive half-forgotten emotional associations. However in spite of Mr. Chesterton's prophecy in "The Napoleon of Notting Hill," very few Londoners have learnt to think primarily as citizens of their boroughs. Town Halls are built which they never see, coats of arms are invented which they would not recognize; and their boroughs are mere electoral wards in which they vote for a list of unknown names grouped under the general title adopted by their political party.

The party is, in fact, the most effective political entity in the modern national State. It has come into existence with the appearance of representative government on a large scale; its development has been unhampered by legal or constitutional traditions, and it represents the most vigorous attempt which has been made to adapt the form of our political institutions to the actual facts of human nature. In a modern State there may be ten million or more voters. Every one of them has equal right to come forward as a candidate and to urge either as candidate or agitator the particular views which he may hold on any possible political question. But to each citizen, living as he does in the infinite stream of things, only a few of his million fellow-citizens could exist as separate objects of political thought or feeling, even if each one of them held only one opinion on one subject without change during his life. Something is required simpler and more permanent, something which can be loved and trusted, and which can be recognized at successive elections as being the same thing that

was loved and trusted before; and a party is such a
thing.

The origin of any particular party may be due to a
deliberate intellectual process.   It may be formed, as
Burke said, by "a body of men united for promoting by
their joint endeavours the national interest upon some
particular principle in which they are all agreed."[1]

But when a party has once come into existence its
fortunes depend upon facts of human nature of
which deliberate thought is only one.   It is primarily a
name, which, like other names, calls up when it is heard
or seen an "image" that shades imperceptibly into the
voluntary realization of its meannig.   As in other cases,
emotional reactions can be set up by the name and its
automatic mental associations.   It is the business of
the party managers to secure that these automatic
associations shall be as clear as possible, shall be shared
by as large a number as possible, and shall call up as
many and as strong emotions as possible.   For this
purpose nothing is more generally useful than the party
colour.   Our distant ancestors must have been able to
recognize colour before they recognized language, and
the simple and stronger emotions more easily attach
themselves to a colour than to a word.   The poor boy
who died the other day with the ribbon of the Sheffield
Wednesday Football Club on his pillow loved the colour
itself with a direct and intimate affection.

A party tune is equally automatic in its action, and,

[1] *Thoughts on the Present Discontents* (Macmillan, 1902), p. 81.

in the case of people with a musical "ear," even more *music* effective than a party colour as an object of emotion. As long as the Marseillaise, which is now the national tune of France, was the party tune of the revolution its influence was enormous. Even now, outside of France, it is a very valuable party asset. It was a wise suggestion which an experienced political organizer made in the *Westminster Gazette* at the time of Gladstone's death, that part of the money collected in his honour should be spent in paying for the composition of the best possible marching tune, which should be identified for all time with the Liberal Party.[1] One of the few mistakes made by the very able men who organised Mr. Chamberlain's Tariff Reform Campaign was their failure to secure even a tolerably good tune.

Only less automatic than those of colour or tune *names* are the emotional associations called up by the first and simplest meaning of the word or words used for the party name. A Greek father called his baby "Very Glorious" or "Good in Council," and the makers of parties in the same way chose names whose primary meanings possess established emotional associations. From the beginning of the existence and activity of a party new associations are, however, being created which tend to take the place, in association, of the original meaning of the name. No one in America when he uses the terms Republican or Democrat thinks of their dictionary meaning. Any one, indeed, who did so

[1] *Westminster Gazette*, June 11, 1898.

would have acquired a mental habit as useless and as annoying as the habit of reading Greek history with a perpetual recognition of the original meanings of names like Aristobulus and Theocritus. Long and precise names which make definite assertions as to party policy are therefore soon shortened into meaningless syllables with new associations derived from the actual history of the party. The Constitutional Democrats in Russia become Cadets, and the Independent Labour Party becomes the I.L.P. On the other hand, the less conscious emotional associations which are automatically excited by less precise political names may last much longer. The German National Liberals were valuable allies for Bismarck during a whole generation because their name vaguely suggested a combination of patriotism and freedom. When the mine-owners in the Transvaal decided some years ago to form a political party they chose, probably after considerable discussion, the name of "Progressive." It was an excellent choice. In South Africa the original associations of the word were apparently soon superseded, but elsewhere it long suggested that Sir Percy Fitzpatrick and his party had the same sort of democratic sympathies as Mr. M'Kinnon Wood and his followers on the London County Council. No one speaking to an audience whose critical and logical faculties were fully aroused would indeed contend that because a certain body of people had chosen to call themselves Progressives, therefore a vote against them was necessarily a vote against progress. But in the dim and shadowy region of emotional association a good name, if its associations are sufficiently subconscious, has a real political value.

Conversely, the opponents of a party attempt to label it with a name that will excite feelings of opposition. The old party terms of Whig and Tory are striking instances of such names given by opponents and lasting perhaps half a century before they lost their original abusive associations. More modern attempts have been less successful, because they have been more precise. "Jingo" had some of the vague suggestiveness of an effectively bad name, but "Separatist," "Little Englander," "Food Taxer," remain as assertions to be consciously accepted or rejected.

The whole relation between party entities and political impulse can perhaps be best illustrated from the art of advertisement. In advertisement the intellectual process can be watched apart from its ethical implications, and advertisement and party politics are becoming more and more closely assimilated in method. The political poster is placed side by side with the trade or theatrical poster on the hoardings, it is drawn by the same artist, and follows the same empirical rules of art. Let us suppose, therefore, that a financier thinks that there is an opening for a large advertising campaign in connection, say, with the tea trade. The actual tealeaves in the world are as varied and unstable as the actual political opinions of mankind. Every leaf in every tea-garden is different from every other leaf, and

a week of damp weather may change the whole stock
in any warehouse. What therefore should the advertiser do to create a commercial "entity," a "tea" which
men can think and feel about? A hundred years ago he
would have made a number of optimistic and detailed
statements with regard to his opportunities and methods
of trade. He would have printed in the newspapers a
statement that "William Jones, assisted by a staff of
experienced buyers, will attend the tea-sales of the East
India Company, and will lay in parcels from the best
Chinese Gardens, which he will retail to his customers
at a profit of not more than five per centum." This, however, is an open appeal to the critical intellect, and by
the critical intellect it would now be judged. We should
not consider Mr. Jones to be an unbiassed witness as to
the excellence of his choice, or think that he would have
sufficient motive to adhere to his pledge about his rate
of profit if he thought he could get more.

Nowadays, therfore, such an advertiser would practise on our automatic and sub-conscious associations.
He would choose some term, say "Parramatta Tea,"
which would produce in most men a vague suggestion
of the tropical East, combined with the sub-conscious
memory of a geography lesson on Australia. He would
then proceed to create in connection with the word an
automatic picture-image having previous emotional
associations of its own. By the time that a hundred thousand pounds had been cleverly spent, no one
in England would be able to see the word "Parramatta"

on a parcel without a vague impulse to buy, founded on
a day-dream recollection of his grandmother, or of the
British fleet, or of a pretty young English matron, or
of any other subject that the advertiser had chosen for
its associations with the emotions of trust or affection.
When music plays a larger part in English public
education it may be possible to use it effectively for
advertisement, and a "Parramatta Motif" would in that
case appear in all the pantomimes, in connection, say,
with a song about the Soldier's Return, and would be
squeaked by a gramophone in every grocer's shop.

This instance has the immense advantage, as an aid
to clearness of thought, that up to this point no Parramatta Tea exists, and no one has even settled what
sort of tea shall be provided under that name.   Parramatta tea is still a commercial entity pure and simple.
It may later on be decided to sell very poor tea at a
large profit until the original associations of the name
have been gradually superseded by the association of
disappointment.   Or it may be decided to experiment
by selling different teas under that name in different
places, and to push the sale of the flavour which "takes
on."   But there are other attractive names of teas on the
hoardings, with associations of babies, and bull-dogs,
and the Tower of London.   If it is desired to develop
a permanent trade in competition with these it will probably be found wisest to supply tea of a fairly uniform
quality, and with a distinctive flavour which may act
as its "meaning."   The great difficulty will then come

when there is a change of public taste, and when the sales fall off because the chosen flavour no longer pleases. The directors may think it safest to go on selling the old flavour to a diminishing number of customers, or they may gradually substitute another flavour, taking the risk that the number of housewives who say, "This is not the real Parramatta Tea," may be balanced by the number of those who say, "Parramatta Tea has improved." If people will not buy the old flavour at all, and prefer to buy the new flavour under a new name, the Parramatta Tea Company must be content to disappear, like a religion which has made an unsuccessful attempt to put new wine into old bottles.

All these conditions are as familiar to the party politician as they are to the advertiser. The party candidate is, at his first appearance, to most of his constituents merely a packet with the name of Liberal or Conservative upon it. That name has associations of colour and music, of traditional habit and affection, which, when once formed, exist independently of the party policy. Unless he bears the party label—unless he is, as the Americans say, a "regular" candidate—not only will those habits and affections be cut off from him, but he will find it extraordinarily difficult to present himself as a tangible entity to the electors at all. A proportion of the electors, varying greatly at different times and at different places, will vote for the "regular" nominee of their party without reference to his program, though to the rest of them, and always to the nominating committee, he must also present a program which can be identified with the party policy. But, in any case, as long as he is a party candidate, he must remember that it is in that character that he speaks and acts. *party candidates* The party prepossessions and party expectations of his constituents alone make it possible for them to think and feel with him. When he speaks there is between him and his audience the party mask, larger and less mobile than his own face, like the mask which enabled actors to be seen and heard in the vast open-air theatres of Greece. If he can no longer act the part with sincerity he must either leave the stage or present himself in the mask of another party.

Party leaders, again, have always to remember that the organization which they control is an entity with an existence in the memory and emotions of the electors, independent of their own opinions and actions. This does not mean that party leaders cannot be sincere. As individuals they can indeed only preserve their political life by being in constant readiness to lose it. Sometimes they must even risk the existence of their party itself. When Sir Robert Peel was converted to Free Trade in 1845, he had to decide whether he and his friends should shatter the Tory Party by leaving it, or should so transform its policy that it might not be recognized, even in the half conscious logic of habit and association, as that entity for which men had voted and worked four years before. In either case Peel was doing something other and more serious than the expression of his individual opinion on a question of the moment. And yet, if, recognizing this, he had gone on advocating corn duties for the sake of his party, his whole personal force as a politician, and therefore even his party value, would have been lost.

If a celestial intelligence were now to look down from heaven on to earth with the power of observing every fact about all human beings at once, he might ask, as the newspaper editors are asking as I write, what that Socialism is which influences so many lives? He might answer himself with a definition which could be clumsily translated as "a movement towards greater social equality, depending for its force upon three main factors, the growing political power of the working classes, the growing social sympathy of many members of all classes, and the belief, based on the growing authority of scientific method, that social arrangements can be transformed by means of conscious and deliberate contrivance." He would see men trying to forward this movement by proposals as to taxation, wages, and regulative or collective administration; some of which proposals would prove to be successfully adapted to the facts of human existence, and some would in the end be abandoned, either because no nation could be persuaded to try them, or because when tried they failed. But he would also see that this definition of a many-sided and ever-varying movement drawn by abstraction from innumerable socialistic proposals and desires is not a description of "Socialism" as it exists for the greater number of its supporters. The need of something which one may love and for which one may work has created for thousands of working men a personified "Socialism," a winged goddess with stern eyes and drawn sword, to be the hope of the world and the protector of those that suffer. The need of some engine of thought which one may use with absolute faith and certainty has also created another Socialism, not a personification, but a final and authoritative creed. Such a creed appeared in England in 1884, and William Morris took it down in his beautiful handwriting from Mr. Hyndman's lectures. It was the revelation which made a little dimly educated working man say to me three years later, with tears of genuine humility in his eyes, "How strange it is that this glorious truth has been hidden from all the clever and learned men of the world and shown to me."

Meanwhile Socialism is always a word, a symbol used in common speech and writing. A hundred years hence it may have gone the way of its predecessors—Leveller, Saint-Simonism, Communism, Chartism—and may survive only in histories of a movement which has since undergone other transformation and borne other names. It may, on the other hand, remain, as Republic has remained in France, to be the title on coins and public buildings of a movement which, after many disappointments and disillusionments, has succeeded in establishing itself as a government.

But the use of a word in common speech is only the resultant of its use by individual men and women, and particularly by those who accept it as a party name. Each one of them, as long as the movement is really alive, will find that while the word must be used, because otherwise the movement will have no political existence, yet its use creates a constant series of difficult problems in conduct. Any one who applies the name to himself or others in a sense so markedly different from common use as to make it certain or probable that he is creating a false impression is rightly charged with want of ordinary veracity. And yet there are cases where enormous practical results may depend upon keeping wide the use of a word which is tending to be narrowed. The "Modernist" Roman Catholic who has studied the history of religion uses the term "Catholic Church" to mean a society which has gone through various intellectual stages in the past, and which depends for its vitality upon the existence of reasonable freedom of change in the future. He therefore, calls himself a Catholic. To the Pope and his advisers, on the other hand, the Church is an unchanging miracle based on an unchanging revelation. Father Tyrrell, when he says that he "believes" in the Catholic Church, though he obviously disbelieves in the actual occurrence of most of the facts which constitute the original revelation, seems to them to be simply a liar, who is stealing their name for his own fraudulent purposes. They can no more understand him than can the Ultramontanes among the German Social-Democrats understand Bernstein and his Modernist allies.   Bernstein himself, on the other hand, has to choose whether he ought to try to keep open the common use of the name Socialist, or whether in the end he will have to abandon it, because his claim to use it merely creates bad feeling and confusion of thought.

Sometimes a man of exceptional personal force and power of expression is, so to speak, a party—a political entity—in himself.   He may fashion a permanent and recognizable mask for himself as "Honest John" or "The Grand Old Man."   But this can as a rule only be done by those who learn the main condition of their task, the fact that if an individual statesman's intellectual career is to exist for the mass of the present public at all, it must be based either on an obstinate adherence to unchanging opinions or on a development, slow, simple, and consistent.   The indifferent and half-attentive mind which most men turn towards politics is like a very slow photograph plate.   He who wishes to be clearly photographed must stand before it in the same attitude for a long time.   A bird that flies across the plate leaves no mark.

"Change of opinion," wrote Gladstone in 1868, "in those to whose judgment the public looks more or less to assist its own, is an evil to the country, although a much smaller evil than their persistence in a course which they know to be wrong.   It is not always to be blamed. But it is always to be watched with vigillance; always to be challenged and put upon its trial." [1] Most statesmen avoid this choice between the loss of force resulting from a public change of opinion, and the loss of character resulting from the public persistence in an opinion privately abandoned, not only by considering carefully every change in their own conclusions, but by a delay, which often seems cowardly and absurd, in the public expression of their thoughts upon all questions except those which are ripe for immediate action. The written or reported word remains, and becomes part of that entity outside himself which the stateman is always building or destroying or transforming.

newspapers

The same conditions affect other political entities besides parties and statemen. If a newspaper is to live as a political force it must impress itself on men's minds as holding day by day to a consistent view. The writers, not only from editorial discipline, but from the instinctive desire to be understood, write in the character of their paper's personality. If it is sold to a proprietor holding or wishing to advocate different opinions, it must either frankly proclaim itself as a new thing or must make it appear by slow and solemn argumentative steps that the new attitude is a necessary development of the old. It is therefore rightly felt that a capitalist who buys a paper for the sake of using its old influence to strengthen a new movement is doing something to be

[1] *Gleanings*, vol. vii. p. 100, quoted in Morley's *Life*, vol. i. p. 211.

judged by other moral standards than those which apply to the purchase of so much printing-machinery and paper. He may be destroying something which has been a stable and intelligible entity for thousands of plain people living in an otherwise unintelligible world, and which has collected round it affection and trust as real as was ever inspired by an orator or a monarch.

CHAPTER III

NON-RATIONAL INFERENCE
IN POLITICS

THE assumption—which is so closely interwoven with our habits of political and economic thought—that men always act on a reasoned opinion as to their interests, may be divided into two separate assumptions: first, that men always act on some kind of inference as to the best means of reaching a preconceived end, and secondly, that all inferences are of the same kind, and are produced by a uniform process of "reasoning."

In the two preceding chapters I dealt with the first assumption, and attempted to show that it is important for a politician to realize that men do not always act on inferences as to means and ends. I argued that men often act in politics under the immediate stimulus of affection and instinct, and that affection and instinct may be directed towards political entities which are very different from those facts in the world around us which we can discover by deliberate observation and analysis.

In this chapter I propose to consider the second assumption, and to inquire how far it is true that men, when they do form inferences as to the result of their political actions, always form them by a process of reasoning.

In such an inquiry one meets the preliminary difficulty that it is very hard to arrive at a clear definition of reasoning. Any one who watches the working of his own mind will find that it is by no means easy to trace these sharp distinctions between various mental states, which seem so obvious when they are set out in little books on psychology. The mind of man is like a harp, all of whose strings throb together; so that emotion, impulse, inference, and the special kind of inference called reasoning, are often simultaneous and intermingled aspects of a single mental experience.

This is especially true in moments of action and excitement; but when we are sitting in passive contemplation we would often find it hard to say whether our successive states of consciousness are best described as emotions or inferences. And when our thought clearly belongs to the type of inference it is often hard to say whether its steps are controlled by so definite a purpose of discovering truth that we are entitled to call it reasoning.

Even when we think with effort and with a definite purpose, we do not always draw inferences or form beliefs of any kind. If we forget a name we say the alphabet over to ourselves, and pause at each letter to see if the name we want will be suggested to us. When we receive bad news we strive to realize it by allowing successive mental associations to arise of themselves, and waiting to discover what the news will mean for us. A poet broods with intense creative effort on the images which appear in his mind, and arranges them, not in order to discover truth, but in order to attain an artistic and dramatic end.   In Prospero's great speech in "The Tempest" the connection between the successive images —the baseless fabric of this vision—the cloud-capped towers—the gorgeous palaces—the solemn temples— the great globe itself—is, for instance, one not of infer- ence but of reverie, heightened by creative effort, and subordinated to poetic intention.

Most of the actual inferences which we draw during any day belong, indeed, to a much humbler type of thought than do some of the higher forms of non- inferential association.   Many of our inferences, like the quasi-instinctive impulses which they accompany and modify, take place when we are making no con- scious effort at all.   In such a purely instinctive action as leaping backwards from a falling stone, the impulse to leap and the inference that there is danger, are simply two names for a single automatic and uncon- scious process.   We can speak of instinctive inference as well as of instinctive impulse; we draw, for instance, by an instinctive mental process, inferences as to the distance and solidity of objects from the movements of our eye-muscles in focussing, and from the difference between the images on our two retinas.   We are unaware of the method by which we arrive at these inferences, and even when we know that the double photograph in the stereoscope is flat, or that the conjurer has placed two converging sheets of looking-glass beneath his table, we can only say that the photograph "looks" solid, or that we "seem" to see right under the table.

The whole process of inference, rational or non-rational, is indeed built up from the primary fact that one mental state may call up another, either because the two have been associated together in the history of the individual, or because a connection between the two has proved useful in the history of the race. If a man and his dog stroll together down the street they turn to the right hand or the left, hesitate or hurry in crossing the road, recognize and act upon the bicycle bell and the cabman's shout, by using the same process of inference to guide the same group of impulses. Their inferences are for the most part effortless, though sometimes they will both be seen to pause until they have settled some point by wordless deliberation. It is only when a decision has to be taken affecting the more distant purposes of his life that the man enters on a region of definitely rational thought where the dog cannot follow him, in which he uses words, and is more or less conscious of his own logical methods.

But the weakness of inference by automatic association as an instrument of thought consists in the fact that either of a pair of associated ideas may call up the other without reference to their logical connection. The effect calls up the cause as freely as the cause calls up the effect. A patient under a hypnotic trance is wonderfully rapid and fertile in drawing inferences, but he hunts the scent backward as easily as he does forward. Put a dagger in his hand and he believes that he has committed a murder. The sight of an empty plate convinces him that he has had dinner. If left to himself he will probably go through routine actions well enough. But any one who understands his condition can make him act absurdly.

In the same way when we dream we draw absurd inferences by association. The feeling of discomfort due to slight indigestion produces a belief that we are about to speak to a large audience and have mislaid our notes, or are walking along the Brighton Parade in a night-shirt. Even when men are awake, those parts of their mind to which for the moment they are not giving full attention are apt to draw equally unfounded inferences. A conjurer who succeeds in keeping the attention of his audience concentrated on the observation of what he is doing with his right hand can make them draw irrational conclusions from the movements of his left hand. People in a state of strong religious emotion sometimes become conscious of a throbbing sound in their ears, due to the increased force of their circulation. An organist, by opening the thirty-two foot pipe, can create the same sensation, and can thereby induce in the congregation a vague and half-conscious belief that they are experiencing religious emotion.

The political importance of all this consists in the fact that most of the political opinions of most men are the result, not of reasoning tested by experience, but of unconscious or half-conscious inference fixed by habit.

It is indeed mainly in the formation of tracks of thought that habit shows its power in politics. In our other activities habit is largely a matter of muscular adaptation, but the bodily movements of politics occur so seldom that nothing like a habit can be set up by them. One may see a respectable voter, whose political opinions have been smoothed and polished by the mental habits of thirty years, fumbling over the act of marking and folding his ballot paper like a child with its first copybook.

Some men even seem to reverence most those of their opinions whose origin has least to do with deliberate reasoning. When Mr. Barrie's Bowie Haggart said: "I am of opeenion that the works of Burns is of an immoral tendency. I have not read them myself, but such is my opeenion," [1] he was comparing the merely rational conclusion which might have resulted from a reading of Burns's works with the conviction about them which he found ready-made in his mind, and which was the more sacred to him and more intimately his own, because he did not know how it was produced.

Opinion thus unconsciously formed is a fairly safe guide in the affairs of our daily life. The material world does not often go out of its way to deceive us, and our final convictions are the resultant of many hundreds of independent fleeting inferences, of which the valid are more numerous and more likely to survive than the fallacious. But even in our personal affairs

[1] *Auld Licht Idylls*, p. 220.

our memory is apt to fade, and we can often remember
the association between two ideas, while forgetting the
cause which created that association.   We discover in
our mind a vague impression that Simpson is a drunk-
ard, and cannot recollect whether we ever had any reason to believe it, or whether some one once told us that
Simpson had a cousin who invented a cure for drunkenness.   When the connection is remembered in a telling phrase, and when its origin has never been consciously noticed, we may find ourselves with a really
vivid belief for which we could, if cross-examined, give
no account whatever.   When, for instance, we have
heard an early-Victorian bishop called "Soapy Sam"
half a dozen times we get a firm conviction of his
character without further evidence.

Under ordinary circumstances not much harm is
done by this fact; because a name would not be likely
to "catch on" unless a good many people really thought
it appropriate, and unless it "caught on" we should not
be likely to hear it more than once or twice. But in
politics, as in the conjuring trade, it is often worth while
for some people to take a great deal of trouble in order
to produce such an effect without waiting for the idea to
enforce itself by merely accidental repetition.   I have
already said that political parties try to give each other
bad names by an organized system of mental suggestion.
If the word "Wastrel," for instance, appears on the contents bills of the *Daily Mail* one morning as a name for
the Progressives during a County Council election, a

passenger riding on an omnibus from Putney to the Bank will see it half-consciously at least a hundred times, and will have formed a fairly stable mental association by the end of the journey. If he reflected, he would know that only one person has once decided to use the word, but he does not reflect, and the effect on him is the same as if a hundred persons had used it independently of each other. The contents-bills, indeed, of the newspapers, which were originally short and pithy merely from consideration of space, have developed in a way which threatens to turn our streets (like the advertisement pages of an American magazine) into a psychological laboratory for the unconscious production of permanent associations. "Another German Insult," "Keir Hardie's Crime," "Balfour Backs Down," are intended to stick and do stick in the mind as ready-made opinions.

In all this again the same rule holds as in the production of impulse. Things that are nearer sense, nearer to our more ancient evolutionary past, produce a readier inference as well as a more compelling impulse. When a new candidate on his first appearance smiles at his constituents exactly as if he were an old friend, not only does he appeal, as I said in an earlier chapter, to an ancient and immediate instinct of human affection, but he produces at the same time a shadowy belief that he is an old friend; and his agent may even imply this, provided that he says nothing definite enough to arouse critical and rational attention. By the end of the meeting one can safely go as far as to call for three cheers for "good old Jones."[1]

Mr. G. K. Chesterton some years ago quoted from a magazine article on American elections a sentence which said: "A little sound common-sense often goes further with an audience of American working men than much high-flown argument. A speaker who, as he brought forward his points, hammered nails into a board, won hundreds of votes for his side at the last Presidential election." [1] The "sound common-sense" consisted, not, as Mr. Chesterton pretended to believe, in the presentation of the hammering as a logical argument, but in the orator's knowledge of the way in which force is given to non-logical inference and his willingness to use that knowledge.

When a vivid association has been once formed it sinks into the mass of our mental experience, and may then undergo developments and transformations with which deliberate ratiocination had very little to do. I have been told that when an English agitation against the importation of Chinese contract labour into South Africa was proposed, an important personage said that

[1] Three-quarters of the art of the trained salesman depends upon his empirical knowledge of this group of psychological facts. A small girl of my acquaintance, explaining why she had brought back from her first independent shopping expedition a photograph frame which she herself found to be distressing, said: "The shopman seemed to suppose I had chosen it, and so I paid for it and came away." But her explanation was the result of memory and reflection. At the moment, in a shadowy way which was sufficient for the shopman, she supposed that she had chosen it.

[1] *Heretics*, p. 122.

"there was not a vote in it." But the agitation was set on foot, and was based on a rational argument that the conditions enacted by the Ordinance amounted to a rather cruel kind of slavery imposed upon unusually intelligent Asiatics. Any one, however, who saw much of politics in the winter of 1905–6 must have noticed that the pictures of Chinamen on the hoardings aroused among very many of the voters an immediate hatred of the Mongolian racial type. This hatred was transferred to the Conservative party, and towards the end of the general election of 1906 a picture of a China-man thrown suddenly on a lantern screen before a working-class audience would have aroused an instan-taneous howl of indignation against Mr. Balfour.

After the election, however, the memory of the Chinese faces on the posters tended slowly to identify itself, in the minds of the Conservatives, with the Liberals who had used them. I had at the general election worked in a constituency in which many such posters were displayed by my side, and where we were beaten. A year later I stood for the London County Council in the same constituency. An hour before the close of the poll I saw, with the unnatural clearness of polling-day fatigue, a large white face at the window of the ward committee-room, while a hoarse voice roared: "Where's your bloody pigtail? We cut it off last time: and now we'll put it round your bloody neck and strangle you."

In February 1907, during the County Council election, there appeared on the London hoardings thousands of posters which were intended to create a belief that the Progressive members on the Council made their personal livelihood by defrauding the rate-payers. If a statement had been published to that effect it would have been an appeal to the critical intellect, and could have been met by argument, or in the law courts. But the appeal was made to the process of sub-conscious inference. The poster consisted of a picture of a man supposed to represent the Progressive Party, pointing a foreshortened finger, and saying, with sufficient ambiguity to escape the law of libel: "It's your money we want." Its effectiveness depended on its exploitation of the fact that most men judge of the truth of a charge of fraud by a series of rapid and unconscious inferences from the appearance of the man accused. The person represented was, if judged by the shape of his hat, the fashion of his watch-chain and ring, the neglected condition of his teeth, and the redness of his nose, obviously a professional sharper. He was, I believe, drawn by an American artist, and his face and clothes had a vaguely American appearance, which, in the region of sub-conscious association, further suggested to most onlookers the idea of Tammany Hall. This poster was brilliantly successful, but, now that the election is over, it, like the Chinese pictures, seems likely to continue a career of irrational transference. One notices that one Progressive evening paper uses a reduced copy of it whenever it wishes to imply that the Moderates are influenced by improper pecuniary motives. I myself find that it tends to associate itself in my mind with the energetic politician who induced the railway companies and others to pay for it, and who, for all I know, may in his own personal appearance recall the best traditions of the English gentleman.

Writers on the "psychology of the crowd" have pointed out the effect of excitement and numbers in substituting non-rational for rational inference. Any cause, however, which prevents a man from giving full attention to his mental processes may produce the phenomena of non-rational inference in an extreme degree. I have often watched in some small sub-committee the method by which either of the two men with a real genius for committee work whom I know could control his colleagues. The process was most successful towards the end of an afternoon, when the members were tired, and somewhat dazed with the effort of following a rapid talker through a mass of unfamiliar detail. If at that point the operator slightly quickened the flow of his information, and slightly emphasized the assumption that he was being thoroughly understood, he could put some at least of his colleagues into a sort of walking trance, in which they would have cheerfully assented to the proposition that the best means of securing, *e.g.*, the permanence of private schools was a large and immediate increase in the number of public schools.

It is sometimes argued that such non-rational inferences are merely the loose fringe of our political thinking, and that responsible decisions in politics, whether they are right or wrong, are always the result of conscious ratiocination.   American political writers, for instance, of the traditional intellectualist type are sometimes faced with the fact that the delegates to national party conventions, when they select candidates and adopt programs for Presidential elections, are not in a condition in which they are likely to examine the logical validity of their own mental processes.   Such writers fall back on the reflection that the actual choice of President is decided not by excited conventions, but by voters coming straight from the untroubled sanctuary of the American home.

President Garfield illustrated this point of view in an often-quoted passage of his speech to the Republican Convention of 1880:—

"I have seen the sea lashed into fury and tossed into spray, and its grandeur moves the soul of the dullest man.   But I remember that it is not the billows, but the calm level of the sea from which all heights and depths are measured. . . .   Not here, in this brilliant circle where fifteen thousand men and women are gathered, is the destiny of the Republic to be decreed for the next four years . . . but by four millions of Republican firesides, where the thoughtful voters, with wives and children about them, with the calm thoughts inspired by love of home and country, with the history of the past, the hopes of the future, and knowledge of the great men who have adorned and blessed our nation in days gone by. There God prepares the verdict that shall determine the wisdom of our work tonight." [1]

But the divine oracle, whether in America or in England, turns out, too often, only to be a tired house-holder, reading the headlines and personal paragraphs of his party newspaper, and half-consciously forming mental habits of mean suspicion or national arrogance. Sometimes, indeed, during an election, one feels that it is, after all, in big meetings, where big thoughts can be given with all their emotioned force, that the deeper things of politics have the best chance of recognition.

The voter as he reads his newspaper may adopt by suggestion, and make habitual by repetition, not only political opinions but whole trains of political argument; and he does not necessarily feel the need of comparing them with other trains of argument already in his mind. A lawyer or a doctor will on quite general principles argue for the most extreme trade-unionism in his own profession, while he thoroughly agrees with a denunciation of trade-unionism addressed to him as a railway shareholder or ratepayer. The same audience can sometimes be led by way of "parental rights" to cheer for denominational religious instruction, and by way of "religious freedom" to hoot it. The most skilled political observer that I know, speaking of an organised newspaper attack, said, "As far as I can make out every argument used in attack and in defense has its separate

[1] *Life of J. A. Garfield*, by R. H. Conwell, p. 328.

and independent effect.   They hardly ever meet, even if they are brought to bear upon the same mind." From the purely tactical point of view there is therefore much to be said for Lord Lyndhurst's maxim, "Never defend yourself before a popular assemblage except with and by retorting the attack; the hearers, in the pleasure which the assault gives them, will forget the previous charge." [1]

[1] Morley's *Life of Gladstone*, vol. i. p. 122.

CHAPTER IV

THE MATERIAL OF POLITICAL
REASONING

BUT man is fortunately not wholly dependent in his political thinking upon those forms of inference by immediate association which come so easily to him, and which he shares with the higher brutes. The whole progress of human civilization beyond its earliest stages has been made possible by the invention of methods of thought which enable us to interpret and forecast the working of nature more successfully than we could if we merely followed the line of least resistance in the use of our minds.

These methods, however, when applied in politics, still represent a difficult and uncertain art rather than a science producing its effects with mechanical accuracy.

When the great thinkers of Greece laid down rules for valid reasoning, they had, it is true, the needs of politics specially in their minds. After the prisoners in Plato's cave of illusion should be unbound by true philosophy it was to the service of the State that they were to devote themselves, and their first triumph was to be the control of passion by reason in the sphere of government. Yet if Plato could visit us now, he would learn that while our glass-makers proceed by rigorous and confident processes to exact results, our statesmen, like the glass-makers of ancient Athens, still trust to empirical maxims and personal skill.   Why is it, he would ask us, that valid reasoning has proved to be so much more difficult in politics than in the physical sciences?

Our first answer might be found in the character of the material with which political reasoning has to deal. The universe which presents itself to our reason is the same as that which presents itself to our feelings and impulses—an unending stream of sensations and memories, every one of which is different from every other, and before which, unless we can select and recognize and simplify, we must stand helpless and unable either to act or think.   Man has therefore to create entities that shall be the material of his reasoning, just as he creates entities to be the object of his emotions and the stimulus of his instinctive inferences.

Exact reasoning requires exact comparison, and in the desert or the forest there were few things which our ancestors could compare exactly.   The heavenly bodies seem, indeed, to have been the first objects of consciously exact reasoning, because they were so distant that nothing could be known of them except position and movement, and their position and movement could be exactly compared from night to night.

In the same way the foundation of the terrestrial sciences came from two discoveries, first, that it was possible to abstract single qualities, such as position and movement, in all things however unlike, from the other qualities of those things and to compare

them exactly; and secondly, that it was possible
artificially to create actual uniformities for the purpose
of comparison, to make, that is to say, out of unlike
things, things so like that valid inferences could ·be
drawn as to their behaviour under like circumstances.
Geometry, for instance, came into the service of man
when it was consciously realized that all units of land
and water were exactly alike in so far as they were
extended surfaces. Metallurgy, on the other hand,
only became a science when men could actually take
two pieces of copper ore, unlike in shape and appearance and chemical constitution, and extract from them
two pieces of copper so nearly alike that they would
give the same results when treated in the same way.

This second power over his material the student of
politics can never possess. He can never create an
artificial uniformity in man. He cannot, after twenty
generations of education or breeding render even two
human beings sufficiently like each other for him to
prophesy with any approach to certainty that they will
behave alike under like circumstances.

How far has he the first power? How far can he
abstract from the facts of man's state qualities in respect
of which men are sufficiently comparable to allow of
valid political reasoning?

On April 5th, 1788, a year before the taking of the
Bastille, John Adams, then American Ambassador to
England, and afterwards President of the United States,
wrote to a friend describing the "fermentation upon the

subject of government" throughout Europe. "Is Government a science or not?" he describes men as asking. "Are there any principles on which it is founded? What are its ends? If indeed there is no rule, no standard, all must be accident and chance. If there is a standard, what is it?" [1]

Again and again in the history of political thought men have believed themselves to have found this "standard," this fact about man which should bear the same relation to politics which the fact that all things can be weighed bears to physics, and the fact that all things can be measured bears to geometry.

Some of the greatest thinkers of the past have looked for it in the final causes of man's existence. Every man differed, it is true, from every other man, but these differences all seemed related to a type of perfect manhood which, though few men approached, and none attained it, all were capable of conceiving. May not, asked Plato, this type be the pattern—the "idea"—of man formed by God and laid up "in a heavenly place"? If so, men would have attained to a valid science of politics when by careful reasoning and deep contemplation they had come to know that pattern. Henceforward all the fleeting and varying things of sense would be seen in their due relation to the eternal and immutable purposes of God.

Or the relation of man to God's purpose was thought of not as that between the pattern and the copy, but

[1] *Memoir of T. Brand Hollis*, by J. Disney, p. 32.

as that between the mind of a legislator as expressed in enacted law, and the individual instance to which the law is applied. We can, thought Locke, by reflecting on the moral facts of the world, learn God's law. That law confers on us certain rights which we can plead in the Court of God, and from which a valid political science can be deduced. We know our rights with the same certainty that we know his law.

"Men," wrote Locke, "being all the workmanship of one omnipotent and infinitely wise maker, all the servants of one sovereign master, sent into the world by his order and about his business; they are his property whose workmanship they are, made to last during his, not one another's, pleasure: and being furnished with like faculties, sharing all in one community of nature, there cannot be supposed any such subordination among us that may authorize us to destroy another as if we were made for one another's uses as the inferior ranks of creatures are for ours." [1]

When the leaders of the American revolution sought for certainty in their argument against George the Third they too found it in the fact that men "are endowed by their Creator with certain unalienable rights."

Rousseau and his French followers rested these rights on a presumed social contract. Human rights stood upon that contract as the elephant in the Indian parable stood upon the tortoise, though the contract itself, like the tortoise, was apt to stand upon nothing at all.

[1] Locke, Second Treatise of Government, 1690, ed. 1821, p. 191.

At this point Bentham, backed by the sense of humour of mankind, swept aside the whole conception of
a science of politics deduced from natural right.
"What sort of thing," he asked, "is a natural right,
and where does the maker live, particularly in Atheist's
Town, where they are most rife?" [1]

Bentham himself believed that he had found the
standard in the fact that all men seek pleasure and
avoid pain. In that respect men were measurable
and comparable. Politics and jurisprudence could
therefore be made experimental sciences in exactly
the same sense as physics or chemistry. "The present
work," wrote Bentham, "as well as any other work of
mine that has been or will be published on the subject
of legislation or any other branch of moral science, is
an attempt to extend the experimental method of reasoning from the physical branch to the moral." [2]

Bentham's standard of "pleasure and pain" constituted in many ways an important advance upon "natural
right." It was in the first place founded upon a universally accepted fact; all men obviously do feel both pleasure and pain. That fact was to a certain extent measurable. One could, for instance, count the number of
persons who suffered this year from an Indian famine,
and compare it with the number of those who suffered
last year. It was clear also that some pains and pleas-

[1] *Escheat vice Taxation*, Bentham's Works, vol. ii. p. 598.
[2] MS, in University College, London, quoted by Halévy, *La Jeunesse de
Bentham*, pp. 289-290.

ures were more intense than others, and that therefore the same man could in a given number of seconds experience varying amounts of pleasure or pain.   Above all, the standard of pleasure and pain was one external to the political thinker himself.   John Stuart Mill quotes Bentham as saying of all philosophies which competed with his Utilitarianism: "They consist, all of them, in so many contrivances for avoiding the obligation of appealing to any external standard, and for prevailing upon the reader to accept the author's sentiment or opinion as a reason for itself." [1]

A "Benthamite," therefore, whether he was a member of Parliament like Grote or Molesworth, or an official like Chadwick, or an organizing politician like Francis Place, could always check his own feeling about "rights of property," "mischievous agitators," "spirit of the Constitution," "insults to the flag," and so on, by examining statistical facts as to the numerical proportion, the income, the hours of work, and the death rate from disease, of the various classes and races who inhabited the British Empire.

But as a complete science of politics Benthamism is no longer possible.   Pleasure and pain are indeed facts about human nature, but they are not the only facts which are important to the politician.   The Benthamites, by straining the meaning of words, tried to classify such motives as instinctive impulse, ancient

[1] Bentham's *Works*, vol i. p. 8, quoted in Lytton's *England and the English* (1833), p. 469.   This passage was written by Mill, cf. preface.

tradition, habit, or personal and racial idiosyncrasy as being forms of pleasure and pain. But they failed; and the search for a basis of valid political reasoning has to begin again, among a generation more conscious than were Bentham and his disciples of the complexity of the problem, and less confident of absolute success.

In that search one thing at least is becoming clear. We must aim at finding as many relevant and measurable facts about human nature as possible, and we must attempt to make all of them serviceable in political reasoning. In collecting, that is to say, the material for a political science, we must adopt the method of the biologist, who tries to discover how many common qualities can be observed and measured in a group of related beings, rather than that of the physicist, who constructs, or used to construct, a science out of a single quality common to the whole material world.

The facts when collected must, because they are many, be arranged. I believe that it would be found convenient by the political student to arrange them under three main heads: descriptive facts as to the human type; quantitative facts as to inherited variations from that type observed either in individuals or groups of individuals; and facts, both quantitative and descriptive, as to the environment into which men are born, and the observed effect of that environment upon their political actions and impulses.

A medical student already attempts to master as many as possible of those facts about the human type that are relevant to his science. The descriptive facts, for instance, of typical human anatomy alone which he has to learn before he can hope to pass his examinations must number many thousands. If he is to remember them so that he can use them in practice, they must be carefully arranged in associated groups. He may find, for instance, that he remembers the anatomical facts about the human eye most easily and correctly by associating them with their evolutionary history, or the facts about the bones of the hand by associating them with the visual image of a hand in an X-ray photograph.

The quantitative facts as to variations from the anatomical human type are collected for him in statistical form, and he makes an attempt to acquire the main facts as to hygienic environment when and if he takes the Diploma of Public Health.

The student teacher, too, during his period of training acquires a series of facts about the human type, though in his case they are as yet far less numerous, less accurate, and less conveniently arranged than those in the medical text-books.

If the student of politics followed such an arrangement, he would at least begin his course by mastering a treatise on psychology, containing all those facts about the human type which have been shown by experience to be helpful in politics, and so arranged that the student's knowledge could be most easily recalled when wanted.

political science training

At present, however, the politician who is trained for his work by reading the best-known treatises on political theory is still in the condition of the medical student trained by the study of Hippocrates or Galen. He is taught a few isolated, and therefore distorted, facts about the human type, about pleasure and pain, perhaps, and the association of ideas, or the influence of habit. He is told that these are selected from the other facts of human nature in order that he may think clearly on the hypothesis of there being no others. What the others may be he is left to discover for himself; but he is likely to assume that they cannot be the subject of effective scientific thought. He learns also a few empirical maxims about liberty and caution and the like, and, after he has read a little of the history of institutions, his political education is complete. It is no wonder that the average layman prefers old politicians, who have forgotten their book-learning, and young doctors who remember theirs.[1]

A political thinker so trained is necessarily apt to preserve the conception of human nature which he learnt in his student days in a separate and sacred com-

---

[1] In the winter of 1907-8 I happened, on different occasions, to discuss the method of approaching political science with two young Oxford students. In each case I suggested that it would be well to read a little psychology. Each afterwards told me that he had consulted his tutor, and had been told that psychology was "useless" or "nonsense." One tutor, a man of real intellectual distinction, was said to have added the curiously scholastic reason that psychology was "neither science nor philosophy."

partment of his mind, into which the facts of experience, however laboriously and carefully gathered, are not permitted to enter.   Professor Ostrogorski published, for instance, in 1902, an important and extraordinarily interesting book on "Democracy and the Organization of Political Parties," containing the results of fifteen years close observation of the party system in America and England.   The instances given in the book might have been used as the basis of a fairly full account of those facts in the human type which are of importance to the politician—the nature of our impulses, the necessary limitations of our contact with the external world, and the methods of that thinking brain which was evolved in our distant past, and which we have now to put to such new and strange uses.   But no indication was given that Professor Ostrogorski's experience had altered in the least degree the conception of human nature with which he started.   The facts observed are throughout regretfully contrasted with "free reason," [1] "the general idea of liberty," [2] "the sentiments which inspired the men of 1848," [3] and the book ends with a sketch of a proposed constitution in which the voters are to be required to vote for candidates known to them through declarations of policy "from which all mention of party is rigorously excluded." [4]   One seems to be reading a series of conscientious observations of the Copernican heavens by a loyal but saddened believer in the Ptolemaic astronomy.

[1] *Passim, e.g.*, vol. ii. p. 728.   [2] *Ibid.*, p. 649.
[3] *Ibid*, p. 442.   [4] *Ibid*, p. 756.

Professor Ostrogorski was a distinguished member of the Constitutional Democratic Party in the first Duma of Nicholas II, and must have learnt for himself that if he and his fellows were to get force enough behind them to contend on equal terms with the Russian autocracy they must be a party, trusted and obeyed as a party, and not a casual collection of free individuals. Some day the history of the first Duma will be written, and we shall then know whether Professor Ostrogorski's experience and his faith were at last fused together in the heat of that great struggle.

The English translation of Professor Ostrogorski's book is prefaced by an introduction from Mr. James Bryce. This introduction shows that even in the mind of the author of "The American Constitution" the conception of human nature which he learnt at Oxford still dwells apart.

"In the ideal democracy," says Mr. Bryce, "every citizen is intelligent, patriotic, disinterested. His sole wish is to discover the right side in each contested issue, and to fix upon the best man among competing candidates. His common sense, aided by a knowledge of the constitution of his country, enables him to judge wisely between the arguments submitted to him, while his own zeal is sufficient to carry him to the polling booth." [1]

A few lines further on Mr. Bryce refers to "the

[1] Ostrogorski, voL i. p. xliv.

democratic ideal of the intelligent independence of the individual voter, an ideal far removed from the actualities of any State."

What does Mr. Bryce mean by "ideal democracy"? If it means anything it means the best form of democracy which is consistent with the facts of human nature. But one feels, on reading the whole passage, that Mr. Bryce means by those words the kind of democracy which might be possible if human nature were as he himself would like it to be, and as he was taught at Oxford to think that it was. If so, the passage is a good instance of the effect of our traditional course of study in politics. No doctor would now begin a medical treatise by saying, "the ideal man requires no food, and is impervious to the action of bacteria, but this ideal is far removed from the actualities of any known population." No modern treatise on pedagogy begins with the statement that "the ideal boy knows things without being taught them, and his sole wish is the advancement of science, but no boys at all like this have ever existed."

And what, in a world where causes have effects and effects causes, does "intelligent independence" mean?

Mr. Herman Merivale, successively Professor of Political Economy at Oxford, under-Secretary for the Colonies, and under-secretary for India, wrote in 1861:

"To retain or to abandon a dominion is not an issue which will ever be determined on the mere balance of profit and loss; or on the more refined but even less powerful motives supplied by abstract political philosophy. The sense of national honour; the pride of blood, the tenacious spirit of self-defence, the sympathies of kindred communities, the instincts of a dominant race, the vague but generous desire to spread our civilization and our religion over the world; these are impulses which the student in his closet may disregard, but the statesman dares not. . . ." [1]

What does "abstract political philosophy" here mean? No medical writer would speak of an "abstract" anatomical science in which men have no livers, nor would he add that though the student in his closet may disregard the existence of the liver the working physician dares not.

Apparently Merivale means the same thing by "abstract" political philosophy that Mr. Bryce means by "ideal" democracy. Both refer to a conception of human nature constructed in all good faith by certain eighteenth-century philosophers, which is now no longer exactly believed in, but which, because nothing else has taken its place, still exercises a kind of shadowy authority in a hypothetical universe.

The fact that this or that writer speaks of a conception of human nature in which he is ceasing to believe as "abstract" or "ideal" may seem to be of merely aca-

[1] Herman Merivale, *Colonization*, 1861, 2nd edition. The Book is a re-issue, largely re-written, of lectures given at Oxford in 1837. The passage quoted forms part of the 1861 additions, p. 675.

demic interest.   But such half-beliefs produce immense practical effects.   Because Merivale saw that the political philosophy which his teachers studied in their closets was inadequate, and because he had nothing to substitute for it, he frankly abandoned any attempt at valid thought on so difficult a question as the relation of the white colonies to the rest of the British Empire.   He therefore decided in effect that it ought to be settled by the rule-of-thumb method of "cutting the painter"; and, since he was the chief official in the Colonial Office at a critical time, his decision, whether it was right or wrong, was not unimportant.

Mr. Bryce has been perhaps prevented by the presence in his mind of such a half-belief from making that constructive contribution to general political science for which he is better equipped than any other man of his time.   "I am myself," he says in the same Introduction, "an optimist, almost a professional optimist, as indeed politics would be intolerable were not a man grimly resolved to see between the clouds all the blue sky he can." [1]   Imagine an acknowledged leader in chemical research, who, finding that experiment did not bear out some traditional formula, should speak of himself as nevertheless "grimly resolved" to see things from the old and comfortable point of view!

The next step in the course of political training which I am advocating would be the quantitative study of the inherited variations of individual men when compared

---

[1] *Loc. cit.*, p. xliii.

with the "normal" or "average" man who has so far served for the study of the type.

How is the student to approach this part of the course? Every man differs quantitatively from every other man in respect of every one of his qualities. The student obviously cannot carry in his mind or use for the purposes of thought all the variations even of a single inherited quality which are to be found among the fifteen hundred millions or so of human beings who at any one moment are in existence. Much less can he ascertain or remember the inter-relation of thousands of inherited qualities in the past history of a race in which individuals are at every moment dying and being born.

Mr. H. G. Wells faces this fact in that extremely stimulating essay on "Scepticism of the Instrument," which he has appended to his "Modern Utopia." His answer is that the difficulty is "of the very smallest importance in all the practical affairs of life, or indeed in relation to anything but philosophy and wide generalizations. But in philosophy it matters profoundly. If I order two new-laid eggs for breakfast, up come two unhatched but still unique avian individuals, and the chances are they serve my rude physiological purpose." [1]

To the politician, however, the uniqueness of the individual is of enormous importance, not only when he is dealing with "philosophy and wide generaliza-

[1] *A Modern Utopia*, p. 381.

tions" but in the practical affairs of his daily activity. Even the fowl-breeder does not simply ask for "two eggs" to put under a hen when he is trying to establish a new variety, and the politician, who is responsible for actual results in an amazingly complicated world, has to deal with more delicate distinctions than the breeder.   A statesman who wants two private secretaries, or two generals, or two candidates likely to receive equally enthusiastic support from nonconformists and trade-unionists, does not ask for "two men."

On this point, however, most writers on political science seem to suggest that after they have described human nature as if all men were in all respects equal to the average man, and have warned their readers of the inexactness of their description, they can do no more. All knowledge of individual variations must be left to individual experience.

John Stuart Mill, for instance, in the section on the Logic of the Moral Sciences at the end of his "System of Logic," implies this, and seems also to imply that any resulting in exactness in the political judgments and forecasts made by students and professors of politics does not involve a large element of error.

"Excepting," he says, "the degree of uncertainty, which still exists as to the extent of the natural differences of individual minds, and the physical circumstances on which these may be dependent, (considerations which are of secondary importance when we are considering mankind in the average or *en masse*), I believe most competent judges will agree that the general laws of the different constituent elements of human nature are even now sufficiently understood to render it possible for a competent thinker to deduce from those laws, with a considerable approach to certainty, the particular type of character which would be formed, in mankind generally, by any assumed set of circumstances." [1]

Few people nowadays would be found to share Mill's belief. It is just because we feel ourselves unable to deduce with any "approach to certainty" the effect of circumstances upon character, that we all desire to obtain, if it is possible, a more exact idea of human variation than can be arrived at by thinking of mankind "in the average or *en masse*."

Fortunately the mathematical students of biology, of whom Professor Karl Pearson is the most distinguished leader, are already showing us that facts of inherited variation can be so arranged that we can remember them without having to get by heart millions of isolated instances. Professor Pearson and the other writers in the periodical *Biometrika* have measured innumerable beech leaves, snails' tongues, human skulls, etc., etc., and have recorded in each case the variations of any quality in a related group of individuals by that which Professor Pearson calls an "observation frequency polygon," but which I, in my own thinking, find that I call (from a vague memory of its shape) a "cocked hat."

[1] *System of Logic*, Book vi. vol. ii. (1875), p. 462.

Here is a tracing of such a figure, founded on the actual measurement of 25,878 recruits for the United States army.

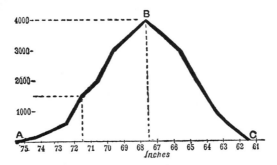

The line *ABC* records, by its distance at successive points from the line *AC*, the number of recruits reaching successive inches of height. It shows, *e.g.* (as indicated by the dotted lines) that the number of recruits between 5 ft. 11. in. and 6 ft. was about 1500, and the number of those between 5 ft. 7 in. and 5 ft. 8 in. about 4000. [1]

Such figures, when they simply record the results of the fact that the likeness of the offspring to the parent in evolution is constantly inexact, are (like the records

[1] This figure is adapted (by the kind permission of the publishers) from one given in Professor K. Pearson's *Chances of Death*, vol. i. p. 277. For the relation between such records of actual observation and the curves resulting from mathematical calculation of the known causes of variations, see *ibid.*, chap. viii., the paper by the same author on "Contributions to the Mathematical Theory of Evolution," in vol. 186 (A) of the *Royal Society's Philosophical Transactions* (1896), and the chapters on evolution in his *Grammar of Science*, 2nd edition.

of other cases of "chance" variation) fairly symmetrical, the greatest number of instances being found at the mean, and the descending curves of those above and those below the mean corresponding pretty closely with each other.   Boot manufacturers, as the result of experience, construct in effect such a curve, making a large number of boots of the sizes which in length or breadth are near the mean, and a symmetrically diminishing number of the sizes above and below it.

In the next chapter I shall deal with the use in reasoning of such curves, either actually "plotted" or roughly imagined.   In this chapter I point out, firstly, that they can be easily remembered (partly because our visual memory is extremely retentive of the image made by a black line on a white surface) and that we can in consequence carry in our minds the quantitative facts as to a number of variations enormously beyond the possibility of memory if they were treated as isolated instances; and secondly, that we can by imagining such curves form a roughly accurate idea of the character of the variations to be expected as to any inherited quality among groups of individuals not yet born or not yet measured.

The third and last division under which knowledge of man can be arranged for the purposes of political study consists of the facts of man's environment, and of the effect of environment upon his character and actions.   The extreme instability and uncertainty of this element constitutes a special difficulty of politics. The human type and the quantitative distribution of its variations are for the politician, who deals with a few generations only, practically permanent. Man's environment changes with ever-increasing rapidity. The inherited nature of every human being varies indeed from that of every other, but the relative frequency of the most important variations can be forecasted for each generation. The difference, on the other hand, between one man's environment and that of other men can be arranged on no curve and remembered or forecasted by no expedient. Buckle, it is true, attempted to explain the present and prophesy the future intellectual history of modern nations by the help of a few generalizations as to the effect of that small fraction of their environment which consisted of climate. But Buckle failed, and no one has attacked the problem again with anything like his confidence.

We can, of course, see that in the environment of any nation or class at any given time there are some facts which constitute for all its members a common experience, and therefore a common influence. Climate is such a fact, or the discovery of America, or the invention of printing, or the rates of wages and prices. All nonconformists are influenced by their memory of certain facts of which very few churchmen are aware, and all Irishmen by facts which most Englishmen try to forget. The student of politics must therefore read history, and particularly the history of those events and habits of thought in the immediate past which are

likely to influence the generation in which he will
work. But he must constantly be on his guard against
the expectation that his reading will give him much
power of accurate forecast. Where history shows him
that such and such an experiment has succeeded or
failed he must always attempt to ascertain how far
success or failure was due to facts of the human type,
which he may assume to have persisted into his own
time, and how far to facts of environment. When he
can show that failure was due to the ignoring of some
fact of the type, and can state definitely what that fact
is, he will be able to attach a real meaning to the
repeated and unheeded maxims by which the elder
members of any generation warn the younger that their
ideas are "against human nature." But if it is possible
that the cause was one of mental environment, that is
to say, of habit or tradition or memory, he should be
constantly on his guard against generalizations about
national or racial "character."

One of the most fertile sources of error in modern
political thinking consists, indeed, in the ascription to
collective habit of that comparative permanence which
only belongs to biological inheritance. A whole science
can be based upon easy generalizations about Celts and
Teutons, or about East and West, and the facts from
which the generalizations are drawn may all disappear
in a generation. National habits used to change
slowly in the past, because new methods of life were
seldom invented and only gradually introduced, and

because the means of communicating ideas between man and man or nation and nation were extremely imperfect; so that a true statement about a national habit might, and probably would, remain true for centuries. But now an invention which may produce profound changes in social or industrial life is as likely to be taken up with enthusiasm in some country on the other side of the globe as in the place of its origin. A statesman who has anything important to say says it to an audience of five hundred millions next morning, and great events like the Battle of the Sea of Japan begin to produce their effects thousands of miles off within a few hours of their happening. Enough has already occurred under these new conditions to show that the unchanging East may tomorrow enter upon a period of revolution, and that English indifference to ideas or French military ambition are habits which, under a sufficiently extended stimulus, nations can shake off as completely as can individual men.

CHAPTER V

THE METHOD OF POLITICAL REASONING

THE traditional method of political reasoning has inevitably shared the defects of its subject-matter. In thinking about politics we seldom penetrate behind those simple entities which form themselves so easily in our minds, or approach in earnest the infinite complexity of the actual world. Political abstractions, such as Justice, or Liberty, or the State, stand in our minds as things having a real existence. The names of political species, "governments" or "rights," or "Irishmen," suggest to us the idea of single "type specimens"; and we tend, like mediaeval naturalists, to assume that all the individual members of a species are in all respects identical with the type specimen and with each other.

In politics a true proposition in the form of "All A is B" almost invariably means that a number of individual persons or things possess the quality B in degrees of variation as numerous as are the individuals themselves. We tend, however, under the influence of our words and the mental habits associated with them to think of A either as a single individual possessing the qualitiy B, or as a number of individuals equally

156

possessing that quality.   As we read in the newspaper that "the educated Bengalis are disaffected" we either see, in the half-conscious substratum of visual images which accompanies our reading, a single Babu with a disaffected expression or the vague suggestion of a long row of identical Babus all equally disaffected.

These personifications and uniformities, in their turn, tempt us to employ in our political thinking that method of *a priori* deduction from large and untried generalizations against which natural science from the days of Bacon has always protested.   No scientist now argues that the planets move in circles, because planets are perfect, and the circle is a perfect figure, or that any newly discovered plant must be a cure for some disease because nature has given healing properties to all plants.   But "logical" democrats still argue in America that, because all men are equal, political offices ought to go by rotation, and "logical" collectivists sometimes argue from the "principle" that the State should own all the means of production to the conclusion that all railway managers should be elected by universal suffrage.

this does not follow from that (not parallel examples)

In natural science, again, the conception of the plurality and interaction of causes has become part of our habitual mental furniture; but in politics both the book-learned student and the man in the street may be heard to talk as if each result had only one cause.   If the question, for instance, of the Anglo-Japanese alliance is raised, any two politicians, whether they are tramps on the outskirts of a Hyde Park crowd or Heads of Colleges writing to the *Times*, are not unlikely to argue, one, that all nations are suspicious, and that therefore the alliance must certainly fail, and the other that all nations are guided by their interest, and that therefore the alliance must certainly succeed. The landlord of the "Rainbow" in "Silas Marner" had listened to many thousands of political discussions before he adopted his formula, "The truth lies atween you: you're both right and both wrong, as I allays say."

In Economics the danger of treating abstract and uniform words as if they were equivalent to abstract and uniform things has now been recognized for the last half century. When this recognition began, it was objected by the followers of the "classical" Political Economy that abstraction was a necessary condition of thought, and that all dangers arising from it would be avoided if we saw clearly what it was that we were doing. Bagehot, who stood at the meeting-point of the old Economics and the new, wrote about 1876:—

"Political Economy...is an abstract science, just as statics and dynamics are deductive sciences. And in consequence, it deals with an unreal and imaginary subject,...not with the entire real man as we know him in fact, but with a simpler imaginary man...." [1]

He goes on to urge that the real and complex man can be depicted by printing on our minds a succession of different imaginary simple men. "The maxim of

[1] *Economic Studies* (Longmans, 1895), p. 97.

science," he says, "is that of common-sense—simple
cases first; begin with seeing how the main force acts
when there is as little as possible to impede it, and
when you thoroughly comprehend that, add to it in succession the separate effects of each of the encumbering
and interfering agencies." [1]

But this process of mental chromolithography, though
it is sometimes a good way of learning a science, is not
a way of using it; and Bagehot gives no indication
how his complex picture of man, formed from successive
layers of abstraction, is to be actually employed in forecasting economic results.

When Jevons published his "Theory of Political
Economy" in 1871, it was already widely felt that a
simple imaginary man, or even a composite picture
made up of a series of different simple imaginary men,
although useful in answering examination questions,
was of very little use in drafting a Factory Act or
arbitrating on a sliding scale of wages. Jevons therefore based his economic method upon the variety and
not the uniformity of individual instances. He arranged
the hours of labour in a working day, or the units of
satisfaction from spending money, on curves of increase
and decrease, and employed mathematical methods to
indicate the point where one curve, whether representing an imaginary estimate or a record of ascertained
facts, would cut the others to the best advantage.

Here was something which corresponded, however

[1] *Economic Studies* (Longmans, 1895), p. 98.

roughly, to the process by which practical people arrived at practical and responsible results.   A railway manager who wishes to discover the highest rate of charges which his traffic will bear is not interested if he is told that the rate when fixed will have been due to the law that all men seek to obtain wealth with as little effort as possible, modified in its working by men's unwillingness to break an established business habit.   He wants a method which, instead of merely providing him with a verbal "explanation" of what has happened, will enable him to form a quantitative estimate of what under given circumstances will happen.   He can, however, and, I believe, now often does, use the Jevonian method to work out definite results in half-pennies and tons from the intersection of plotted curves recording actual statistics of rates and traffic.

Since Jevons's time the method which he initiated has been steadily extended; economic and statistical processes have become more nearly assimilated, and problems of fatigue or acquired skill, of family affection and personal thrift, of management by the *entrepreneur* or the paid official, have been stated and argued in quantitative form.   As Professor Marshall said the other day, *qualitative* reasoning in economics is passing away and *quantitative* reasoning is beginning to take its place.[1]

[1] *Journal of Economics*, March 1907, pp. 7 and 8. "What by chemical analogy may be called qualitative analysis has done the greater part of its work. . . . Much less progress has indeed been made towards the quantitative determination of the relative strength of different enconomic

How far is a similar change of method possible in the discussion not of industrial and financial processes but of the structure and working of political institutions?

It is of course easy to pick out political questions which can obviously be treated by quantitative methods. One may take, for instance, the problem of the best size for a debating hall, to be used, say, by the Federal Deliberative Assembly of the British Empire—assuming that the shape is already settled. The main elements of the problem are that the hall should be large enough to accommodate with dignity a number of members sufficient both for the representation of interests and the carrying out of committee work, and not too large for each member to listen without strain to a debate. The resultant size will represent a compromise among these elements, accommodating a number smaller than would be desirable if the need of representation and dignity alone were to be considered, and larger than it would be if the convenience of debate alone were considered.

A body of economists could agree to plot out or imagine a succession of "curves" representing the advantages to be obtained from each additional unit of size in dignity, adequacy of representation, supply of members for committee work, healthiness, etc., and the disadvantage of each additional unit of size as affect-

forces. That higher and more difficult task must wait upon the slow growth of thorough realistic statistics."

ing convenience of debate, etc. The curves of dignity and adequacy might be the result of direct estimation. The curve of marginal convenience in audibility would be founded upon actual "polygons of variation" recording measurements of the distance at which a sufficient number of individuals of the classes and ages expected could hear and make themselves heard in a room of that shape. The economists might further, after discussion, agree on the relative importance of each element to the final decision, and might give effect to their agreement by the familiar statistical device of "weighting."

The answer would perhaps provide fourteen square feet on the floor in a room twenty-six feet high for each of three hundred and seventeen members. There would, when the answer was settled, be a "marginal" man in point of hearing (representing, perhaps, an average healthy man of seventy-four), who would be unable or just able to hear the "marginal" man in point of clearness of speech—who might represent (on a polygon specially drawn up by the Oxford Professor of Biology) the least audible but two of the tutors at Balliol. The marginal point on the curve of the decreasing utility of successive increments of members from the point of view of committee work might show, perhaps, that such work must either be reduced to a point far below that which is usual in national parliaments, or must be done very largely by persons not members of the assembly itself. The aesthetic curve

of dignity might be cut at the point where the President
of the Society of British Architects could just be induced
not to write to the *Times*.

Any discussion which took place on such lines, even
although the curves were mere forms of speech, would
be real and practical. Instead of one man reiterating
that the Parliament Hall of a great empire ought to
represent the dignity of its task, and another man
answering that a debating assembly which cannot debate
is of no use, both would be forced to ask "How much
dignity"? and "How much debating convenience"? As
it is, this particular question seems often to be settled
by the architect, who is deeply concerned with aesthetic
effect, and not at all concerned with debating convenience. The reasons that he gives in his reports seem
convincing, because the other considerations are not
in the minds of the Building Committee, who think of
one element only of the problem at a time, and make
no attempt to co-ordinate all the elements. Otherwise
it would be impossible to explain the fact that the Debating Hall, for instance, of the House of Representatives
at Washington is no more fitted for debates carried on
by human beings than would a spoon ten feet broad be
fitted for the eating of soup. The able leaders of the
National Congress movement in India made the same
mistake in 1907, when they arranged, with their minds
set only on the need of an impressive display, that
difficult and exciting questions of tactics should be discussed by about fifteen hundred delegates in a huge tent,

and in the presence of a crowd of nearly ten thousand spectators. I am afraid that it is not unlikely that the London County Council may also despise the quantitative method of reasoning on such questions, and may find themselves in 1912 provided with a new hall admirably adapted to illustrate the dignity of London and the genius of their architect, but unfitted for any other purpose.

Nor is the essence of the quantitative method changed when the answer is to be found, not in one, but in several "unknown quantities." Take, for instance, the question as to the best types of elementary school to be provided in London. If it were assumed that only one type of school was to be provided, the problem would be stated in the same form as that of the size of the Debating Hall. But it is possible in most London districts to provide within easy walking distance of every child four or five schools of different types, and the problem becomes that of so choosing a limited number of types as to secure that the degree of "misfit" between child and curriculum shall be as small as possible. If we treat the general aptitude (or "cleverness") of the children as differing only by more or less, the problem becomes one of fitting the types of school to a fairly exactly ascertainable polygon of intellectual variation. It might appear then that the best results would come from the provision, say, of five types of schools, providing respectively for the 2 per cent. of greatest natural cleverness, the succeeding 10 per cent., the intermediate 76 per cent., the comparatively sub-normal 10 per cent., and the 2 per cent. of "mentally deficient." That is to say the local authority would have to provide in that proportion Secondary, Higher Grade, Ordinary, Sub-Normal; and Mentally Deficient schools.

A general improvement in nutrition and other home circumstances might tend to "steepen" the polygon of variation, i. e. to bring more children near the normal, or it might increase the number of children with exceptional inherited cleverness who were able to reveal that fact, and so "flatten" it; and either case might make a change desirable in the best proportion between the types of schools or even in the number of the types.

It would be more difficult to induce a committee of politicians to agree on the plotting of curves, representing the social advantage to be obtained by the successive increments of satisfaction in an urban industrial population of those needs which are indicated by the terms Socialism and Individualism. They could, however, be brought to admit that the discovery of curves for that purpose is a matter of observation and inquiry, and that the best possible distribution of social duties between the individual and the state would cut both at some point or other. For many Socialists and Individualists the mere attempt to think in such a way of their problem would be an extremely valuable exercise. If a Socialist and an Individualist were required

even to ask themselves the question, "How much Socialism?" or "How much Individualism?" a basis of real
discussion would be arrived at—even in the impossible
case that one should answer, "All Individualism and
no Socialism," and the other, "All Socialism and no
Individualism."

The fact, of course, that each step towards either
Socialism or Individualism changes the character of
the other elements in the problem, or the fact that
an invention like printing, or representative government, or Civil Service examinations, or the Utilitarian
philosophy, may make it possible to provide greatly
increased satisfaction both to Socialist and Individualist
desires, complicates the question, but does not alter
its quantitative character. The essential point is that
in every case in which a political thinker is able to
adopt what Professor Marshall calls the quantitative
method of reasoning, his vocabulary and method,
instead of constantly suggesting a false simplicity, warn
him that every individual instance with which he deals
is different from any other, that any effect is a func-
tion of many variable causes, and, therefore, that no
estimate of the result of any act can be accurate unless
all its conditions and their relative importance are taken
into account.

But how far are such quantitative methods possible
when a statesman is dealing, neither with an obviously
quantitative problem, like the building of halls or
schools, nor with an attempt to give quantitative mean-

ing to abstract terms like Socialism or Individualism, but with the enormous complexity of responsible legislation?

In approaching this question we shall be helped if we keep before us a description of the way in which some one statesman has, in fact, thought of a great constitutional problem.

Take, for instance, the indications which Mr. Morley gives of the thinking done by Gladstone on Home Rule during the autumn and winter of 1885–86. Gladstone, we are told, had already, for many years past, pondered anxiously at intervals about Ireland, and now he describes himself as "thinking incessantly about the matter" (vol. iii. p. 264), and "preparing myself by study and reflection" (p. 273).

He has first to consider the state of feeling in England and Ireland, and to calculate to what extent and under what influences it may be expected to change. As to English feeling, "what I expect," he says, "is a healthy slow fermentation in many minds working towards the final product" (p. 261). The Irish desire for self-government, on the other hand, will not change, and must be taken, within the time-limit of his problem, as "fixed" (p. 240). In both England and Ireland, however, he believes that "mutual attachment" may grow (p. 292).

Before making up his mind in favour of some kind of Home Rule, he examines every thinkable alternative, especially the development of Irish County Government, or a Federal arrangement in which all three of the united kingdoms would be concerned. Here and there he finds suggestions in the history of Austria-Hungary, of Norway and Sweden, or of the "colonial type" of government. Nearly every day he reads Burke, and exclaims "what a magazine of wisdom on Ireland and America" (p. 280). He gets much help from "a chapter on semi-sovereign assemblies in Dicey's "Law of the Constitution" (p. 280). He tries to see the question from fresh points of view in intimate personal discussions, and by imagining what "the civilized world" (p. 225) will think. As he gets nearer to his subject, he has definite statistical reports made for him by "Welby and Hamilton on the figures" (p. 306), has "stiff conclaves about finance and land" (p. 298), and nearly comes to a final split with Parnell on the question whether the Irish contribution to Imperial taxation shall be a fifteenth or a twentieth.

Time and persons are important factors in his calculation. If Lord Salisbury will consent to introduce some measure of Irish self-government, the problem will be fundamentally altered, and the same will happen if the general election produces a Liberal majority independent of both Irish and Conservatives; and Mr. Morley describes as underlying all his calculations "the irresistible attraction for him of all the grand and eternal commonplaces of liberty and self-government" (p. 260).

It is not likely that Mr. Morley's narrative touches

on more than a fraction of the questions which must have been in Gladstone's mind during these months of incessant thought. No mention is made, for instance, of religion, or of the military position, or of the permanent possibility of enforcing the proposed restrictions on self-government. But enough is given to show the complexity of political thought at that stage when a statesman, still uncommitted, is considering what will be the effect of a new political departure.

What then was the logical process by which Gladstone's final decision was arrived at?

Did he for instance deal with a succession of simple problems or with one complex problem? It is, I think, clear that from time to time isolated and comparatively simple trains of reasoning were followed up; but it is also clear that Gladstone's main effort of thought was involved in the process of co-ordinating all the laboriously collected contents of his mind onto the whole problem. This is emphasized by a quotation in which Mr. Morley, who was closely associated with Gladstone's intellectual toil during this period, indicates his own recollection.

"Historians," he quotes from Professor Gardiner, "coolly dissect a man's thoughts as they please; and label them like specimens in a naturalist's cabinet. Such a thing, they argue, was done for mere personal aggrandizement; such a thing for national objects, such a thing from high religious motives. In real life we may be sure it was not so" (p. 277).

And it is clear that in spite of the ease and delight with which Gladstone's mind moved among "the eternal commonplaces of liberty and self-government," he is seeking throughout for a quantitative solution. "Home Rule" is no simple entity for him. He realizes that the number of possible schemes for Irish government is infinite, and he attempts to make at every point in his own scheme a delicate adjustment between many varying forces.

A large part of this work of complex co-ordination was apparently in Mr. Gladstone's case unconscious. Throughout the chapters one has the feeling—which any one who has had to make less important political decisions can parallel from his own experience—that Gladstone was waiting for indications of a solution to appear in his mind. He was conscious of his effort, conscious also that his effort was being directed simultaneously towards many different considerations, but largely unconscious of the actual process of inference, which went on perhaps more rapidly when he was asleep, or thinking of something else, than when he was awake and attentive. A phrase of Mr. Morley's indicates a feeling with which every politician is familiar. "The reader," he says, "knows in what direction the main current of Mr. Gladstone's thought must have been setting" (p. 236).

That is to say, we are watching an operation rather of art than of science, of long experience and trained faculty rather than of conscious method.

progress in *substituting for art* *science* X

But the history of human progress consists in the gradual and partial substitution of science for art, of the power over nature acquired in youth by study, for that which comes in late middle age as the half-conscious result of experience. Our problem therefore involves the further question, whether those forms of political thought which correspond to the complexity of nature are teachable or not? At present they are not often taught. In every generation thousands of young men and women are attracted to politics because their intellects are keener, and their sympathies wider than those of their fellows. They become followers of Liberalism or Imperialism, of Scientific Socialism or the Rights of Men or Women. To them, at first, Liberalism and the Empire, Rights and Principles, are real and simple things. Or, like Shelley, they see in the whole human race an infinite repetition of uniform individuals, the "millions on millions" who "wait, firm, rapid, and elate." [1]

About all these things they argue by the old *a priori* methods which we have inherited with our political language. But after a time a sense of unreality grows upon them. Knowledge of the complex and difficult world forces itself into their minds. Like the old Chartists with whom I once spent an evening, they tell you that their politics have been "all talk"—all words— and there are few among them, except those to whom politics has become a profession or a career, who hold

[1] Shelley, *Poetical Works* (H. B. Forman), vol. IV. p. 8.

on until through weariness and disappointment they learn new confidence from new knowledge. Most men, after the first disappointment, fall back on habit or party spirit for their political opinions and actions. Having ceased to think of their unknown fellow citizens as uniform repetitions of a simple type, they cease to think of them at all; and content themselves with using party phrases about the mass of mankind, and realizing the individual existence of their casual neighbours.

Wordsworth's "Prelude" describes with pathetic clearness a mental history, which must have been that of many thousands of men who could not write great poetry, and whose moral and intellectual forces have been blunted and wasted by political disillusionment. He tells us that the "man" whom he loved in 1792, when the French Revolution was still at its dawn, was seen in 1798 to be merely "the composition of the brain." After agonies of despair and baffled affection, he saw "the individual man...the man whom we behold with our own eyes." [1]   But in that change from a false simplification of the whole to the mere contemplation of the individual, Wordsworth's power of estimating political forces or helping in political progress was gone for ever.

If this constantly repeated disappointment is to cease, quantitative method must spread in politics and must transform the vocabulary and the associations of

[1] *The Prelude*, Bk. xiii., ll. 81-84.

that mental world into which the young politician enters. Fortunately such a change seems at least to be beginning. Every year larger and more exact collections of detailed political facts are being accumulated; and collections of detailed facts, if they are to be used at all in political reasoning, must be used quantitatively. The intellectual work of preparing legislation, whether carried on by permanent officials or Royal Commissions or Cabinet Ministers takes every year a more quantitative and a less qualitative form.

Compare for instance the methods of the present Commission on the Poor Law with those of the celebrated and extraordinarily able Commission which drew up the New Poor Law in 1833-34. The argument of the earlier Commissioners' Report runs on lines which it would be easy to put in *a priori* syllogistic form. All men seek pleasure and avoid pain. Society ought to secure that pain attaches to anti-social, and pleasure to social conduct. This may be done by making every man's livelihood and that of his children normally dependent upon his own exertions, by separating those destitute persons who cannot do work useful to the community from those who can, and by presenting these last with the alternative of voluntary effort or painful restriction. This leads to "a principle which we find universally admitted, even by those whose practice is at variance with it, that the situation [of the pauper] on the whole shall not be made really or

the 'Old' reasoning of the poor law

apparently so eligible as the situation of the indepen-dent labourer of the lowest class." [1]   The *a priori* argu-ment is admirably illustrated by instances, reported by the sub-commissioners or given in evidence before the Commission, indicating that labouring men will not exert themselves unless they are offered the alternative of starvation or rigorous confinement, though no attempt is made to estimate the proportion of the working popu-lation of England whose character and conduct is represented by each instance.

This *a priori* deduction, illustrated, but not proved by particular instances, is throughout so clear and so easily apprehended by the ordinary man that the revolutionary Bill of 1834, which affected all sorts of vested interests, passed the House of Commons by a majority of four to one and the House of Lords by a majority of six to one.

the 'New' method of the poor law

The Poor Law Commission of 1905, on the other hand, though it contains many members trained in the traditions of 1834, is being driven, by the mere necessity of dealing with the mass of varied evidence before it, onto new lines.   Instead of assuming half consciously that human energy is dependent solely on the working of the human will in the presence of the ideas of pleasure and pain, the Commissioners are forced to tabulate and consider innumerable quantitative observations relating to the very many factors affecting the will of paupers

[1] *First Report of the Poor Law Commission,* 1834 (reprinted 1894), p. 187.

and possible paupers.   They cannot, for instance, avoid
the task of estimating the relative industrial effectiveness
of health, which depends upon decent surroundings; of
hope, which may be made possible by State provision
for old age; and of the imaginative range which is the
result of education; and of comparing all these with the
"purely economic" motive created by ideas of future
pleasure and pain.

The evidence before the Commission is, that is to
say, collected, not to illustrate general propositions
otherwise established, but to provide quantitative
answers to quantitative questions; and instances are in
each case accumulated according to a well-known
statistical rule until the repetition of results shows that
further accumulation would be useless.

In 1834 it was enough, in dealing with the political
machinery of the Poor Law, to argue that, since all men
desire their own interest, the ratepayers would elect
guardians who would, up to the limit of their knowledge,
advance the interests of the whole community; provided
that electoral areas were created in which all sectional
interests were represented, and that voting power were
given to each ratepayer in proportion to his interest.
It did not then seem to matter much whether the areas
chosen were new or old, or whether the body elected
had other duties or not.

In 1908, on the other hand, it is felt to be necessary
to seek for all the causes which are likely to influence
the mind of the ratepayer or candidate during an

election, and to estimate by such evidence as is available their relative importance.   It has to be considered, for instance, whether men vote best in areas where they keep up habits of political action in connection with parliamentary as well as municipal contests; and whether an election involving other points besides poor-law administration is more likely to create interest among the electorate.   If more than one election, again, is held in a district in any year it may be found by the record of the percentage of votes that electoral enthusiasm diminishes for each additional contest along a very rapidly descending curve.

The final decisions that will be taken either by the Commission or by Parliament on questions of administrative policy and electoral machinery must therefore involve the balancing of all these and many other considerations by an essentially quantitative process.   The lines, that is to say, which ultimately cut the curves indicated by the evidence will allow less weight either to anxiety for the future as a motive for exertion, or to personal health as increasing personal efficiency, than would be given to either if it were the sole factor to be considered.   There will be more "bureaucracy" than would be desirable if it were not for the need of economizing the energies of the elected representatives, and less bureaucracy than there would be if it were not desirable to retain popular sympathy and consent. Throughout the argument the population of England will be looked upon not (as John Stuart Mill would

have said) "on the average or en masse," [1] but as consisting of individuals who can be arranged in "polygons
of variation" according to their nervous and physical
strength, their "character" and the degree to which ideas
of the future are likely to affect their present conduct.

Meanwhile the public which will discuss the Report
has changed since 1834. Newspaper writers, in discussing the problem of destitution, tend now to use,
not general terms applied to whole social classes like
the "poor," "the working class," or "the lower orders,"
but terms expressing quantitative estimates of individual
variations, like "the submerged tenth," or the "unem-
ployable"; while every newspaper reader is fairly familiar with the figures in the Board of Trade monthly
returns which record seasonal and periodical variations
of actual unemployment among Trade Unionists.

One could give many other instances of this beginning of a tendency in political thinking to change from
qualitative to quantitative forms of argument. But
perhaps it will be sufficient to give one relating to
international politics. Sixty years ago sovereignty
was a simple question of quality. Austin had demonstrated that there must be a sovereign everywhere, and
that sovereignty, whether in the hands of an autocracy
or a republic, must be absolute. But the Congress
which in 1885 sat at Berlin to prevent the partition of
Africa from causing a series of European wars as long
as those caused by the partition of America, was com-

[1] See p. 132.

pelled by the complexity of the problems before it to approach the question of sovereignty on quantitative lines. Since 1885 therefore every one has become familiar with the terms then invented to express gradations of sovereignty—"Effective occupation," Hinterland," "Sphere of Influence"—to which the Algeciras Conference has perhaps added a lowest grade, "Sphere of Legitimate Aspiration." It is already as unimportant to decide whether a given region is British territory or not, as it is to decide whether a bar containing a certain percentage of carbon should be called iron or steel.

Even in thinking of the smallest subdivisions of observed political fact some men escape the temptation to ignore individual differences. I remember that the man who has perhaps done more than any one else in England to make a statistical basis for industrial legislation possible, once told me that he had been spending the whole day in classifying under a few heads thousands of "railway accidents," every one of which differed in its circumstances from any other; and that he felt like the bewildered porter in *Punch*, who had to arrange the subtleties of nature according to the unsubtle tariff-schedule of his company. "Cats," he quoted the porter as saying, "is dogs, and guineapigs is dogs, but this 'ere tortoise is a hinsect."

But it must constantly be remembered that quantitative thinking does not necessarily or even generally mean thinking in terms of numerical statistics. Number, which obliterates all distinction between the units numbered, is not the only, nor always even the most exact means of representing quantitative facts. A picture, for instance, may be sometimes nearer to quantitative truth, more easily remembered, and more useful for purposes of argument and verification than a row of figures. The most exact quantitative political document that I ever saw was a set of photographs of all the women admitted into an inebriate home. The photographs demonstrated, more precisely than any record of approximate measurements could have done, the varying facts of physical and nervous structure. It would have been easily possible for a committee of medical men to have arranged the photographs in a series of increasing abnormality, and to have indicated the photograph of the "marginal" woman in whose case, after allowing for considerations of expense, and for the desirability of encouraging individual responsibility, the State should undertake temporary or permanent control. And the record was one which no one who had ever seen it could forget.

The political thinker has indeed sometimes to imitate the cabinet-maker, who discards his most finely divided numerical rule for some kinds of specially delicate work, and trusts to his sense of touch for a quantitative estimation. The most exact estimation possible of a political problem may have been contrived when a group of men, differing in origin, education, and mental type, first establish an approximate agreement as to the probable result of a series of possible political

alternatives involving, say, increasing or decreasing
state interference, and then discover the point where
their "liking" turns into "disliking."   Man is the measure of man, and he may still be using a quantitative process even though he chooses in each case that method of
measurement which is least affected by the imperfection
of his powers.   But it is just in the cases where numerical calculation is impossible or unsuitable that the
politician is likely to get most help by using consciously quantitative conceptions.

An objection has been urged against the adoption
of political reasoning either implicitly or explicitly
quantitative, that it involves the balancing against each
other of things essentially disparate.   How is one, it
is asked, to balance the marginal unit of national honour involved in the continuance of a war with that marginal unit of extra taxation which is supposed to be its
exact equivalent?   How is one to balance the final
sovereign spent on the endowment of science with the
final sovereign spent on a monument to a deceased
scientist, or on the final detail in a scheme of old age
pensions?   The obvious answer is that statesmen have
to act, and that whoever acts does somehow balance all
the alternatives which are before him.   The Chancellor
of the Exchequer, in his annual allocation of grants and
remissions of taxations, balances no stranger things than
does the private citizen, who, having a pound or two
to spend at Christmas, decides between subscribing to
a Chinese Mission and providing a revolving hatch
between his kitchen and his dining-room.

A more serious objection is that we ought not to allow ourselves to think quantitatively in politics, that to do so fritters away the plain consideration of principle. "Logical principles" may be only an inadequate representation of the subtlety of nature, but to abandon them is, it is contended, to become a mere opportunist.

In the minds of these objectors the only alternative to deductive thought from simple principles seems to be the attitude of Prince Bülow, in his speech in the Reichstag on universal suffrage. He is reported to have said:—"Only the most doctrinaire Socialists still regarded universal and direct suffrage as a fetish and as an infallible dogma. For his own part he was no worshipper of idols, and he did not believe in political dogmas. The welfare and the liberty of a country did not depend either in whole or in part upon the form of its Constitution or of its franchise. Herr Bebel had once said that on the whole he preferred English conditions even to conditions in France. But in England the franchise was not universal, equal, and direct. Could it be said that Mecklenburg, which had no popular suffrage at all, was governed worse than Haiti, of which the world had lately heard such strange news, although Haiti could boast of possessing universal suffrage?" [1]

But what Prince Bülow's speech showed, was that he was either deliberately parodying a style of scholastic reasoning with which he did not agree, or he was incapable of grasping the first conception of quantitative

[1] *Times*, March 27, 1908.

political thought. If the "dogma" of universal suffrage means the assertion that all men who have votes are thereby made identical with each other in all respects, and that universal suffrage is the one condition of good government, then, and then only, is his attack on it valid. If, however, the desire for universal suffrage is based on the belief that a wide extension of political power is one of the most important elements in the conditions of good government—racial aptitude, ministerial responsibility, and the like, being other elements—then the speech is absolutely meaningless.

But Prince Bülow was making a parliamentary speech, and in parliamentary oratory that change from qualitative to quantitative method which has so deeply affected the procedure of Conferences and Commissions has not yet made much progress. In a "full-dress" debate even those speeches which move us most often recall Mr. Gladstone, in whose mind, as soon as he stood up to speak, his Eton and Oxford training in words always contended with his experience of things, and who never made it quite clear whether the "grand and eternal commonplaces of liberty and self government" meant that certain elements must be of great and permanent importance in every problem of Church and State, or that an *a priori* solution of all political problems could be deduced by all good men from absolute and authoritative laws.

PART II

POSSIBILITIES OF PROGRESS

CHAPTER I

POLITICAL MORALITY

In the preceding chapters I have argued that the efficiency of political science, its power, that is to say, of forecasting the results of political causes, is likely to increase. I based my argument on two facts, firstly, that modern psychology offers us a conception of human nature much truer, though more complex, than that which is associated with the traditional English political philosophy; and secondly, that, under the influence and example of the natural sciences, political thinkers are already beginning to use in their discussions and inquiries quantitative rather than merely qualitative words and methods, and are able therefore both to state their problems more fully and to answer them with a greater approximation to accuracy.

In this argument it was not necessary to ask how far such an improvement in the science of politics is likely to influence the actual course of political history. Whatever may be the best way of discovering truth will remain the best, whether the mass of mankind choose to follow it or not.

But politics are studied, as Aristotle said, "for the sake of action rather than of knowledge," [1] and the

[1] *Ethics*, Bk. i. ch. iii.(6).

student is bound, sooner or later, to ask himself what will be the effect of a change in his science upon that political world in which he lives and works.

One can imagine, for instance, that a professor of politics in Columbia University, who had just taken part as a "Mugwump" in a well-fought but entirely unsuccessful campaign against Tammany Hall, might say: "The finer and more accurate the processes of political science become, the less do they count in politics. Astronomers invent every year more delicate methods of forecasting the movements of the stars, but cannot with all their skill divert one star an inch from its course. So we students of politics will find that our growing knowledge brings us only a growing sense of helplessness. We may learn from our science to estimate exactly the forces exerted by the syndicated newspaper press, by the liquor saloons, or by the blind instincts of class and nationality and race; but how can we learn to control them? The fact that we think about these things in a new way will not win elections or prevent wars."

I propose, therefore, in this second part of my book to discuss how far the new tendencies which are beginning to transform the science of politics are likely also to make themselves felt as a new political force. I shall try to estimate the probable influence of these tendencies, not only on the student or the trained politician, but on the ordinary citizen whom political science reaches only at second or third hand; and, with that intention, shall

treat in successive chapters their relation to our ideals
of political morality, to the form and working of the
representative and official machinery of the State, and to
the possibilities of international and inter-racial understanding.

This chapter deals from that point of view with their
probable influence on political morality.   In using that
term I do not mean to imply that certain acts are moral
when done from political motives which would not be
moral if done from other motives, or vice versa, but to
emphasize the fact that there are certain ethical questions
which can only be studied in close connection with political science.   There are, of course, points of conduct
which are common to all occupations.   We must all try
to be kind, and honest, and industrious, and we expect
the general teachers of morals to help us to do so.   But
every occupation has also its special problems, which
must be stated by its own students before they can be
dealt with by the moralist at all.

In politics the most important of these special questions of conduct is concerned with the relation between
the process by which the politician forms his own opinions and purposes, and that by which he influences the
opinions and purposes of others.

A hundred or even fifty years ago, those who worked
to create a democracy of which they had had as yet no
experience felt no misgivings on this point.   They
looked on reasoning, not as a difficult and uncertain
process, but as the necessary and automatic working

of man's mind when faced by problems affecting his interest. They assumed, therefore, that the citizens under a democracy would necessarily be guided by reason in the use of their votes, that those politicians would be most successful who made their own conclusions and the grounds for them most clear to others, and that good government would be secured if the voters had sufficient opportunities of listening to free and sincere discussion.

A candidate today who comes fresh from his books to the platform almost inevitably begins by making the same assumption. He prepares his speeches and writes his address with the conviction that on his demonstration of the relation between political causes and effects will depend the result of the election. Perhaps his first shock will come from that maxim which every professional agent repeats over and over again to every candidate, "Meetings are no good." Those who attend meetings are, he is told, in nine cases out of ten, already loyal and habitual supporters of his party. If his speeches are logically unanswerable the chief political importance of that fact is to be found, not in his power of convincing those who are already convinced, but in the greater enthusiasm and willingness to canvass which may be produced among his supporters by their admiration of him as a speaker.

Later on he learns to estimate the way in which his printed "address" and that of his opponent appeal to the constituents. He may, for instance, become suddenly aware of the attitude of mind with which he himself opens the envelopes containing other candidates' addresses in some election (of Poor Law Guardians, for instance), in which he is not specially interested, and of the fact that his attention is either not aroused at all, or is only aroused by words and phrases which recall some habitual train of thought. By the time that he has become sufficiently confident or important to draw up a political program for himself, he understands the limits within which any utterance must be confined that is addressed to large numbers of voters—the fact that proposals are only to be brought "within the sphere of practical politics" which are simple, striking, and carefully adapted to the half-conscious memories and likes and dislikes of busy men.

All this means that his own power of political reasoning is being trained. He is learning that every man differs from every other man in his interest, his intellectual habits and powers, and his experience, and that success in the control of political forces depends on a recognition of this and a careful appreciation of the common factors of human nature. But meanwhile it is increasingly difficult for him to believe that he is appealing to the same process of reasoning in his hearers as that by which he reaches his own conclusions. He tends, that is to say, to think of the voters as the subject-matter rather than the sharers of his thoughts. He, like Plato's sophist, is learning what the public is, and is beginning to understand "the passions and desires" of

that "huge and powerful brute, how to approach and han-
dle it, at what times it becomes fiercest and most gentle,
on what occasions it utters its several cries, and what
sounds made by others soothe or irritate it." [1]   If he
resolutely guards himself against the danger of passing
from one illusion to another, he may still remember that
he is not the only man in the constituency who has
reasoned and is reasoning about politics.   If he does
personal canvassing he may meet sometimes a middle-
aged working man, living nearer than himself to the
facts of life, and may find that this constituent of his has
reasoned patiently and deeply on politics for thirty
years, and that he himself is a rather absurd item in the
material of that reasoning.   Or he may talk with a
business man, and be forced to understand some one who
sees perhaps more clearly than himself the results of his
proposals, but who is separated from him by the gulf of
a difference of desire: that which one hopes the other
fears.

Yet however sincerely such a candidate may respect
the process by which the more thoughtful both of those
who vote for him and of those who vote against him
reach their conclusions, he is still apt to feel that his own
part in the election has little to do with any reasoning
process at all.   I remember that before my first election my most experienced political friend said to me,
"Remember that you are undertaking a six weeks' advertising campaign."   Time is short, there are innumerable

---

[1] Plato, *Republic*, p. 493.

details to arrange, and the candidate soon returns from the rare intervals of mental contact with individual electors to that advertising campaign which deals with the electors as a whole. As long as he is so engaged, the maxim that it is wrong to appeal to anything but the severest process of logical thought in his constituents will seem to him, if he has time to think of it, not so much untrue as irrelevant.

After a time, the politician may cease even to desire to reason with his constituents, and may come to regard them as purely irrational creatures of feeling and opinion, and himself as the purely rational "overman" who controls them. It is at this point that a resolute and able statesman may become most efficient and most dangerous. Bolingbroke, while he was trying to teach his "Patriot King" how to govern men by understanding them, spoke in a haunting phrase of "that staring timid creature man." [1] A century before Darwin he, like Swift and Plato, was able by sheer intellectual detachment to see his fellow-men as animals. He himself, he thought, was one of those few "among the societies of men . . . who engross almost the whole reason of the species, who are born to instruct, to guide, and to preserve, who are designed to be the tutors and the guardians of human kind." [2] For the rest, "Reason has small effect upon numbers: a turn of imagination, often as violent and as sudden as a gust of wind, determines their conduct." [3]

[1] *Letters on the Spirit of Patriotism*, etc. (ed. of 1785), p. 70.
[2] *Ibid.*, p. 2.   [3] *Ibid.*, p. 165.

The greatest of Bolingbroke's disciples was Disraeli, who wrote, 'We are not indebted to the Reason of man for any of the great achievements which are the landmarks of human action and human progress.... Man is only truly great when he acts from the passions; never irresistible but when he appeals to the imagination. Even Mormon accounts more votaries than Bentham." [4] It was Disraeli who treated Queen Victoria "like a woman," and Gladstone, with the Oxford training from which he never fully recovered, who treated her "like a public meeting."

In spite of Disraeli's essentially kindly spirit, his calculated play upon the instincts of the nation which he governed seemed to many in his time to introduce a cold and ruthless element into politics, which seemed colder and more ruthless when it appeared in the less kindly character of his disciple Lord Randolph Churchill. But the same ruthlessness is often found now, and may perhaps be more often found in the future, whenever any one is sufficiently concentrated on some political end to break through all intellectual or ethical conventions that stand in his way. I remember a long talk, a good many years ago, with one of the leaders of the Russian terrorist movement. He said, "It is no use arguing with the peasants even if we were permitted to do so. They are influenced by events not words. If we kill a Tzar, or a Grand Duke, or a minister, our movement becomes something which exists and ccunts

4 *Coningsby*, ch. xiii.

with them, otherwise, as far as they are concerned, it does not exist at all."

In war, the vague political tradition that there is something unfair in influencing the will of one's fellow-men otherwise than by argument does not exist. This was what Napoleon meant when he said, "À la guerre, tout est moral, et le moral et l'opinion font plus de la moitié de la réalité." [1]   And it is curious to observe that when men are consciously or half-consciously determining to ignore that tradition they drop into the language of warfare. Twenty years ago, the expression "Class-war" was constantly used among English Socialists to justify the proposal that a Socialist party should adopt those methods of parliamentary terrorism (as opposed to parliamentary argument) which had been invented by Parnell. When Lord Lansdowne in 1906 proposed to the House of Lords that they should abandon any calculation of the good or bad administrative effect of measures sent to them from the Liberal House of Commons, and consider only the psychological effect of their acceptance or rejection on the voters at the next general election, he dropped at once into military metaphor. "Let us" he said, "be sure that if we join issue we do so upon ground which is as favourable as possible to ourselves. In this case I believe the ground would be unfavourable to this House, and I believe the juncture is one when, even if we were to win for the moment, our victory would be fruitless in the end." [2]

[1] *Maximes de Guerre et Penseés de Napoleon Ier* (Chapelot), p. 230.
[2] Hansard (Trades Disputes Bill, House of Lords, Dec. 4, 1906), p. 703.

At first sight, therefore, it might appear that the change in political science which is now going on will simply result in the abandonment by the younger politicians of all ethical traditions, and the adoption by them, as the result of their new book-learning, of those methods of exploiting the irrational elements of human nature which have hitherto been the trade secret of the elderly and the disillusioned.

I have been told, for instance, that among the little group of women who in 1906 and 1907 brought the question of Women's Suffrage within the sphere of practical politics, was one who had received a serious academic training in psychology, and that the tactics actually employed were in large part due to her plea that in order to make men think one must begin by making them feel.[1]

A Hindoo agitator, again, Mr. Chandra Pal, who also had read psychology, imitated Lord Lansdowne a few months ago by saying, "Applying the principles of psychology to the consideration of political problems we find it necessary that we . . . should do nothing that will make the Government a power for us. Because if the Government becomes easy, if it becomes pleasant, if it becomes good government, then our signs of separation from it will be gradually lost." [2]   Mr. Chandra Pal,

[1] Mrs. Pankhurst is reported in the *Observer* of July 26, 1908, to have said, "Whatever the women who are called Suffragists might be, they at least understood how to bring themselves in touch with the public. They had caught the spirit of the age, learnt the art of advertising."

[2] Quoted in *Times*, June 3, 1907.

unlike Lord Lansdowne, was shortly afterwards im-
prisoned, but his words have had an important political
effect in India.

If this mental attitude and the tactics based on it
succeed, they must, it may be argued, spread with constantly increasing rapidity; and just as, by Gresham's
Law in commerce, base coin, if there is enough of it,
must drive out sterling coin, so in politics, must the
easier and more immediately effective drive out the
more difficult and less effective method of appeal.

One cannot now answer such an argument by a
mere statement that knowledge will make men wise.
It was easy in the old days to rely on the belief that
human life and conduct would become perfect if men
only learnt to know themselves.   Before Darwin, most
political speculators used to sketch a perfect polity
which would result from the complete adoption of their
principles, the republics of Plato and of More, Bacon's
Atlantis, Locke's plea for a government which should
consciously realize the purposes of God, or Bentham's
Utilitarian State securely founded upon the Table of
the Springs of Action.   We, however, who live after
Darwin, have learnt the hard lesson that we must not
expect knowledge, however full, to lead us to perfection.   The modern student of physiology believes that
if his work is successful, men may have better health
than they would have if they were more ignorant, but
he does not dream of producing a perfectly healthy
nation; and he is always prepared to face the discovery

that biological causes which he cannot control may be tending to make health worse.   Nor does the writer on education now argue that he can make perfect characters in his schools.   If our imaginations ever start on the old road to Utopia, we are checked by remembering that we are blood-relations of the other animals, and that we have no more right than our kinsfolk to suppose that the mind of the universe has contrived that we can find a perfect life by looking for it.   The bees might to-morrow become conscious of their own nature, and of the waste of life and toil which goes on in the best ordered hive.   And yet·they might learn that no greatly improved organization was possible for creatures hampered by such limited powers of observation and inference, and enslaved by such furious passions. They might be forced to recognize that as long as they were bees their life must remain bewildered and violent and short.   Political inquiry deals with man as he now is, and with the changes in the organization of his life that can be made during the next few centuries. It may be that some scores of generations hence, we shall have discovered that the improvements in government which can be brought about by such inquiry are insignificant when compared with the changes which will be made possible when, through the hazardous experiment of selective breeding we have altered the human type itself.

But however anxious we are to see the facts of our existence without illusion, and to hope nothing with-

out cause, we can still draw some measure of comfort
from the recollection that during the few thousand
years through which we can trace political history in
the past, man, without changing his nature, has made
enormous improvements in his polity, and that those
improvements have often been the result of new moral
ideals formed under the influence of new knowledge.

The ultimate and wider effect on our conduct of
any increase in our knowledge may indeed be very
different from, and more important than, its immediate
and narrower effect. We each of us live our lives in
a pictured universe, of which only a small part is
contributed by our own observation and memory, and
by far the greater part by what we have learnt from
others. The changes in that mental picture of our
environment made for instance by the discovery of
America, or the ascertainment of the true movements
of the nearer heavenly bodies, exercised an influence on
men's general conception of their place in the universe,
which proved ultimately to be more important than
their immediate effect in stimulating explorers and
improving the art of navigation. But none of the
changes of outlook in the past have approached in
their extent and significance those which have been
in progress during the last fifty years, the new history
of man and his surroundings, stretching back through
hitherto unthought-of ages, the substitution of an
illimitable vista of ever changing worlds for the
imagined perfection of the ordered heavens, and above

198 HUMAN NATURE IN POLITICS

all the intrusion of science into the most intimate regions of ourselves. The effects of such changes often come, it is true, more slowly than we hope. I was talking not long ago to one of the ablest of those who were beginning their intellectual life when Darwin published the "Origin of Species." He told me how he and his philosopher brother expected that at once all things should become new, and how unwillingly as the years went on they had accepted their disappointment. But though slow, they are far-reaching.

To myself it seems that the most important political result of the vast range of new knowledge started by Darwin's work may prove to be the extension of the idea of conduct so as to include the control of mental processes of which at present most men are either unconscious or unobservant. The limits of our conscious conduct are fixed by the limits of our self-knowledge. Before men knew anger as something separable from the self that knew it, and before they had made that knowledge current by the invention of a name, the control of anger was not a question of conduct. Anger was a part of the angry man himself, and could only be checked by the invasion of some other passion, love, for instance, or fear, which was equally, while it lasted, a part of self. The man survived to continue his race if anger or fear or love came upon him at the right time, and with the right intensity. But when man had named his anger, and could stand outside it in thought, anger came within the region of conduct. Henceforth, in that respect, man could choose either the old way of half-conscious obedience to an impulse which on the whole had proved useful in his past evolution, or the new way of fully conscious control directed by a calculation of results.

A man who has become conscious of the nature of fear, and has acquired the power of controlling it, if he sees a boulder bounding towards him down a torrent bed, may either obey the immediate impulse to leap to one side, or may substitute conduct for instinct, and stand where he is because he has calculated that at the next bound the course of the boulder will be deflected. If he decides to stand he may be wrong. It may prove by the event that the immediate impulse of fear was, owing to the imperfection of his powers of conscious inference, a safer guide than the process of calculation. But because he has the choice, even the decision to follow impulse is a question of conduct. Burke was sincerely convinced that men's power of political reasoning was so utterly inadequate to their task, that all his life long he urged the English nation to follow prescription, to obey, that is to say, on principle their habitual political impulses. But the deliberate following of prescription which Burke advocated was something different, because it was the result of choice, from the uncalculated loyalty of the past. Those who have eaten of the tree of knowledge cannot forget.

In other matters than politics the influence of the fruit of that tree is now spreading further over our lives.

Whether we will or not, the old unthinking obedience to appetite in eating is more and more affected by our knowledge, imperfect though that be, of the physiological results of the quantity and kind of our food. Mr. Chesterton cries out, like the Cyclops in the play, against those who complicate the life of man, and tells us to eat "caviare on impulse," instead of "grape nuts on principle." [1]   But since we cannot unlearn our knowledge, Mr. Chesterton is only telling us to eat caviare on principle.   The physician, when he knows the part which mental suggestion plays in the cure of disease, may hate and fear his knowledge, but he cannot divest himself of it.   He finds himself watching the unintended effects of his words and tones and gestures, until he realizes that in spite of himself he is calculating the means by which such effects can be produced.   After a time, even his patients may learn to watch the effect of "a good bedside manner" on themselves.

So in politics, now that knowledge of the obscurer impulses of mankind is being spread (if only by the currency of new words), the relation both of the politician and the voter to those impulses is changing.   As soon as American politicians called a certain kind of specially paid orator a "spell-binder," the word penetrated through the newspapers from politicians to audiences.   The man who knows that he has paid two dollars to sit in a hall and be "spell-bound," feels, it is true, the old sensations, but feels them with a subtle

[1] *Heretics*, 1905, p. 136.

and irrevocable difference. The English newspaper reader who has once heard the word "sensational," may try to submit every morning the innermost sanctuary of his consciousness to the trained psychologists of the halfpenny journals. He may, according to the suggestion of the day, loathe the sixty million crafty scoundrels who inhabit the German Empire, shudder at a coming comet, pity the cowards on the Government Front Bench, or tremble lest a pantomime lady should throw up her part. But he cannot help the existence in the background of his consciousness of a self which watches, and, perhaps, is a little ashamed of his "sensations." Even the rapidly growing psychological complexity of modern novels and plays helps to complicate the relation of the men of our time to their emotional impulses. The young tradesman who has been reading either "Evan Harrington," or a novel by some writer who has read "Evan Harrington," goes to shake hands with a countess at an entertainment given by the Primrose League, or the Liberal Social Council, conscious of pleasure, but to some degree critical of his pleasure. His father, who read "John Halifax, Gentleman," would have been carried away by a tenth part of the condescension which is necessary in the case of the son. A voter who has seen "John Bull's Other Island" at the theatre, is more likely than his father, who only saw "The Shaughraun," to realize that one's feelings on the Irish question can be thought about as well as felt.

In so far as this change extends, the politician may

find in the future that an increasing proportion of his constituents half-consciously "see through" the cruder arts of emotional exploitation.

But such an unconscious or half-conscious extension of self-knowledge is not likely of itself to keep pace with the parallel development of the political art of controlling impulse. The tendency, if it is to be effective, must be strengthened by the deliberate adoption and inculcation of new moral and intellectual conceptions— new ideal entities to which our affections and desires may attach themselves.

"Science" has been such an entity ever since Francis Bacon found again, without knowing it, the path of Aristotle's best thought. The conception of "Science," of scientific method and the scientific spirit, was built up in successive generations by a few students. At first their conception was confined to themselves. Its effects were seen in the discoveries which they actually made; but to the mass of mankind they seemed little better than magicians. Now it has spread to the whole world. In every class-room and laboratory in Europe and America the conscious idea of Science forms the minds and wills of thousands of men and women who could never have helped to create it. It has penetrated, as the political conceptions of Liberty or of Natural Right never penetrated, to non-European races. Arab engineers in Khartoum, doctors and nurses and generals in the Japanese army, Hindoo and Chinese students make of their whole lives an intense activity inspired by absolute submission to Science, and not only English or American or German town working men, but villagers in Italy or Argentina are learning to respect the authority and sympathize with the methods of that organized study which may double at any moment the produce of their crops or check a plague among their cattle.

"Science" however, is associated by most men, even in Europe, only with things exterior to themselves, things that can be examined by test-tubes and microscopes. They are dimly aware that there exists a science of the mind, but that knowledge suggests to them, as yet, no ideal of conduct.

It is true that in America, where politicians have learnt more successfully than elsewhere the art of controlling other men's unconscious impulses from without, there have been of late some noteworthy declarations as to the need of conscious control from within. Some of those especially who have been trained in scientific method at the American Universities are now attempting to extend to politics the scientific concep-tion of intellectual conduct. But it seems to me that much of their preaching misses its mark, because it takes the old form of an opposition between "reason" and "passion." The President of the University of Yale said, for instance, the other day in a powerful address, "Every man who publishes a newspaper which appeals to the emotions rather than to the intelligence of its readers...attacks our political life at a most vulnerable point." [1]   If forty years ago Huxley had in this way merely preached "intelligence" as against "emotions" in the exploration of nature, few would have listened to him.   Men will not take up the "intolerable disease of thought" unless their feelings are first stirred, and the strength of the idea of Science has been that it does touch men's feelings, and draws motive power for thought from the passions of reverence, of curiosity, and of limitless hope.

The President of Yale seems to imply that in order to reason men must become passionless.   He would have done better to have gone back to that section of the Republic where Plato teaches that the supreme purpose of the State realizes itself in men's hearts by a "harmony" which strengthens the motive force of passion, because the separate passions no longer war among themselves, but are concentrated on an end discovered by the intellect. [2]

In politics, indeed, the preaching of reason as opposed to feeling is peculiarly ineffective, because the feelings of mankind not only provide a motive for political thought but also fix the scale of values which must be used in political judgment.   One finds oneself, when trying to realize this, falling back (perhaps because one gets so little help from current language) upon Plato's favourite metaphor of the arts.   In music the

---

[1] A. T. Hadley in *Munsey's Magazine*, 1907.
[2] Cf. Plate's *Republic*, Book IV.

noble and the base composers are not divided by the fact that the one appeals to the intellect and the other to the feelings of his hearers. Both must make their appeal to feeling, and both must therefore realize intensely their own feelings. The conditions under which they succeed or fail are fixed, for both, by facts in our emotional nature which they cannot change. One, however, appeals by easy tricks to part only of the nature of his hearers, while the other appeals to their whole nature, requiring of those who would follow him that for the time their intellect should sit enthroned among the strengthened and purified passions.

But what, besides mere preaching, can be done to spread the conception of such a harmony of reason and passion, of thought and impulse, in political motive? One thinks of education, and particularly of scientific education. But the imaginative range which is necessary if students are to transfer the conception of intellectual conduct from the laboratory to the public meeting is not common. It would perhaps more often exist if part of all scientific education were given to such a study of the lives of scientific men as would reveal their mental history as well as their discoveries, if, for instance, the young biologist were set to read the correspondence between Darwin and Lyell, when Lyell was preparing to abandon the conclusions on which his great reputation was based, and suspending his deepest religious convictions, in the cause of a truth not yet made clear.

But most school children, if they are to learn the facts on which the conception of intellectual conduct depends, must learn them even more directly. I myself believe that a very simple course on the well-ascertained facts of psychology would, if patiently taught, be quite intelligible to any children of thirteen or fourteen who had received some small preliminary training in scientific method. Mr. William James's chapter on Habit in his "Principles of Psychology" would, for instance, if the language were somewhat simplified, come well within their range. A town child again, lives nowadays in the constant presence of the psychological art of advertisement, and could easily be made to understand the reason why, when he is sent to get a bar of soap, he feels inclined to get that which is most widely advertised, and what relation his inclination has to that mental process which is most likely to result in the buying of good soap. The basis of knowledge necessary for the conception of intellectual duty could further be enlarged at school by the study in pure literature of the deeper experiences of the mind, A child of twelve might understand Carlyle's "Essay on Burns" if it were carefully read in class, and a good "sixth form" might learn much from Wordsworth's "Prelude."

The whole question, however, of such deliberate instruction in the emotional and intellectual facts of man's nature as may lead men to conceive of the co-ordination of reason and passion as a moral ideal is one on which much steady thinking and observation is still required.   The instincts of sex, for instance, are becoming in all civilized countries more and more the subject of serious thought.   Conduct based upon a calculation of results is in that sphere claiming to an ever increasing degree control over mere impulse.   Yet no one is sure that he has found the way to teach the barest facts as to sexual instincts either before or during the period of puberty, without prematurely exciting the instincts themselves.

Doctors, again, are more and more recognizing that nutrition depends not only upon the chemical composition of food but upon our appetite, and that we can become aware of our appetite and to some extent control and direct it by our will.   Sir William Macewen said not long ago, "We cannot properly digest our food unless we give it a warm welcome from a free mind with the prospect of enjoyment."[1]   But it would not be easy to create by teaching that co-ordination of the intellect and impulse at which Sir William Macewen hints.   If you tell a boy that one reason why food is wholesome is because we like it, and that it is therefore our duty to like that food which other facts of our nature have made both wholesome and likeable, you may find yourself stimulating nothing except his sense of humour.

So, in the case of the political emotions, it is very easy to say that the teacher should aim first at making

[1] *British Medical Journal,* Oct. 8, 1904.

his pupils conscious of the existence of those emotions, then at increasing their force, and finally at subordinating them to the control of deliberate reasoning on the consequences of political action.   But it is extraordinarily difficult to discover how this can be done under the actual conditions of school teaching.   Mr. Acland, when he was Education Minister in 1893, introduced into the Evening School Code a syllabus of instruction on the Life and Duties of the Citizen.   It consisted of statements of the part played in social life by the rate-collector, the policeman, and so on, accompanied by a moral for each section, such as "serving personal interest is not enough," "need of public spirit and intelligence for good Government," "need of honesty in giving a vote," "the vote a trust as well as a right." Almost every school publisher rushed out a text-book on the subject, and many School Boards encouraged its introduction; and yet the experiment, after a careful trial, was an acknowledged failure.   The new text-books (all of which I had at the time to review), constituted perhaps the most worthless collection of printed pages that have ever occupied the same space on a bookshelf, and the lessons, with their alternations of instruction and edification, failed to stimulate any kind of interest in the students.   If our youths and maidens are to be stirred as deeply by the conception of the State as were the pupils of Socrates, teachers and the writers of text-books must apparently approach their   task   with   something   of

Socrates' passionate love of truth and of the searching courage of his dialectic.

If again, at an earlier age, children still in school are to be taught what Mr. Wells calls "the sense of the State"[1] we may, by remembering Athens, get some indication of the conditions on which success depends. Children will not learn to love London while getting figures by heart as to the millions of her inhabitants and the miles of her sewers. If their love is to be roused by words, the words must be as beautiful and as simple as the chorus in praise of Athens in the "Oedipus Coloneus." But such words are not written except by great poets who actually feel what they write, and perhaps before we have a poet who loves London as Sophocles loved Athens it may be necessary to make London itself somewhat more lovely.

The emotions of children are, however, most easily reached not by words but by sights and sounds. If therefore, they are to love the State, they should either be taken to see the noblest aspects of the State or those aspects should be brought to them. And a public building or ceremony, if it is to impress the unflinching eyes of childhood, must, like the buildings of Ypres or Bruges or the ceremonies of Japan, be in truth impressive. The beautiful aspect of social life is fortunately not to be found in buildings and ceremonies only, and no Winchester boy used to come back uninfluenced from a

[1] *The Future in America,* chapter ix.

visit to Father Dolling in the slums of Landport; though boys' eyes are even quicker to see what is genuine in personal motive than in external pomp.

More subtle are the difficulties in the way of the deliberate intensification by adult politicians of their own political emotions. A life-long worker for education on the London School Board once told me that when he wearied of his work—when the words of reports become mere words, and the figures in the returns mere figures—he used to go down to a school and look closely at the faces of the children in class after class, till the freshness of his impulse came back. But for a man who is about to try such an experiment on himself even the word "emotion" is dangerous. The worker in full work should desire cold and steady, not hot and disturbed impulse, and should perhaps keep the emotional stimulus of his energy, when it is once formed, for the most part below the level of full consciousness. The surgeon in a hospital is stimulated by every sight and sound in the long rows of beds and would be less devoted to his work if he only saw a few patients brought to his house. But all that he is conscious of during the working hours is the one purpose of healing, on which the half-conscious impulses of brain and eye and hand are harmoniously concentrated.

Perhaps indeed most adult politicians would gain rather by becoming conscious of new vices than of new virtues. Some day, for instance, the word "opinion" itself may become the recognized name of the most dangerous political vice. Men may teach themselves by habit and association to suspect those inclinations and beliefs which, if they neglect the duty of thought, appear in their minds they know not how, and which, as long as their origin is not examined, can be created by any clever organizer who is paid to do so. The most easily manipulated State in the world would be one inhabited by a race of Nonconformist business men who never followed up a train of political reasoning in their lives, and who, as soon as they were aware of the existence of a strong political conviction in their minds, should announce that it was a matter of "conscience" and therefore beyond the province of doubt or calculation.

But, it may be still asked, is it not Utopian to suppose that Plato's conception of the Harmony of the Soul—the intensification both of passion and of thought by their conscious co-ordination—can ever become a part of the general political ideals of a modern nation? Perhaps most men before the war between Russia and Japan would have answered, Yes. Many men would now answer, No. The Japanese are apparently in some respects less advanced in their conceptions of intellectual morality than, say, the French. One hears, for instance, of incidents which seem to show that liberty of thought is not always valued in Japanese universities. But both during the years of preparation for the war, and during the war itself, there was something in what one was told of the combined emotional and intellectual attitude of the Japanese, which to a European seemed wholly new. Napoleon contended against the "idéo-logues" who saw things as they wished them to be, and until he himself submitted to his own illusions he ground them to powder. But we associate Napoleon's clearness of vision with personal selfishness. Here was a nation in which every private soldier outdid Napoleon in his determination to see in warfare not great principles nor picturesque traditions, but hard facts; and yet the fire of their patriotism was hotter than Gambetta's. Something of this may have been due to the inherited organization of the Japanese race, but more seemed to be the effect of their mental environment. They had whole-heartedly welcomed that conception of Science which in Europe, where it was first elaborated, still struggles with older ideals. Science with them had allied, and indeed identified, itself with that idea of natural law which, since they learnt it through China from Hindustan, had always underlain their various religions.[1] They had acquired, therefore, a mental outlook which was determinist without being fatalist, and which combined the most absolute submission to nature with untiring energy in thought and action.

One would like to hope that in the West a similiar fusion might take place between the emotional and philosophical traditions of religion, and the new conception of intellectual duty introduced by Science. The political effect of such a fusion would be enormous.

[1] See Okakura, *The Japanese Spirit* (1905).

But for the moment that hope is not easy. The inevitable conflict between old faith and new knowledge has produced, one fears, throughout Christendom, a division not only between the conclusions of religion and science, but also between the religious and the scientific habit of mind. The scientific men of to-day no longer dream of learning from an English Bishop, as their predecessors learnt from Bishop Butler, the doctrine of probability in conduct, the rule that while belief must never be fixed, must indeed always be kept open for the least indication of new evidence, action, where action is necessary, must be taken as resolutely on imperfect knowledge, if that is the best available, as on the most perfect demonstration. The policy of the last Vatican Encyclical will leave few Abbots who are likely to work out, as Abbot Mendel worked out in long years of patient observation, a new biological basis for organic evolution. Mental habits count for more in politics than do the acceptance or rejection of creeds or evidences. When an English clergyman sits at his breakfast-table reading his *Times* or *Mail*, his attitude towards the news of the day is conditioned not by his belief or doubt that he who uttered certain commandments about non-resistance and poverty was God Himself, but by the degree to which he has been trained to watch the causation of his opinions. As it is, Dr. Jameson's prepared manifesto on the Johannesburg Raid stirred most clergymen like a trumpet, and the sugges·

tion that the latest socialist member of Parliament is not a gentleman, produces in them a feeling of genuine disgust and despair.

It may be therefore that the effective influence in politics of new ideals of intellectual conduct will have to wait for a still wider change of mental attitude, touching our life on many sides. Some day the conception of a harmony of thought and passion may take the place, in the deepest regions of our moral consciousness, of our present dreary confusion and barren conflicts. If that day comes much in politics which is now impossible will become possible. The politician will be able not only to control and direct in himself the impulses of whose nature he is more fully aware, but to assume in his hearers an understanding of his aim. Ministers and Members of Parliament may then find their most effective form of expression in that grave simplicity of speech which in the best Japanese State papers rings so strangely to our ears, and citizens may learn to look to their representatives, as the Japanese army looked to their generals, for that unbought effort of the mind by which alone man becomes at once the servant and the master of nature.

CHAPTER II

REPRESENTATIVE GOVERNMENT

But our growing knowledge of the causation of political impulse, and of the conditions of valid political reasoning, may be expected to change not only our ideals of political conduct but also the structure of our political institutions.

I have already pointed out that the democratic movement which produced the constitutions under which most civilized nations now live, was inspired by a purely intellectual conception of human nature which is becoming every year more unreal to us. If, it may then be asked, representative democracy was introduced under a mistaken view of the conditions of its working, will not its introduction prove to have been itself a mistake?

Any defender of representative democracy who rejects the traditional democratic philosophy can only answer this question by starting again from the beginning, and considering what are the ends representation is intended to secure, and how far those ends are necessary to good government.

The first end may be roughly indicated by the word consent. The essence of a representative government is that it depends on the periodically renewed consent of a considerable proportion of the inhabitants; and the degree of consent required may shade from the mere acceptance of accomplished facts, to the announcement of positive decisions taken by a majority of the citizens, which the government must interpret and obey.

The question, therefore, whether our adoption of representative democracy was a mistake, raises the preliminary question whether the consent of the members of a community is a necessary condition of good government. To this question Plato, who among the political philosophers of the ancient world stood at a point of view nearest to that of a modern psychologist, unhesitatingly answered, No. To him it was incredible that any stable polity could be based upon the mere fleeting shadows of popular opinion. He proposed, therefore, in all seriousness, that the citizens of his Republic should live under the despotic government of those who by "slaving for it"[1] had acquired a knowledge of the reality which lay behind appearance. Comte, writing when modern science was beginning to feel its strength, made, in effect, the same proposal. Mr. H. G. Wells, in one of his sincere and courageous speculations, follows Plato. He describes a Utopia which is the result of the forcible overthrow of representative government by a voluntary aristocracy of trained men of science. He appeals, in a phrase consciously influenced by Plato's metaphysics, to "the idea

[1] *Republic*, p. 494.

of a comprehensive movement of disillusioned and illuminated men behind the shams and patriotisms, the spites and personalities of the ostensible world. . . ."[1] There are some signs, in America as well as in England, that an increasing number of those thinkers who are both passionately in earnest in their desire for social change and disappointed in their experience of democracy, may, as an alternative to the cold-blooded manipulation of popular impulse and thought by professional politicians, turn "back to Plato"; and when once this question is started, neither our existing mental habits nor our loyalty to democratic tradition will prevent it from being fully discussed.

To such a discussion we English, as the rulers of India, can bring an experiment in government without consent larger than any other that has ever been tried under the conditions of modern civilization. The Covenanted Civil Service of British India consists of a body of about a thousand trained men. They are selected under a system which ensures that practically all of them will not only possess exceptional mental force, but will also belong to a race, which, in spite of certain intellectual limitations, is strong in the special

---

[1] Wells, *A Modern Utopia*, p. 263. " I know of no case for the elective Democratic government of modern States that cannot be knocked to pieces in five minutes. It is manifest that upon countless important public issues there is no collective will, and nothing in the mind of the average man except blank indifference; that an electional system simply places power in the hands of the most skilful electioneers. . . ." Wells, *Anticipations*, p. 147.

faculty of government; and they are set to rule, under a system approaching despotism, a continent in which the most numerous races, in spite of their intellectual subtlety, have given little evidence of ability to govern.

Our Indian experiment shows, however, that all men, however carefully selected and trained, must still inhabit "the ostensible world." The Anglo-Indian civilian during some of his working hours—when he is toiling at a scheme of irrigation, or forestry, or famine-prevention—may live in an atmosphere of impersonal science which is far removed from the jealousies and superstitions of the villagers in his district. But an absolute ruler is judged not merely by his efficiency in choosing political means, but also by that outlook on life which decides his choice of ends; and the Anglo-Indian outlook on life is conditioned, not by the problem of British India as history will see it a thousand years hence, but by the facts of daily existence in the little government stations, with their trying climates, their narrow society, and the continual presence of an alien and possibly hostile race. We have not, it is true, yet followed the full rigour of Plato's system, and chosen the wives of Anglo-Indian officials by the same process as that through which their husbands pass. But it may be feared that even if we did so, the lady would still remain typical who said to Mr. Nevinson, "To us in India a pro-native is simply a rank outsider."[1]

What is even more important is the fact that, be-

[1] *The Nation,* December 21, 1907.

cause those whom the Anglo-Indian civilian governs are also living in the ostensible world, his choice of means on all questions involving popular opinion depends even more completely than if he were a party politician at home, not on things as they are, but on things as they can be made to seem. The avowed tactics of our empire in the East have therefore always been based by many of our high officials upon psychological and not upon logical considerations. We hold Durbars, and issue Proclamations, we blow men from guns, and insist stiffly on our own interpretation of our rights in dealing with neighbouring Powers, all with reference to "the moral effect upon the native mind." And, if half what is hinted at by some ultra-imperialist writers and talkers is true, racial and religious antipathy between Hindus and Mohammedans is sometimes welcomed, if not encouraged, by those who feel themselves bound at all costs to maintain our dominant position.

The problem of the relation between reason and opinion is therefore one that would exist at least equally in Plato's corporate despotism as in the most complete democracy. Hume, in a penetrating passage in his essay on *The First Principles of Government,* says: "It is . . . on opinion only that government is founded; and this maxim extends to the most despotic and most military governments as well as to the most free and the most popular."[1] It is when a Czar or a bureaucracy find themselves forced to govern in opposition to a

[1] Hume's *Essays,* chap. iv.

vague national feeling, which may at any moment create an overwhelming national purpose, that the facts of man's sublogical nature are most ruthlessly exploited. The autocrat then becomes the most unscrupulous of demagogues, and stirs up racial, or religious, or social hatred, or the lust for foreign war, with less scruple than does the proprietor of the worst newspaper in a democratic State.

Plato, with his usual boldness, faced this difficulty, and proposed that the loyalty of the subject-classes in his Republic should be secured once for all by religious faith. His rulers were to establish and teach a religion in which they need not believe. They were to tell their people "one magnificent lie"; [1] a remedy which in its ultimate effect on the character of their rule might have been worse than the disease which it was intended to cure.

But even if it is admitted that government without consent is a complicated and ugly process, it does not follow either that government by consent is always possible, or that the machinery of parliamentary representation is the only possible, or always the best possible, method of securing consent.

Government by a chief who is obeyed from custom, and who is himself restrained by custom from mere tyranny, may at certain stages of culture be better than anything else which can be substituted for it. And representation, even when it is possible, is not an

[1] Republic, p. 414.

unchanging entity, but an expedient capable of an infinite number of variations. In England at this moment we give the vote for a sovereign parliament to persons of the male sex above twenty-one years of age, who have occupied the same place of residence for a year; and enrol them for voting purposes in constituencies based upon locality. But in all these respects, age, sex, qualification, and constituency, as well as in the political power given to the representative, variation is possible.

If, indeed, there should appear a modern Bentham, trained not by Fénelon and Helvétius, but by the study of racial psychology, he could not use his genius and patience better than in the invention of constitutional expedients which should provide for a real degree of government by consent in those parts of the British Empire where men are capable of thinking for themselves on political questions, but where the machinery of British parliamentary government would not work. In Egypt, for instance, one is told that at elections held in ordinary local constituencies only two per cent. of those entitled to vote go to the poll.[1] As long as that is the case representative government is impossible. A slow process of education might increase the proportion of voters, but meanwhile it would surely be possible for men who understand the way in which Egyptians or Arabs think and feel to discover other methods by which the vague desires of the native population can be

[1] *Times,* January 6, 1908.

ascertained, and the policy of the government made in some measure to depend on them.

The need for invention is even more urgent in India, and that fact is apparently being realized by the Indian Government itself. The inventive range of Lord Morley and his advisers does not, however, for the moment appear to extend much beyond the adaptation of the model of the English House of Lords to Indian conditions, and the organization of an "advisory Council of Notables"; [1] with the possible result that we may be advised by the hereditary rent-collectors of Bengal in our dealings with the tillers of the soil, and by the factory owners of Bombay in our regulation of factory labour.

In England itself, though great political inventions are always a glorious possibility, the changes in our political structure which will result from our new knowledge are likely, in our own time, to proceed along lines laid down by slowly acting and already recognizable tendencies.

A series of laws have, for instance, been passed in the United Kingdom during the last thirty or forty years, each of which had little conscious connection with the rest, but which, when seen as a whole, show that government now tends to regulate, not only the process of ascertaining the decision of the electors, but also the more complex process by which that decision is formed;

[1] Mr. Morley in the House of Commons. Hansard, June 6, 1907, p. 885.

and that this is done not in the interest of any particular body of opinion, but from a belief in the general utility of right methods of thought, and the possibility of securing them by regulation.

The nature of this change may perhaps be best understood by comparing it with the similar but earlier and far more complete change that has taken place in the conditions under which that decision is formed which is expressed in the verdict of a jury. Trial by jury was, in its origin, simply a method of ascertaining, from ordinary men whose veracity was secured by religious sanctions, their real opinions on each case.[1] The various ways in which those opinions might have been formed were matters beyond the cognizance of the royal official who called the jury together, swore them, and registered their verdict. Trial by jury in England might therefore have developed on the same lines as it did in Athens, and have perished from the same causes. The number of the jury might have been increased, and the parties in the case might have hired advocates to write or deliver for them addresses containing distortions of fact and appeals to prejudice as audacious as those in the "Private Orations" of Demosthenes. It might have become more important that the witnesses should burst into passionate weeping than that they should tell what they knew, and the final verdict might have been taken by a show of hands, in a crowd that was rapidly degenerating into a mob. If such an institution had lasted up

[1] See, e.g., Stephen, *History of the Criminal Law*, vol. i. pp. 260-72.

to our time, the newspapers would have taken sides in every important case. Each would have had its own version of the facts, the most telling points of which would have been reserved for the final edition on the eve of the verdict, and the fate of the prisoner or defendant would often have depended upon a strictly party vote.

But in the English jury trial it has come to be assumed, after a long series of imperceptible and forgotten changes, that the opinion of the jurors, instead of being formed before the trial begins, should be formed in court. The process, therefore, by which that opinion is produced has been more and more completely controlled and developed, until it, and not the mere registration of the verdict, has become the essential feature of the trial.

The jury are now separated from their fellow-men during the whole case. They are introduced into a world of new emotional values. The ritual of the court, the voices and dress of judge and counsel, all suggest an environment in which the petty interests and impulses of ordinary life are unimportant when compared with the supreme worth of truth and justice. They are warned to empty their minds of all preconceived inferences and affections. The examination and cross-examination of the witnesses are carried on under rules of evidence which are the result of centuries of experience, and which give many a man as he sits on a jury his first lesson in the fallibility of the unobserved and uncontrolled inferences of the human brain. The "said I's," and "thought I's," and "said he's," which are the material of his ordinary reasoning, are here banished on the ground that they are "not evidence," and witnesses are compelled to give a simple account of their remembered sensations of sight and hearing.

The witnesses for the prosecution and the defence, if they are well-intentioned men, often find themselves giving, to their own surprise, perfectly consistent accounts of the events at issue. The barristers' tricks of advocacy are to some extent restrained by professional custom and by the authority of the judge, and they are careful to point out to the jury each other's fallacies. Newspapers do not reach the jury box, and in any case are prevented by the law as to contempt of court from commenting on a case which is under trial. The judge sums up, carefully describing the conditions of valid inference on questions of disputed fact, and warning the jury against those forms of irrational and unconscious inference to which experience has shown them to be most liable. They then retire, all carrying in their minds the same body of simplified and dissected evidence, and all having been urged with every circumstance of solemnity to form their conclusions by the same mental process. It constantly happens therefore that twelve men, selected by lot, will come to a unanimous verdict as to a question on which in the outside world they would have been hopelessly divided, and that that verdict, which may depend upon questions of fact so difficult as to leave the practised intellect of the judge undecided, will very generally be right. An English law court is indeed during a well-governed jury trial a laboratory in which psychological rules of valid reasoning are illustrated by experiment; and when, as threatens to occur in some American States and cities, it becomes impossible to enforce those rules, the jury system itself breaks down.[1]

At the same time, trial by jury is now used with a certain degree of economy, both because it is slow and expensive, and because men do not make good jurors if they are called upon too often. In order that popular consent may support criminal justice, and that the law may not be unfairly used to protect the interests or policy of a governing class or person, no man, in most civilized countries, may be sentenced to death or to a long period of imprisonment, except after the verdict of a jury. But the overwhelming majority of other judicial decisions are now taken by men selected not by lot, but, in theory at least, by special fitness for their task.

In the light of this development of the jury trial we may now examine the tentative changes which, since the Reform Act of 1867, have been introduced into the law of elections in the United Kingdom. Long before that date, it had been admitted that the State ought

[1] On the jury system see Mr. Wells's *Mankind in the Making*, chapter vii. He suggests the use of juries in many administrative cases where it is desirable that government should be supported by popular consent.

not to stretch the principle of individual liberty so far as to remain wholly indifferent as to the kind of motives which candidates might bring to bear upon electors. It was obvious that if candidates were allowed to practise open bribery the whole system of representation would break down at once. Laws, therefore, against bribery had been for several generations on the statute books, and all that was required in that respect was the serious attempt, made after the scandals at the general election of 1880, to render them effective. But without entering into definite bargains with individual voters, a rich candidate can by lavish expenditure on his electoral campaign, both make himself personally popular, and create an impression that his connection with the constituency is good for trade. The Corrupt Practices Act of 1883 therefore fixed a maximum of expenditure for each candidate at a parliamentary election. By the same Act of 1883, and by earlier and later Acts, applying both to parliamentary and municipal elections, intimidation of all kinds, including the threatening of penalties after death, is forbidden. No badges or flags or bands of music may be paid for by, or on behalf of, a candidate. In order that political opinion may not be influenced by thoughts of the simpler bodily pleasures, no election meeting may be held in a building where any form of food or drink is habitually sold, although that building may be only a Co-operative Hall with facilities for making tea in an ante-room.

The existing laws against Corrupt Practices repre-

sent, it is true, rather the growing purpose of the State
to control the conditions under which electoral opinion
is formed, than any large measure of success in carrying out that purpose.   A rapidly increasing proportion
of the expenditure at any English election is now in-
curred by bodies enrolled outside the constituency, and
nominally engaged, not in winning the election for a
particular candidate, but in propagating their own
principles.   Sometimes   the   candidate   whom   they
support, and whom they try to commit as deeply as
possible, would be greatly relieved if they withdrew.
Generally their agents are an integral part of his fighting organization, and often the whole of their expenditure at an election is covered by a special subscription
made by him to the central fund.   Every one sees that
this system drives a coach and horses through those
clauses in the Corrupt Practices Act which restrict
election expenses and forbid the employment of paid
canvassers, though no one as yet has put forward any
plan for preventing it.   But it is acknowledged that
unless the whole principle is to be abandoned, new
legislation must take place; and Lord Robert Cecil talks
of the probable necessity for a "stringent and far-
reaching Corrupt Practices Act." [1]   If, however, an act
is carried stringent enough to deal effectually with the
existing development of electoral tactics, it will have
to be drafted on lines involving new and hitherto un-

[1] *Times*, June 26, 1907.

thought-of forms of interference with the liberty of political appeal.

A hundred years ago a contested election might last in any constituency for three or four weeks of excitement and horseplay, during which the voters were every day further removed from the state of mind in which serious thought on the probable results of their votes was possible. Now no election may last more than one day, and we may soon enact that all the polling for a general election shall take place on the same day. The sporting fever of the weeks during which a general election even now lasts, with the ladder-climbing figures outside the newspaper offices, the flash-lights at night, and the cheering or groaning crowds in the party clubs, are not only waste of energy but an actual hindrance to effective political reasoning.

A more difficult psychological problem arose in the discussion of the Ballot. Would a voter be more likely to form a thoughtful and public-spirited decision if, after it was formed, he voted publicly or secretly? Most of the followers of Bentham advocated secrecy. Since men acted in accordance with their ideas of pleasure and pain, and since landlords and employers were able, in spite of any laws against intimidation, to bring "sinister" motives to bear upon voters whose votes were known, the advisability of secret voting seemed to follow as a corollary from utilitarianism. John Stuart Mill, however, whose whole philosophical life consisted of a slowly developing revolt of feeling against the utilitarian philosophy to which he gave nominal allegiance till the end, opposed the Ballot on grounds which really involved the abandonment of the whole utilitarian position. If ideas of pleasure and pain be taken as equivalent to those economic motives which can be summed up as the making or losing money, it is not true, said Mill, that even under a system of open voting such ideas are the main causes which induce the ordinary citizen to vote. "Once in a thousand times, as in the case of peace or war, or of taking off taxes, the thought may cross him that he shall save a few pounds or shillings in his year's expenditure if the side he votes for wins." He votes as a matter of fact in accordance with ideas of right or wrong. "His motive, when it is an honourable one, is the desire to do right. We will not term it patriotism or moral principle, in order not to ascribe to the voter's frame of mind a solemnity that does not belong to it." But ideas of right and wrong are strengthened and not weakened by the knowledge that we act under the eyes of our neighbours. "Since then the real motive which induces a man to vote honestly is for the most part not an interested motive in any form, but a social one, the point to be decided is whether the social feelings connected with an act and the sense of social duty in performing it, can be expected to be as powerful when the act is done in secret, and he can neither be admired for disinterested, nor blamed for mean and selfish conduct.

But this question is answered as soon as stated. When in every other act of a man's life which concerns his duty to others, publicity and criticism ordinarily improve his conduct, it cannot be that voting for a member of parliament is the single case in which he will act better for being sheltered against all comment."[1]

Almost the whole civilized world has now adopted the secret Ballot; so that it would seem that Mill was wrong, and that he was wrong in spite of the fact that, as against the consistent utilitarians, his description of average human motive was right. But Mill, though he soon ceased to be in the original sense of the word a utilitarian, always remained an intellectualist, and he made in the case of the Ballot the old mistake of giving too intellectual and logical an account of political impulses. It is true that men do not act politically upon a mere stock-exchange calculation of material advantages and disadvantages. They generally form vague ideas of right and wrong in accordance with vague trains of inference as to the good or evil results of political action. If an election were like a jury trial, such inferences might be formed by a process which would leave a sense of fundamental conviction in the mind of the thinker, and might be expressed under conditions of religious and civic solemnity to which publicity would lend an added weight, as it

---

[1] Letter to the *Reader*, Ap. 29, 1865, signed J. S. M., quoted as Mill's by Henry Romilly in pamphlet, *Public Responsibility and Vote by Ballot*, pp. 89, 90.

does in those "acts of a man's life which concern his duty to others," to which Mill refers—the paying of a debt of honour, for instance, or the equitable treatment of one's relatives. But under existing electoral conditions, trains of thought, formed as they often are by the half-conscious suggestion of newspapers or leaflets, are weak as compared with the things of sense. Apart from direct intimidation, the voice of the canvasser, the excitement of one's friends, the look of triumph on the face of one's opponents, or the vague indications of disapproval by the rulers of one's village, are all apt to be stronger than the shadowy and uncertain conclusions of one's thinking brain. To make the ultimate vote secret, gives therefore thought its best chance, and at least requires the canvasser to produce in the voter a belief which, however shadowy, shall be genuine, rather than to secure by the mere manipulation of momentary impulse a promise which is shamefacedly carried out in public because it is a promise.

Lord Courtney is the last survivor in public life of the personal disciples of Mill, and at present he is devoting himself to a campaign in favor of "proportional representation," in which, as it seems to me, the old intellectualist misconceptions reappear in another form. He proposes to deal with two difficulties, first, that under the existing system of the "single ballot" a minority in any single-member constituency may, if there are more candidates than two, return its representative, and secondly, that certain citizens who think for themselves instead of allowing party leaders to think for them—the Free-Trade Unionists, for instance, or the High-Church Liberals—have, as a rule, no candidate representing their own opinions for whom they can vote. He proposes, therefore, that each voter shall mark in order of preference a ballot paper containing lists of candidates for large constituences each of which returns six or seven members, Manchester with eight seats being given as an example.

This system, according to Lord Courtney, "will lead to the dropping of the fetters which now interfere with free thought, and will set men and women on their feet, erect, intelligent, independent."[1]   But the arguments used in urging it all seem to me to suffer from the fatal defect of dwelling solely on the process by which opinion is ascertained, and ignoring the process by which opinion is created.   If at the assizes all the jurors summoned were collected into one large jury, and if they all voted Guilty or Not Guilty on all the cases, after a trial in which all the counsel were heard and all the witnesses were examined simultaneously, verdicts would indeed no longer depend on the accidental composition of the separate juries; but the process of forming verdicts would be made, to a serious degree, less effective.

The English experiment on which the Proportional Representation Society mainly relies is an imaginery election, held in November 1906 by means of ballot

[1] Address delivered by Lord Courtney at the Mechanics Institute, Stockport, March 22, 1907, p. 6.

papers distributed through members and friends of the society and through eight newspapers. "The constituency," we are told, "was supposed to return five members; the candidates, twelve in number, were politicians whose names might be expected to be known to the ordinary newspaper reader, and who might be considered as representative of some of the main divisions of public opinion."[1] The names were, in fact, Sir A. Acland Hood, Sir H. Campbell-Bannerman, Sir Thomas P. Whittaker, and Lord Hugh Cecil, with Messrs. Richard Bell, Austen Chamberlain, Winston Churchill, Haldane, Keir Hardie, Arthur Henderson, Bonar Law, and Philip Snowden. In all, 12,418 votes were collected.

I was one of the 12,418, and in my case the ballot papers were distributed at the end of a dinner party. No discussion of the various candidates took place, with the single exception that, finding my memory of Mr. Arthur Henderson rather vague, I whispered a question about him to my next neighbor. We were all politicians, and nearly all the names were those of persons belonging to that small group of forty or fifty whose faces the caricaturists of the Christmas numbers expect their readers to recognise.

At our dinner party not much unreality was introduced by the intellectualist assumption that the names on the list were, as a Greek might have said, the same, "to us," as they were "in themselves." But an ordinary list of candidates' names presented to an ordinary voter

[1] Proportional Representation Pamphlet, No. 4, p. 6.

is "to him" simply a piece of paper with black marks on it, with which he will either do nothing or do as he is told.

The Proportional Representation Society seem to assume that a sufficient preliminary discussion will be carried on in the newspapers, and that not only the names and party programs but the reasons for the selection of a particular person as candidate and for all the items in his program will be known to the "ordinary newspaper reader," who is assumed to be identical with the ordinary citizen. But even if one neglects the political danger arising from the modern concentration of newspaper property in the hands of financiers who may use their control for frankly financial purposes, it is not true that each man now reads or is likely to read a newspaper devoted to a single candidature or to the propaganda of a small political group. Men read newspapers for news, and, since the collection of news is enormously costly, nine-tenths of the electorate read between them a small number of established papers advocating broad party principles. These newspapers, at any rate during a general election, only refer to those particular contests in which the party leaders are not concerned as matters of casual information, until, on the day of the poll, they issue general directions "How to vote." The choice of candidates is left by the newspapers to the local party organizations, and if any real knowledge of the personality of a candidate or of the details of his program is to be made part of the consciousness of the

ordinary voter, this must still be done by local electioneering in each constituency, *i.e.* by meetings and
canvassing and the distribution of "election literature."
Lord Courtney's proposal, even if it only multiplied
the size of the ordinary constituency by six, would multiply by at least six the difficulty of effective electioneering, and even if each candidate were prepared to
spend six times as much money at every contest, he
could not multiply by six the range of his voice or the
number of meetings which he could address in a day.

These considerations were brought home to me by
my experience of the nearest approximation to Proportional Representation which has ever been actually
adopted in England.   In 1870 Lord Frederick Caven-
dish induced the House of Commons to adopt "plural
voting" for School Board elections.   I fought in three
London School Board elections as a candidate and in
two others as a political worker.   In London the legal
arrangement was that each voter in eleven large districts should be given about five or six votes, and that
the same number of seats should be assigned to the district.   In the provinces a town or parish was given a
number of seats from five to fifteen.   The voter might
"plump" all his votes on one candidate, or might distribute them as he liked among any of them.

This left the local organizers both in London and the
country with two alternatives.   They might form the
list of party candidates in each district into a recognizable entity like the American "ticket" and urge all

voters to vote, on party lines, for the Liberal or Conservative "eight" or "five" or "three." If they did this they were saved the trouble involved in any serious attempt to instruct voters as to the individual personalities of the members of the list. Or they might practically repeal the plural voting law, split up the constituency by a voluntary arrangement into single member sections, and spend the weeks of the election in making one candidate for each party known in each section. The first method was generally adopted in the provinces, and had all the good and bad effects from a party point of view of the French *scrutin de liste*. The second method was adopted in London, and perhaps tended to make the London elections turn more than they otherwise would have done upon the qualities of individual candidates. Whichever system was adopted by the party leaders was acted upon by practically all the voters, with the exception of the well-organized Roman Catholics, who voted for a Church and not a person, and of those who plumped for representatives of the special interests of the teachers or school-keepers.

If Lord Courtney's proposal is adopted for parliamentary elections, it is the "ticket" system which, owing to the intensity of party feeling, will be generally used. Each voter will bring into the polling booth a printed copy of the ballot paper marked with the numbers 1, 2, 3, etc., according to the decision of his party association, and will copy the numbers onto the unmarked official paper. The essential fact, that is to say, on

which party tactics would depend under Lord Courtney's scheme is not that the votes would finally be added
up in this way or in that, but that the voter would be
required to arrange in order more names than there is
time during the election to turn for him into real persons.

Lord Courtney, in speaking on the second reading of
his Municipal Representation Bill in the House of
Lords, [1] contrasted his proposed system with that used
in the London Borough Council elections, according to
which a number of seats are assigned to each ward, and
the voter may give one vote each, without indication of
preference, to that number of candidates.   It is true that
the electoral machinery for the London Boroughs is the
worst to be found anywhere in the world outside of
America.   I have before me my party ballot-card in-
structing me how to vote at the last Council election in
my present borough.   There were six seats to be filled
in my ward and fifteen candidates.   I voted as I was
told by my party organization, giving one vote each to
six names, not one of which I remembered to have seen
before.   If there had been one seat to be filled, and
say, three candidates, I should have found out enough
about one candidate at least to give a more or less independent vote; and the local party committees would have
known that I and others would do so.   Each party would
then have circulated a portrait and a printed account of
their candidate and of his principles, and would have
had a strong motive for choosing a thoroughly reputa-

[1] April 30, 1907.

ble person. But I could not give the time necessary for forming a real opinion on fifteen candidates, who volunteered no information about themselves. I therefore, and probably twenty-nine out of every thirty of those who voted in the borough, voted a "straight ticket." If for any reason the party committee put, to use an Americanism, a "yellow dog" among the list of names, I voted for the yellow dog.

Under Lord Courtney's system I should have had to vote on the same ticket, with the same amount of knowledge, but should have copied down different marks from my party card. On the assumption, that is to say, that every name on a long ballot paper represents an individual known to every voter there would be an enormous difference between Lord Courtney's proposed system and the existing system in the London Boroughs. But if the fact is that the names in each case are mere names, there is little effective difference between the working of the two systems until the votes are counted.

If the sole object of an election were to discover and record the exact proportion of the electorate who are prepared to vote for candidates nominated by the several party organizations Lord Courtney's scheme might be adopted as a whole. But English experience, and a longer experience in America, has shown that the personality of the candidate nominated is at least as important as his party allegiance, and that a parliament of well-selected members who represent somewhat roughly the opinions of the nation is better than a parliament of ill-selected members who, as far as their party labels are concerned, are, to quote Lord Courtney, "a distillation, a quintessence, a microcosm, a reflection of the community."[1]

To Lord Courtney the multi-member constituency, which permits of a wide choice, and the preferential vote, which permits of full use of that choice, are equally essential parts of his plan; and that plan will soon be seriously discussed, because parliament, owing to the rise of the Labour Party and the late prevalence of "three-cornered" contests, will soon have to deal with the question. It will then be interesting to see whether the growing substitution of the new quantitative and psychological for the old absolute and logical way of thinking about elections will have advanced sufficiently far to enable the House of Commons to distinguish between the two points. If so, they will adopt the transferable vote, and so get over the difficulty of three-cornered elections, while retaining single-member constituencies, and therewith the possibility of making the personality of a candidate known to the whole of his constituents.

A further effect of the way in which we are beginning to think of the electoral process is that, since 1888, parliament, in reconstructing the system of English local government, has steadily diminished the number of elections, with the avowed purpose of increasing their efficiency. The Local Government Acts of 1888 and 1894 swept away thousands of elections for Improve-

---

[1] Address at Stockport, p. 11.

ment Boards, Burial Boards, Vestries, etc. In 1902 the separately elected School Boards were abolished, and it is certain that the Guardians of the Poor will soon follow them. The Rural Parish Councils, which were created in 1894, and which represented a reversion by the Liberal Party to the older type of democratic thought, have been a failure, and will either be abolished or will remain ineffective, because no real administrative powers will be given to them. But if we omit the rural districts, the inhabitant of a "county borough" will soon vote only for parliament and his borough council, while the inhabitant of London or of an urban district or non-county borough will only vote for parliament, his county, and his district or borough council. On the average, neither will be asked to vote more than once a year.

In America one notices a similiar tendency towards electoral concentration as a means of increasing electoral responsibility. In Philadelphia I found that this concentration had taken a form which seemed to me to be due to a rather elementary quantitative mistake in psychology. Owing to the fact that the reformers had thought only of economizing political force, and had ignored the limitations of political knowledge, so many elections were combined on one day that the Philadelphia "blanket-ballot" which I was shown, with its parallel columns of party "tickets," containing some four hundred names. The resulting effects on the *personnel* of Philadelphian politics were as obvious as they were lamentable. In other American cities, however, concentration often takes the form of the abolition of many of the elected boards and officials, and the substitution for them of a single elected Mayor, who administers the city by nominated commissions, and whose personality it is hoped can be made known during an election to all the voters, and therefore must be seriously considered by his nominators.

One noticed again the growing tendency to substitute a quantitative and psychological for an absolute and logical view of the electoral process in the House of Commons debate on the claim set up by the House of Lords in 1907 to the right of forcing a general election (or a referendum) at any moment which they thought advantageous to themselves. Mr. Herbert Samuel, for instance, argued that this claim, if allowed, would give a still further advantage in politics to the electoral forces of wealth, acting, at dates carefully chosen by the House of Lords, both directly and through the control of the Press. Lord Robert Cecil alone, whose mind is historical in the worst sense of that term, objected "What a commentary was that on the 'will of the people' " [1] and thought it somehow illegitimate that Mr. Samuel should not defend democracy according to the philosophy of Thomas Paine, so that he could answer in the style of Canning. The present quarrel between the two Houses may indeed result in a further step in the public control of the methods of producing political opinion by the substitution of

[1] *Times*, June 25, 1907.

General Elections occurring at regular intervals for our present system of sudden party dissolutions at moments of national excitement.

But in the electoral process, as in so many other cases, one dares not hope that these slow and half-conscious changes in the general intellectual attitude will be sufficient to suggest and carry through all the improvements of machinery necessary to meet our growing difficulties, unless they are quickened by a conscious purpose. At my last contest for the London County Council I had to spend the half hour before the close of the vote in one of the polling stations of a very poor district. I was watching the proceedings, which in the crush at the end are apt to be rather irregular, and at the same time was thinking of this book. The voters who came in were the result of the "final rally" of the canvassers on both sides. They entered the room in rapid but irregular succession, as if they were jerked forward by a hurried and inefficient machine. About half of them were women, with broken straw hats, pallid faces, and untidy hair. All were dazed and bewildered, having been snatched away in carriages or motors from the making of match-boxes, or button-holes, or cheap furniture, or from the public house, or, since it was Saturday evening, from bed. Most of them seemed to be trying, in the unfamiliar surroundings, to be sure of the name for which, as they had been reminded at the door, they were to vote. A few were drunk, and one man, who was apparently a supporter of my own, clung to my neck while he tried to tell me of some vaguely tremendous fact which just eluded his power of speech. I was very anxious to win, and inclined to think I had won, but my chief feeling was an intense conviction that this could not be accepted as even a decently satisfactory method of creating a government for a city of five million inhabitants, and that nothing short of a conscious and resolute facing of the whole problem of the formation of political opinion would enable us to improve it.

Something might be done, and perhaps will be done in the near future, to abolish the more sordid details of English electioneering. Public houses could be closed on the election day, both to prevent drunkenness and casual treating, and to create an atmosphere of comparative seriousness. It is a pity that we cannot have the elections on a Sunday as they have in France. The voters would then come to the poll after twenty or twenty-four hours' rest, and their own thoughts would have some power of asserting themselves even in the presence of the canvasser, whose hustling energy now inevitably dominates the tired nerves of men who have just finished their day's work. The feeling of moral responsibility half consciously associated with the religious use of Sunday would also be so valuable an aid to reflection that the most determined anti-clerical might be willing to risk the chance that it would add to the political power of the churches. It may cease to be true that in England the Christian day of rest, in spite of the recorded protest of the founder of Christianity, is still too much hedged about by the traditions of prehistoric taboo to be available for the most solemn act of citizenship. It might again be possible to lend to the polling-place some of the dignity of a law court, and if no better buildings were available, at least to clean and decorate the dingy schoolrooms now used. But such improvements in the external environment of election day, however desirable they may be in themselves, can only be of small effect.

Some writers argue or imply that all difficulties in the working of the electoral process will disappear of themselves as men approach to social equality. Those who are now rich will, they believe, have neither motive for corrupt electoral expenditure, nor superfluity of money to spend on it; while the women and the working men who are now unenfranchised or politically inactive, will bring into politics a fresh stream of unspoilt impulse.

If our civilization is to survive, greater social equality must indeed come. Men will not continue to live peacefully together in huge cities under conditions that are intolerable to any sensitive mind, both among those who profit, and those who suffer by them. But no one who is near to political facts can believe that the immediate effect either of greater equality or of the extension of the suffrage will be to clear away

all moral and intellectual difficulties in political organization.

A mere numerical increase in the number of persons
in England who are interested in politics would indeed
itself introduce a new and difficult political factor.
The active politicians in England, those who take
any part in politics beyond voting, are at present a
tiny minority. I was to speak not long ago at an
election meeting, and having been misdirected as to
the place where the meeting was to be held, found myself in an unknown part of North London, compelled
to inquire of the inhabitants until I should find the
address either of the meeting-hall or of the party committee-room. For a long time I drew blank, but at
last a cabman on his way home to tea told me that
there was a milkman in his street who was "a politician
and would know." There are in London seven hundred
thousand parliamentary voters, and I am informed by
the man who is in the best position to know that it
would be safe to say that less than ten thousand persons actually attend the annual ward meetings of the
various parties, and that not more than thirty
thousand are members of the party associations. That
division of labour which assigns politics to a special
class of enthusiasts, looked on by many of their neighbours as well-meaning busybodies, is not carried so far
in most other parts of England as in London.
But in no county in England, as far as I am aware,

does the number of persons really active in politics amount to ten per cent. of the electorate.

There are, I think, signs that this may soon cease to be true. The English Elementary Education Act was passed in 1870, and the elementary schools may be said to have become fairly efficient by 1880. Those who entered them, being six years old, at that date are now aged thirty-four. The statistics as to the production and sale of newspapers and cheap books and the use of free libraries, show that the younger working men and women in England read many times as much as their parents did. This, and the general increase of intellectual activity in our cities of which it is only a part, may very probably lead, as the social question in politics grows more serious, to a large extension of electoral interest. If so, the little groups of men and women who now manage the three English parties in the local constituencies will find themselves swamped by thousands of adherents who will insist on taking some part in the choice of candidates and the formation of programs. That will lead to a great increase in the complexity of the process by which the Council, the Executive, and the officers of each local party association are appointed. Parliament indeed may find itself compelled, as many of the American States have been compelled, to pass a series of Acts for the prevention of fraud in the interior government of parties. The ordinary citizen would find then, much

more obviously than he does at present, that an effective
use of his voting power involves not only the marking
of a ballot paper on the day of the election, but an
active share in that work of appointing and controlling
party committtees from which many men whose
opinions are valuable to the State shrink with an
instinctive dread.

But the most important difficulties raised by the
extension of political interest from a very small to a
large fraction of the population would be concerned with
political motive rather than political machinery.
It is astonishing that the early English democrats, who
supposed that individual advantage would be the sole
driving force in politics,¹ assumed, without realizing the
nature of their own assumption, that the representative,
if he were elected for a short term, would inevitably
feel his own advantage to be identical with that of the
community.¹   At present there is a fairly sufficient
supply of men whose imagination and sympathies are
sufficiently quick and wide to make them ready to
undertake the toil of unpaid electioneering and
adminstration for the general good.   But every
organizer of elections knows that the supply is never
more than sufficient, and payment of members, while
it would permit men of good-will to come forward who

¹ *E.g.*, James Mill, *Essay on Government* (1825), " We have seen in
what manner it is possible to prevent in the Representatives the rise of
an interest different from that of the parties who choose them, namely,
by giving them little time not dependent upon the will of those parties"
(p. 27).

are now shut out, would also make it possible for less worthy motives to become more effective. The concentration both of administrative and legislative work in the hands of the Cabinet, while it tends to economy of time and effort, is making the House of Commons yearly a less interesting place; and members have of late often expressed to me a real anxiety lest the *personnel* of the House should seriously deteriorate.

The chief immediate danger in the case of the two older parties is that, owing to the growing expense of electioneering and the growing effect of legislation on commerce and finance, an increasing proportion of the members and candidates may be drawn from the class of "hustling" company-promoters and financiers. The Labour Party, on the other hand, can now draw upon an ample supply of genuine public spirit, and its difficulties in this respect will arise, not from calculated individual selfishness, but from the social and intellectual environment of working-class life. During the last twenty years I have been associated, for some years continuously and afterwards at intervals, with English political working men. They had, it seemed to me, for the most part a great advantage in the fact that certain real things of life were real to them. It is, for instance, the "class-conscious" working men who, in England as on the Continent, are the chief safeguard against the horrors of a general European war. But as their number and responsibility increase they will, I believe, have to learn some rather hard

lessons as to the intellectual conditions of representative government upon a large scale. The town working man lives in a world in which it is very difficult for him to choose his associates. If he is of
an expansive temperament, and it is such men who
become politicians, he must take his mates in the
shop and his neighbours in the tenement house as he
finds them—and he sees them at very close range.
The social virtue therefore which is almost a necessity
of his existence is a good-humoured tolerance of the
defects of average human nature. He is keenly aware
of the uncertainty of his own industrial position,
accustomed to give and receive help, and very unwilling to "do" any man "out of his job."   His parents and
grandparents read very little and he was brought up
in a home with few books. If, as he grows up, he
does not himself read, things beyond his direct observation are apt to be rather shadowy for him, and he
is easily made suspicious of that which he does not
understand.   If, on the other hand, he takes to reading
when he is already a grown man, words and ideas are
apt to have for him a kind of abstract and sharply
outlined reality in a region far removed from his daily
life.

Now the first virtue required in government is the
habit of realizing that things whose existence we infer
from reading are as important as the things observed
by our senses, of looking, for instance, through a list
of candidates for an appointment and weighing the

qualifications of the man whom one has never met by the same standard as those of the man whom one has met, and liked or pitied, the day before; or of deciding on an improvement with complete impartiality as between the district one knows of only on the map and the district one sees every morning. If a representative elected to govern a large area allows personal acquaintance and liking to influence his decisions, his acquaintance and liking will be schemed for and exploited by those who have their own ends to gain. The same difficulty arises in matters of discipline, where the interests of the unknown thousands who will suffer from the inefficiency of an official have to be balanced against those of the known official who will suffer by being punished or dismissed; as well as in those numerous cases in which a working man has to balance the dimly realized interests of the general consumer against his intimate sympathy with his fellow-craftsmen.

The political risk arising from these facts is not, at present, very great in the parliamentary Labour Party. The working men who have been sent to parliament have been hitherto, as a rule, men of picked intelligence and morale and of considerable political experience. But the success or failure of any scheme aiming at social equity will depend chiefly on its administration by local bodies, to which the working classes must necessarily send men of less exceptional ability and experience. I have never myself served on an elected local body the majority of whose members were weekly wage earners.

But I have talked with men, both of working-class and middle-class origin, who have been in that position. What they say confirms that which I have inferred from my own observation, that on such a body one finds a high level of enthusiasm, of sympathy, and of readiness to work, combined with a difficulty in maintaining a sufficiently rigorous standard in dealing with sectional interests and official discipline.

One is told that on such a body many members feel it difficult to realize that the way in which a well intentioned man may deal with his own personal expenditure, his continued patronage, for instance, of a rather in-efficient tradesman because he has a large family, or his refusal to contest an account from a dislike of imputing bad motives, is fatal if applied in the expenditure of the large sums entrusted to a public body. Some-times there are even, one learns, indications of that good-humoured and not ill-meant laxity in expending public money which has had such disastrous results in America, and which lends itself so easily to exploitation by those in whom the habit of giving and taking personal favours has hardened into systematic fraud. When one of the West Ham Guardians, two years ago, committed suicide on being charged with corruption, the *Star* sent down a representative who filled a column with the news. "His death," we are told, "has robbed the district of an indefatigable public worker. County Council, Board of Guardians, and Liberal interests all occupied his leisure time." "One of his friends" is described as saying to the *Star* reporter, "You do not need to go far to learn of his big-souled geniality. The poor folks of the workhouse will miss him badly"[1] When one has waded through masses of evidence on American municipal corruption, that phrase about "big-souled geniality" makes one shudder.

The early history of the co-operative and trade-union movements in England is full of pathetic instances of this kind of failure, and both movements show how a new and more stringent ideal may be slowly built up. Such an ideal will not come of itself without an effort, and must be part of the conscious organized thought of each generation if it is to be permanently effective.

These difficulties have in the past been mainly pointed out by the opponents of democracy. But if democracy is to succeed they must be frankly considered by the democrats themselves; just as it is the engineer who is trying to build the bridge, and not the ferry-owner, who is against any bridge at all, whose duty it is to calculate the strain which the materials will stand. The engineer, when he wishes to increase the margin of safety in his plans, treats as factors in the same quantitative problem both the chemical expedients by which he can strengthen his materials and the structural changes by which the strain on those materials can be diminished. So those who would increase the margin of safety in our democracy must estimate, with no desire except to arrive at truth, both the degree to which the political strength

[1] *Star*, November 28, 1906.

of the individual citizen can, in any given time, be actually increased by moral and educational changes, and the possibility of preserving or extending or inventing such elements in the structure of democracy as may prevent the demand upon him being too great for his strength.

CHAPTER III

OFFICIAL THOUGHT

It is obvious, however, that the persons elected under any conceivable system of representation cannot do the whole work of government themselves.

If all elections are held in single member constituencies of a size sufficient to secure a good supply of candidates; if the number of elections is such as to allow the political workers a proper interval for rest and reflection between the campaigns; if each elected body has an area large enough for effective administration, a number of members sufficient for committee work and not too large for debate, and duties sufficiently important to justify the effort and expense of a contest; then one may take about twenty-three thousand as the best number of men and women to be elected by the existing population of the United Kingdom—or rather less than one to every two thousand of the population.[1]

This proportion depends mainly on facts in the

[1] I arrive at this figure by dividing the United Kingdom into single member parliamentary constituencies, averaging 100,000 in population, which gives a House of Commons of 440—a more convenient number than the existing 670. I take the same unit of 100,000 for the average municipal area. Large towns would contain several parliamentary constituencies, and small towns would, as at present, be separate municipal areas, although only part of a parliamentary constituency. I allow one local council of 50 on the average to each municipal area.

255

psychology of the electors, which will change very slowly
if they change at all.   At present the amount of work
to be done in the way of government is rapidly increasing, and seems likely to continue to increase.   If so,
the number of elected persons available for each unit
of work must tend to decrease.   The number of persons
now elected in the United Kingdom (including, for
instance, the Parish Councillors of rural parishes, and
the Common Council of the City of London) is, of course,
larger than my estimate, though it has been greatly
diminished by the Acts of 1888, 1894, and 1902.
Owing, however, to the fact that areas and powers are
still somewhat uneconomically distributed it represents
a smaller actual working power than would be given
by the plan which I suggest.

On the other hand, the number of persons (excluding
the Army and Navy) given in the Census Returns of
1901 as professionally employed in the central and local
government of the United Kingdom was 161,000.   This
number has certainly grown since 1901 at an increasing
rate, and consists of persons who give on an average at
least four times as many hours a week to their work
as can be expected from the average elected member.

What ought to be the relation between these two bodies,
of twenty-three thousand elected, and say, two hundred
thousand non-elected persons?   To begin with, ought
the elected members to be free to appoint the non-elected
officials as they like?   Most American politicians of
Andrew Jackson's time, and a large number of American

politicians to-day, would hold, for instance, as a direct corollary from democratic principles, that the elected congressman or senator for a district or State has a right to nominate the local federal officials. There may, he would admit, be some risk in that method, but the risk, he would argue, is one involved in the whole scheme of democracy, and the advantages of democracy as a whole are greater than its disadvantages.

Our political logic in England has never been so elementary as that of the Americans, nor has our faith in it been so unflinching. Most Englishmen, therefore, have no feeling of disloyalty to the democratic idea in admitting that it is not safe to allow the efficiency of officials to depend upon the personal character of individual representatives. At the General Election of 1906 there were at least two English constituencies (one Liberal and the other Conservative) which returned candidates whose personal unfitness had been to most men's minds proved by evidence given in the law courts. Neither constituency was markedly unlike the average in any respect. The facts were well known, and in each case an attempt was made by a few public-spirited voters to split the party vote, but both candidates were successful by large majorities. The Borough of Croydon stands, socially and intellectually, well above the average, but Mr. Jabez Balfour represented Croydon for many years, until he was sentenced to penal servitude for fraud. No one in any of these three cases would have desired that the sitting member should appoint, say, the postmasters, or collectors of Inland Revenue for his constituency.

But though the case against the appointment of officials by individual representatives is clear, the question of the part which should be taken by any elected body as a whole in appointing the officials who serve under it is much more difficult, and cannot be discussed without considering what are to be the relative functions of the officials and the representatives after the appointment has taken place. Do we aim at making election in fact as well as in constitutional theory the sole base of political authority, or do we desire that the non-elected officials shall exert some amount of independent influence?

The fact that most Englishmen, in spite of their traditional fear of bureaucracy, would now accept the second of these alternatives, is one of the most striking results of our experience in the working of democracy. We see that the evidence on which the verdict at an election must be given is becoming every year more difficult to collect and present, and further removed from the direct observation of the voters. We are afraid of being entirely dependent on partisan newspapers or election leaflets for our knowledge, and we have therefore come to value, even if for that reason only, the existence of a responsible and more or less independent Civil Service. It is difficult to realize how short a time it is since questions for which we now rely entirely on official statistics were discussed by the ordinary political methods of agitation and advocacy. In the earlier years of George the Third's reign, at a time when population in England was, as we now know, rising with unprecedented rapidity, the question of fact whether it was rising or falling led to embittered political controversy.[1] In the spring of 1830 the House of Commons gave three nights to a confused party debate on the state of the country. The Whigs argued that distress was general, and the Tories (who were, as it happened, right) that it was local.[2] In 1798 or 1830 the "public" who could take part in such discussions numbered perhaps fifty thousand at the most. At least ten million people must, since 1903, have taken part in the present Tariff Reform controversy; and that controversy would have degenerated into mere Bedlam if it had not been for the existence of the Board of Trade Returns, with whose figures both sides had at least to appear to square their arguments.

If official figures did not exist in England, or if they did not possess or deserve authority, it is difficult to estimate the degree of political harm which could be done in a few years by an interested and deliberately dishonest agitation on some question too technical for the personal judgment of the ordinary voter. Suppose, for instance, that our Civil Service were either notoriously inefficient or believed to be dominated by party influence, and that an organized and fraudulent "cur-

[1] Bonar's *Malthus*, chap. vii.
[2] *Hansard*, Feb. 4, 5, 6, 1830.

rency agitation" should suddenly spring up. A powerful press syndicate brings out a series of well-advertised
articles declaring that the privileges of the Bank of
England and the law as to the gold reserve are "stran-
gling British Industry." The contents bills of fifty
newspapers denounce every day the "monopolists" and
the "gold-bugs," the "lies and shams" of the Bank
Returns, and the "paid perjurers of Somerset House."
The group of financiers who control the syndicate stand
to win enormous sums by the creation of a more "elastic"
currency, and subscribe largely to a Free Money League
which includes a few sincere paper-money theorists who
have been soured by the contempt of the professional
economists. A vigorous and well-known member of
parliament—a not very reputable aristocrat perhaps,
or some one loosely connected with the Labor movement
—whom everybody has hitherto feared and no one quite
trusted, sees his opportunity. He puts himself at the
head of the movement, denounces the "fossils" and
"superior persons" who at present lead Conservative
and Liberal and Labour parties alike, and, with the help
of the press syndicate and the subscription fund of the
"Free Money League," begins to capture the local associations, and through them the central office of the party
which is for the moment in opposition.

Can any one be sure that such a campaign, if it were
opposed only by counter-electioneering, might not succeed, even although its proposals were wholly fraudulent,
and its leaders so ignorant or so criminal that they could

only come into power by discrediting two-thirds of the honest politicians in the country, and by replacing them with "hustlers" and "boodlers" and "grafters," and the other species for whom American political science has provided names? How is the ordinary voter—a market-gardener, or a gas-stoker, or a water-colour painter—to distinguish by the help of his own knowledge and reasoning power between the various appeals made to him by the "Reformers" and the "Safe Money Men" as to the right proportion of the gold reserve to the note issue—the "ten per cent." on the blue posters and the "cent. per cent." on the yellow? Nor will his conscience be a safer guide than his judgment. A "Christian Service Wing" of the Free Money League may be formed, and his conscience may be roused by a white-cravatted orator intoxicated by his own eloquence into something like sincerity, who borrows that phrase about "Humanity crucified upon a cross of gold" which Mr. W. J. Bryan borrowed a dozen years ago from some one else. In an optimistic mood one might rely on the subtle network of confidence by which each man trusts, on subjects outside his own knowledge, some honest and better-informed neighbour, who again trusts at several removes the trained thinker. But does such a personal network exist in our vast delocalized urban populations?

It is the vague apprehension of such dangers, quite as much as the merely selfish fears of the privileged classes, which preserves in Europe the relics of past systems of non-elective government, the House of Lords, for instance, in England, and the Monarchy in Italy or Norway. Men feel that a second base in politics is required, consisting of persons independent of the tactics by which electoral opinion is formed and legally entitled to make themselves heard. But political authority founded on heredity or wealth is not in fact protected from the interested manipulation of opinion and feeling. The American Senate, which has come to be representative of wealth, is already absorbed by that financial power which depends for its existence on manufactured opinion; and our House of Lords is rapidly tending in the same direction. From the beginning of history it has been found easier for any skilled politician who set his mind to it, to control the opinions of a hereditary monarch than those of a crowd.

The real "Second Chamber," the real "constitutional check" in England, is provided, not by the House of Lords or the Monarchy, but by the existence of a permanent Civil Service, appointed on a system independent of the opinion or desires of any politician, and holding office during good behaviour. If such a service were, as it is in Russia and to a large extent in India, a sovereign power, it would itself, as I argued in the last chapter, have to cultivate the art of manipulating opinion. But the English Civil servants in their present position have the right and duty of making their voice heard, without the necessity of making their will, by fair means or foul, prevail.

The creation of this Service was the one great
political invention in nineteenth-century England, and
like other inventions it was worked out under the pres-
sure of an urgent practical problem. The method of
appointing the officials of the East India Company had
been a critical question in English politics since 1783.
By that time it had already become clear that we could
not permanently allow the appointment of the rulers
of a great empire kept in existence by the English fleet
and army to depend upon the irresponsible favour of
the Company's directors. Charles James Fox in 1783,
with his usual heedlessness, proposed to cut the knot by
making Indian appointments, in effect, part of 'the
ordinary system of parliamentary patronage; and he
and Lord North were beaten over their India Bill, not
only because George the Third was obstinate and unscrupulous, but because men felt the enormous political
dangers involved in their proposal. The question, in
fact, could only be solved by a new invention. The
expedient of administering an oath to the Directors
that they would make their requirements honestly, proved
to be useless, and the requirements that the nominees
of the Directors should submit to a special training at
Hayleybury, though more effective, left the main evil
of patronage untouched.

As early, therefore, as 1833, the Government Bill
introduced by Macaulay for the renewal and revision
of the Company's charter contained a clause providing
that East India cadetships should be thrown open to

competition.[1] For the time the influence of the Directors was sufficient to prevent so great a change from
being effected, but in 1853, on a further renewal of the
Charter, the system of competition was definitely
adopted, and the first open examination for cadetships
took place in 1855.

In the meantime Sir Charles Trevelyan, a distinguished Indian Civilian who had married Macaulay's
sister, had been asked to inquire, with the help of
Sir Stafford Northcote, into the method of appointment
in the Home Civil Service. His report appeared in
the spring of 1854,[2] and is one of the ablest of those
State Papers which have done so much to mould the
English constitution during the last two generations.
It showed the intolerable effects on the *personnel* of
the existing Service of the system by which the Patronage
Secretary of the Treasury distributed appointments in
the national Civil Service among those members of
parliament whose votes were to be influenced or re-
warded, and it proposed that all posts requiring intellectual qualifications should be thrown open to those
young men of good character who succeeded at a competitive examination in the subjects which then constituted the education of a gentleman.

But to propose that members of parliament should

[1] It would be interesting if Lord Morley, now that he has access to the
records of the East India House, would tell us the true intellectual history of this far-reaching suggestion. For the facts as now known, cf. A.
L. Lowell, *Colonial Civil Service*, pp. 243-256.

[2] *Reports and Papers on the Civil Service*, 1854-5.

give up their own patronage was a very different thing
from asking them to take away the patronage of the
East India Company. Sir Charles Trevelyan, therefore, before publishing his proposal, sent it round to a
number of distinguished persons both inside and outside the Government service, and printed their very
frank replies in an appendix.

Most of his correspondents thought that the idea was
hopelessly impracticable. It seemed like the intrusion
into the world of politics of a scheme of cause and effect
derived from another universe—as if one should propose
to the Stock Exchange that the day's prices should be
fixed by prayer and the casting of lots. Lingen, for
instance, the permanent head of the Education Office,
wrote "considering that, as a matter of fact, patronage
is one element of power, and not by any means an unreal one; considering the long and inestimably valuable
habituation of the people of this country to political
contests in which the share of office . . . reckons among
the legitimate prizes of war; considering that socially
and in the business of life, as well as in Downing Street,
rank and wealth (as a fact, and whether we like it or
not) hold the keys of many things, and that our modes
of thinking and acting proceed, in a thousand ways,
upon this supposition, considering all these things, I
should hesitate long before I advised such a revolution
of the Civil Service as that proposed by yourself and
Sir Stafford Northcote."[1] Sir James Stephen of the

---

[1] *Reports and Papers on the Civil Service*, pp. 104, 105.

Colonial Office put it more bluntly, "The world we live in is not, I think, half moralized enough for the acceptance of such a scheme of stern morality as this." [1] When, a few years later, competition for commissions in the Indian army was discussed, Queen Victoria (or Prince Albert through her) objected that it "reduced the sovereign to a mere signing machine." [2]

In 1870, however, sixteen years after Trevelyan's Report, Gladstone established open competition throughout the English Civil Service, by an order in Council which was practically uncriticized and unopposed; and the parliamentary government of England in one of its most important functions did in fact reduce itself "to a mere signing machine."

The causes of the change in the political atmosphere which made this possible constitute one of the most interesting problems in English history. One cause is obvious. In 1867 Lord Derby's Reform Act had suddenly transferred the ultimate control of the House of Commons from the "ten pound householders" in the boroughs to the working men. The old "governing classes" may well have felt that the patronage which they could not much longer retain would be safer in the hands of an independent Civil Service Commission, interpreting, like a blinded figure of Justice, the verdict of Nature, than in those of the dreaded "caucuses," which Mr. Schnadhorst was already organizing.

[1] *Reports and papers on the Civil Service*, p. 78.
[2] *Life of Queen Victoria*, vol. iii, p. 377 (July 29, 1858).

But one seems to detect a deeper cause of change than the mere transference of voting power. The fifteen years from the Crimean War to 1870 were in England a period of wide mental activity, during which the conclusions of a few penetrating thinkers like Darwin or Newman were discussed and popularized by a crowd of magazine writers and preachers and poets. The conception was gaining ground that it was upon serious and continued thought and not upon opinion that the power to carry out our purposes, whether in politics or elsewhere, must ultimately depend.

Carlyle in 1850 had asked whether "democracy once modelled into suffrages, furnished with ballot-boxes and such-like, will itself accomplish the salutary universal change from Delusive to Real," and had answered, "Your ship cannot double Cape Horn by its excellent plans of voting. The ship may vote this and that, above decks and below, in the most harmonious exquisitely constitutional manner: the ship, to get round Cape Horn, will find a set of conditions already voted for, and fixed with adamantine rigour by the ancient Elemental Powers, who are entirely careless how you vote. If you can, by voting or without voting, ascertain those conditions, and valiantly conform to them, you will get round the Cape: if you cannot—the ruffian Winds will blow you ever back again."[1]

By 1870 Carlyle's lesson was already well started

[1] *Latter Day Pamphlets, No.* 1, *The Present Time.* (Chapman and Hall, 1894, pp. 12 and 14.)

on   its course from paradox to platitude.   The most important single influence in that course had been the growth of Natural Science.   It was, for instance, in 1870 that Huxley's "Lay Sermons" were collected and published.   People who could not in 1850 understand Carlyle's distinction between the Delusive and the Real, could not help understanding Huxley's comparison of life and death to a game of chess with an unseen opponent who never makes a mistake.[1]   And Huxley's impersonal Science seemed a more present aid in the voyage round Cape Horn than Carlyle's personal and impossible Hero.

But the invention of a competitive Civil Service, when it had once been made and adopted, dropped from the region of severe and difficult thought in which it originated, and took its place in our habitual political psychology.   We now half-consciously conceive of the Civil Service as an unchanging fact whose good and bad points are to be taken or left as a whole.   Open competition has by the same process become a "principle," conceived of as applying to those cases to which it has been in fact applied, and to no others.   What is therefore for the moment most needed, if we are to think fruitfully on the subject, is that we should in our own minds break up this fact, and return to the world of infinite possible variations.   We must think of the expedient of competition itself as varying in a thousand

[1] *Lay Sermons*, p. 31, " A Liberal Education " (1868).

different directions, and shading by imperceptible gradations into other methods of appointment; and of the
posts offered for competition as differing each from
all the rest, as overlapping those posts for which competition in some form is suitable though it has not yet
been tried, and as touching, at the marginal point on
their curve, those posts for which competition is unsuitable.

Directly we begin this process one fact becomes obvious. There is no reason why the same system should
not be applied to the appointment of the officials of
the local as to those of the central government. It
is an amazing instance of the intellectual inertia of
the English people that we have never seriously considered this point. In America the term Civil Service
is applied equally to both groups of offices, and "Civil
Service principles" are understood to cover State and
Municipal as well as Federal appointments. The
separation of the two systems in our minds may,
indeed, be largely due to the mere accident that from
historical reasons we call them by different names.
As it is, the local authorities are (with the exception
that certain qualifications are required for teachers and
medical officers) left free to do as they will in making
appointments. Perhaps half a dozen Metropolitan
and provincial local bodies have adopted timid and
limited schemes of open competition. But in all other
cases the local civil servants, who are already probably

as numerous as those of the central government,[1] are appointed under conditions which, if the Government chose to create a Commission of Inquiry, would probably be found to have reproduced many of the evils that existed in the patronage of the central government before 1855.

It would not, of course, be possible to appoint a separate body of Civil Service Commissioners to hold a separate examination for each locality, and difficulties would arise from the selection of officials by a body responsible only to the central government, and out of touch with the local body which controls, pays, and promotes them when appointed. But similiar difficulties have been obviated by American Civil Service Reformers, and a few days' hard thinking would suffice to adapt the system to English local conditions.

One object aimed at by the creation of a competitive Civil Service for the central government in England was the prevention of corruption. It was made more difficult for representatives and officials to conspire together in order to defraud the public, when the official ceased to owe his appointment to the representative. If an English member of parliament desired now to make money out of his position, he would have to corrupt a whole series of officials in no way dependent on his favour, who perhaps intensely dislike the human type to

[1] The figures in the census of 1901 were—National, 90,000; Local, 71, 000. But the local officials since then have, I believe, increased much more rapidly than the national.

which he belongs, and who would be condemned to disgrace or imprisonment years after he had lost his seat if some record of their joint misdoing were unearthed.

This precaution against corruption is needed even more clearly under the conditions of local government. The expenditure of local bodies in the United Kingdom is already much larger than that of the central State, and is increasing at an enormously greater rate, while the fact that most of the money is spent locally, and in comparatively small sums, makes fraud easier. English municipal life is, I believe, on the whole pure, but fraud does occur, and is encouraged by the close connection that may exist between the officials and the representatives. A needy or thick-skinned urban councillor or guardian may at any moment tempt, or be tempted, by a poor relation who helped him at his election, and for whom (perhaps as the result of a tacit understanding that similar favours should be allowed to his colleagues), he obtained a municipal post.

The railway companies, again, in England are coming every year more and more under State control, but no statesman has ever attempted to secure in their case, as was done in the case of the East India Company a century ago, some reasonable standard of purity and impartiality in appointments and promotion. Some few railways have systems of competition for boy clerks, even more inadequate than those carried on by municipalities; but one is told that under most of the companies both appointment and promotion may be influenced by the favour of directors or large shareholders. We regulate the minutiae of coupling and signalling on the railways, but do not realize that the safety of the public depends even more directly upon their systems of patronage.

How far this principle should be extended, and how far, for instance, it would be possible to prevent the head of a great private firm from ruining half a country side by leaving the management of his business to a hopelessly incompetent relation, is a question which depends, among other things, upon the powers of political invention which may be developed by collectivist thinkers in the next fifty years.

We must meanwhile cease to treat the existing system of competition by the hasty writing of answers to unexpected examination questions as an unchangeable entity. That system has certain very real advantages. It is felt by the candidates and their relations to be "fair." It reveals facts about the relative powers of the candidates in some important intellectual qualities which no testimonials would indicate, and which are often unknown, till tested, to the candidates themselves. But if the sphere of independent selection is to be widely extended, greater variety must be introduced into its methods. In this respect invention has stood still in England since the publication of Sir Charles Trevelyan's Report in 1855. Some slight modifications have taken place in the subjects chosen for examination, but the enormous changes in English educational conditions

during the last half century have been for the most part
ignored. It is still assumed that young Englishmen consist of a small minority who have received the nearly
uniform "education of a gentleman," and a large majority who have received no intellectual training at all. The
spread of varied types of secondary schools, the increasing specialization of higher education, and the experience which all the universities of the world have accumulated as to the possibility of testing the genuineness and
intellectual quality of "post graduate" theses have had
little or no effect.

The Playfair Commission of 1875 found that a few
women were employed for strictly subordinate work
in the Post Office. Since then female typewriters and
a few better-paid women have been introduced into
other offices in accordance with the casual impulses
of this or that parliamentary or permanent chief; but
no systematic attempt has been made to enrich the
thinking power of the State by using the trained and
patient intellects of the women who graduate each year
in the newer, and "qualify by examination to graduate,"
in the older Universities.

To the general public, indeed, the adoption of open
competition in 1870 seemed to obviate any necessity
for further consideration not only of the method by
which officials were appointed but also of the system
under which they did their work. The race of Tite
Barnacles, they learnt, was now to become extinct. Appointment was to be made by "merit," and the announce-

ment of the examination results, like the wedding in a middle-Victorian novel, was to be the end of the story. But in a Government office, as certainly as in a law-court or a laboratory, effective thinking will not be done unless adequate opportunities and motives are secured by organization during the whole working life of the appointed officials. Since 1870, however, the organization of the Government Departments has either been left to the casual development of office tradition in each Department or has been changed (as in the case of the War Office) by an agitation directed against one Department only. The official relations, for instance, between the First Division minority and the Second Division majority of the clerks in each office vary, not on any considered principle, but according to the opinions and prejudices of some once-dominant but now forgotten chief. The same is true of the relation between the heads of each section and the officials immediately below them. In at least one office important papers are brought first to the chief. His decision is at once made, and is sent down the hierarchy for elaboration. In other offices the younger men are given invaluable experience, and the elder men are prevented from getting into an official rut, by a system which requires that all papers should be sent first to a junior, who sends them up to his senior accompanied not only by the necessary papers but also by a minute of his own suggesting official action. One of these two types of organization must in fact be better than the other, but no one has systematically compared them.

In the Colonial Office, again, it is the duty of the Librarian to see that the published books as well as the office records on any question are available for every official who has to report on it. In the Board of Trade, which deals with subjects on which the importance of published as compared with official information is even greater, room has only just been found for a technical library which was collected many years ago.[1] The Foreign Office and the India Office have libraries, the Treasury and the Local Government Board have none.

In the Exchequer and Audit Department a deliberate policy has been adopted of training junior officials by transferring them at regular intervals to different branches of the work. The results are said to be excellent, but nothing of the kind is systematically done or has even been seriously discussed in any other Department which I know.

Nearly all departmental officials are concerned with the organization of non-departmental work more directly executive than their own, and part of a wise system of official training would consist in "seconding" young officials for experience in the kind of work which they are to organize. The clerks of the Board of Agriculture should be sent at least once in their career to help in superintending the killing of infected swine and inter-

[1] For a long time the Library of the Board of Trade was kept at the Foreign Office.

viewing actual farmers, while an official in the Railway
section of the Board of Trade should acquire some
personal knowledge of the inside of a railway office.
This principle of "seconding" might well be extended
so as to cover (as is already done in the army) definite
periods of study during which an official, on leave of
absence with full pay, should acquire knowledge useful
to his department; after which he should show the result
of his work, not by the answering of examination questions, but by the presentation of a book or report of
permanent value.

The grim necessity of providing, after the events of
the Boer War, for effective thought in the government
of the British army produced the War Office Council.
The Secretary of State, instead of knowing only of those
suggestions that reach him through the "bottle-neck" of
his senior official's mind, now sits once a week at a
table with half a dozen heads of sub-departments.   He
hears real discussion; he learns to pick men for higher
work; and saves many hours of circumlocutory writing.
At the same time, owing to a well-known fact in the
physiology of the human brain, the men who are tired
of thinking on paper find a new stimulus in the spoken
word and the presence of their fellow human beings,
just as politicians who are tired with talking, find, if
their minds are still uninjured, a new stimulus in the
silent use of a pen.

If this periodical alternation of written and oral
discussion is useful in the War Office, it would pro-

bably be useful in other offices; but no one with sufficient authority to require an answer has ever asked if it is so.

One of the most important functions of a modern Government is the effective publication of information, but we have no Department of Publicity, though we have a Stationery Office; and it is, for instance, apparently a matter of accident whether any particular Department has or has not a Gazette and how and when that Gazette is published. Nor is it any one's business to discover and criticize and if necessary coordinate the statistical methods of the various official publications.

On these points and many others a small Departmental Committee (somewhat on the lines of that Esher Committee which reorganized the War Office in 1904), consisting perhaps of an able manager of an Insurance Company, with an open-minded Civil Servant, and a business man with experience of commercial and departmental organization abroad, might suggest such improvements as would without increase of expense double the existing intellectual output of our Government offices.

But such a Committee will not be appointed unless the ordinary members of parliament, and especially the members who advocate a wide extension of collective action, consider much more seriously than they do at present the organization of collective thought. How, for instance, are we to prevent or minimize the danger that a body of officials will develop "official" habits of thought, and a sense of a corporate interest opposed

to that of the majority of the people?   If a sufficient proportion of the ablest and best equipped young men of
each generation are to be induced to come into the Government service they must be offered salaries which place
them at once among the well-to-do classes.   How are we
to prevent them siding consciously or unconsciously on
all questions of administration with their economic
equals?   If they do, the danger is not only that social
reform will be delayed, but also that working men in
England may acquire that hatred and distrust of highly
educated permanent officials which one notices in any
gathering of working men in America.

We are sometimes told, now that good education
is open to every one, that men of every kind of social
origin and class sympathy will enter to an increasing
extent the higher Civil Service.   If that takes place it
will be an excellent thing, but meanwhile any one who
follows the development of the existing examination
system knows that care is required to guard against the
danger that preference in marking may, if only from
official tradition, be given to subjects like Greek and
Latin composition, whose educational value is not higher
than others, but excellence in which is hardly ever acquired except by members of one social class.

It would, of course, be ruinous to sacrifice intellectual
efficiency to the dogma of promotion from the ranks, and
the statesmen of 1870 were perhaps right in thinking
that promotion from the second to the first division of
the service would be in their time so rare as to be

negligible. But things have changed since then. The competition for the second division has become incomparably more severe, and there is no reasonable test under which some of those second class officials who have continued their education by means of reading and University teaching in the evening would not show, at thirty years of age, a greater fitness for the highest work than would be shown by many of those who had entered by the more advanced examination.

But however able our officials are, and however varied their origin, the danger of the narrowness and rigidity which has hitherto so generally resulted from official life would still remain, and must be guarded against by every kind of encouragement to free intellectual development. The German Emperor did good service the other day when he claimed (in a semi-official communication on the Tweedmouth letter) that the persons who are Kings and Ministers in their official capacity have as Fachmänner (experts) other and wider rights in the republic of thought. One only wishes that he would allow his own officials after their day's work to regroup themselves, in the healthy London fashion, with labour leaders, and colonels, and schoolmasters, and court ladies, and members of parliament, as individualists or socialists, or protectors of African aborigines, or theosophists, or advocates of a free stage or a free ritual.

The intellectual life of the government official is indeed becoming part of a problem which every year touches us all more closely. In literature and science as well as in commerce and industry the independent producer is dying out and the official is taking his place. We are nearly all of us officials now, bound during our working days, whether we write on a newspaper, or teach in a university, or keep accounts in a bank, by restrictions on our personal freedom in the interest of a larger organization. We are little influenced by that direct and obvious economic motive which drives a small shopkeeper or farmer or country solicitor to a desperate intensity of scheming how to outstrip his rivals or make more profit out of his employees. If we merely desire to do as little work and enjoy as much leisure as possible in our lives, we all find that it pays us to adopt that steady unanxious "stroke" which neither advances nor retards promotion.

The indirect stimulus, therefore, of interest and variety, of public spirit and the craftsman's delight in his skill, is becoming more important to us as a motive for the higher forms of mental effort, and threats and promises of decrease or increase of salary less important. And because those higher efforts are needed not only for the advantage of the community but for the good of our own souls we are all of us concerned in teaching those distant impersonal masters of ours who are ourselves how to prevent the opportunity of effective thought from being confined to a tiny rich minority, living, like the Cyclopes, in irresponsible freedom. If we consciously accept the fact that organized work will in the future be the rule and unorganized work the exception, and if we deliberately adjust our methods of working as well as our personal ideals to that condition, we need no longer feel that the direction of public business must be divided between an uninstructed and unstable body of politicians and a selfish and pedantic bureaucracy.

CHAPTER IV

NATIONALITY AND HUMANITY

I HAVE discussed, in the three preceding chapters, the probable effect of certain existing intellectual tendencies on our ideals of political conduct, our systems of representation, and the methods which we adopt for securing intellectual initiative and efficiency among our professional officials—that is to say, on the internal organization of the State.

In this chapter I propose to discuss the effect of the same tendencies on international and interracial relations. But, as soon as one leaves the single State and deals with the interrelation of several States, one meets with the preliminary question, What is a State? Is the British Empire, or the Concert of Europe, one State or many? Every community in either area now exerts political influence on every other, and the telegraph and the steamship have abolished most of the older limitations on the further development and extension of that influence. Will the process of coalescence go on either in feeling or in constitutional form, or are there any permanent causes tending to limit the geographical or racial sphere of effective political solidarity, and therefore the size and composition of States?

Aristotle, writing under the conditions of the ancient world, laid it down that a community whose population extended to a hundred thousand would no more be a State than would one whose population was confined to ten.[1]   He based his argument on measurable facts as to the human senses and the human memory.   The territory of a State must be "visible as a whole" by one man's eye, and the assembly attended by all the full citizens must be able to hear one voice—which must be that of an actual man and not of the legendary Stentor.   The governing officials must be able to remember the faces and characters of all their fellow citizens.[2]   He did not ignore the fact that nearly all the world's surface as he knew it was occupied by States enormously larger than his rule allowed.   But he denied that the great barbarian monarchies were in the truest sense "States" at all.

We ourselves are apt to forget that the facts on which Aristotle relied were both real and important. The history of the Greek and mediæval City-States shows how effective a stimulus may be given to some of the highest activities and emotions of mankind when the whole environment of each citizen comes within the first-hand range of his senses and memory.   It is now only here and there, in villages outside the main stream of civilization, that men know the faces of their neighbours, and see daily as part of one whole the fields and cottages in which they work and rest.   Yet, even now, when a

---

1 *Ethics*, ix., x. 3.
2 Aristotle, *Polit.*, Bk. vii. ch. iv.

village is absorbed by a sprawling suburb or over-
whelmed by the influx of a new industrial population,
some of the older inhabitants feel that they are losing
touch with the deeper realities of life

A year ago I stood with a hard-walking and hard-
thinking old Yorkshire schoolmaster on the high moor-
land edge of Airedale.   Opposite to us was the country-
house where Charlotte Brontë was governess, and below
us ran the railway, linking a string of manufacturing
villages which already were beginning to stretch out
towards each other, and threatened soon to extend through
the valley an unbroken succession of tall chimneys and
slate roofs.   He told me how, within his memory, the
old affection for place and home had disappeared from
the district.   I asked whether he thought that a new
affection was possible, whether, now that men lived in
the larger world of knowledge and inference, rather
than in the narrower world of sight and hearing, a patriotism of books and maps might not appear which should
be a better guide to life than the patriotism of the village
street.

This he strongly denied; as the older feeling went,
nothing, he said, had taken its place, or would take its
place, but a naked and restless individualism, always
seeking for personal satisfaction, and always missing
it.   And then, almost in the words of Morris and Ruskin,
he began to urge that we should pay a cheap price if we
could regain the true riches of life by forgetting steam
and electricity, and returning to the agriculture of the

mediæval village and the handicrafts of the mediæval town.

He knew and I knew that his plea was hopeless. Even under the old conditions the Greek and Italian and Flemish City-States perished, because they were too small to protect themselves against larger though less closely organized communities; and industrial progress is an invader even more irresistible than the armies of Macedon or Spain. For a constantly increasing proportion of the inhabitants of modern England there is now no place where in the old sense they "live." Nearly the whole of the class engaged in the direction of English industry, and a rapidly increasing proportion of the manual workers, pass daily in tram or train between sleeping-place and working-place a hundred times more sights than their eyes can take in or their memory retain. They are, to use Mr. Wells's phrase, "delocalized."[1]

But now that we can no longer take the range of our senses as a basis for calculating the possible area of the civilized State, there might seem to be no facts at all which can be used for such a calculation. How can we fix the limits of effective intercommunication by steam or electricity, or the area which can be covered by such political expedients as representation and federalism? When Aristotle wished to illustrate the relation of the size of the State to the powers of its citizens he compared it to a ship, which, he said, must not be too large to be handled by the muscles of actual men. "A ship of two

---

[1] *Mankind in the Making*, p. 406.

furlongs length would not be a ship at all."[1]   But the
Lusitania is already not very far from a furlong and a
half in length, and no one can even guess what is the
upward limit of size which the ship-builders of a
generation hence will have reached.   If once we assume
that a State may be larger than the field of vision of a
single man, then the merely mechanical difficulty of
bringing the whole earth under a government as effective
as that of the United States or the British Empire has
already been overcome.   If such a government is impossible, its impossibility must be due to the limits not
of our senses and muscles but of our powers of imagination and sympathy.

I have already pointed out[2] that the modern State
must exist for the thoughts and feelings of its citizens,
not as a fact of direct observation but as an entity of
the mind, a symbol, a personification or an abstraction.
The possible area of the State will depend, therefore,
mainly on the facts which limit our creation and use of
such entities.   Fifty years ago the statesmen who were
reconstructing Europe on the basis of nationality thought
that they had found the relevant facts in the causes which
limit the physical and mental homogeneity of nations.   A
State, they thought, if it is to be effectively governed,
must be a homogeneous "nation," because no citizen
can imagine his State or make it the object of his political
affection unless he believes in the existence of a national

---

[1] Aristotle, *Polit.*, Bk. VII. ch. iv.
[2] Part I. ch. ii. pp. 72, 73, and 77-81.

type to which the individual inhabitants of the State are assimilated; and he cannot continue to believe in the existence of such a type unless in fact his fellow-citizens are like each other and like himself in certain important respects.   Bismarck deliberately limited the area of his intended German Empire by a quantitive calculation as to the possibility of assimilating other Germans to the Prussian type.   He always opposed the inclusion of Austria, and for a long time the inclusion of Bavaria, on the ground that while the Prussian type was strong enough to assimilate the Saxons and Hanoverians to itself, it would fail to assimilate Austrians and Bavarians. He said, for instance, in 1866: "We cannot use these Ultramontanes, and we must not swallow more than we can digest."[1]

Mazzini believed, with Bismarck, that no State could be well governed unless it consisted of a homogeneous nation.   But Bismarck's policy of the artificial assimilation of the weaker by the stronger type seemed to him the vilest form of tyranny; and he based his own plans for the reconstruction of Europe upon the purpose of God, as revealed by the existing correspondence of national uniformities with geographical facts.   "God," he said, "divided humanity into distinct groups or nuclei upon the face of the earth. . . .   Evil governments have disfigured the Divine design.   Nevertheless you may still trace it, distinctly marked out—at least as far as Europe is concerned—by the course of the great rivers,

---

[1] *Bismarck* (J. W. Headlam), p. 269.

the direction of the higher mountains, and other geographical conditions."[1]

Both Mazzini and Bismarck, therefore, opposed with all their strength the humanitarianism of the French Revolution, the philosophy which, as Canning said, "reduced the nation into individuals in order afterwards to congregate them into mobs."[2] Mazzini attacked the "cosmopolitans," who preached that all men should love each other without distinction of nationality, on the ground that they were asking for a psychological impossibility. No man, he argued, can imagine, and therefore no one can love, mankind, if mankind means to him all the millions of individual human beings. Already in 1836 he denounced the original Carbonari for this reason: "The cosmopolitan," he then said, "alone in the midst of the immense circle by which he is surrounded, whose boundaries extend beyond the limits of his vision; possessed of no other weapons than the consciousness of his rights (often misconceived) and his individual faculties—which, however powerful, are incapable of extending their activity over the whole sphere of application constituting the aim . . . has but two paths before him. He is compelled to choose between despotism and inertia."[3] He quotes the Breton fisherman who, as he puts out to sea,

---

[1] *Life and Writings* (Smith, Elder, 1891), vol. iv. (written 1858), p. 275.

[2] Canning, *Life* by Stapleton, p. 341 (speech at Liverpool, 1818).

[3] Mazzini, *Life and Writings* (Smith, Elder, 1891), vol. iii. p. 8.

prays to God, "Help me my God!   My boat is so small
and Thy ocean so wide." [1]

For Mazzini the divinely indicated nation stood therefore between the individual man and the unimaginable
multitude of the human race.   A man could comprehend
and love his nation because it consisted of beings like
himself "speaking the same language, gifted with the
same tendencies and educated by the same historical
tradition," [2] and could be thought of as a single national
entity.   The nation was "the intermediate term between
humanity and the individual," [3] and man could only
attain to the conception of humanity by picturing it to
himself as a mosaic of homogeneous nations.   "Nations
are the citizens of humanity as individuals are the citizens
of the nation," [4] and again, "The pact of humanity cannot be signed by individuals, but only by free and equal
peoples, possessing a name, a banner, and the consciousness of a distinct existence." [5]

Nationalism, as interpreted either by Bismarck or by
Mazzini, played a great and valuable part in the development of the political consciousness of Europe
during the nineteenth century.   But it is becoming less
and less possible to accept it as a solution for the
problems of the twentieth century.   We cannot now

[1] Mazzini, *Life and Writings* (Smith, Elder, 1891), vol. iv. p. 274.
[2] *Ibid* vol. iv. p. 276 (written 1858).
[3] *Ibid*, vol. v. p. 273.
[4] *Ibid.*, vol. v. p. 274 (written 1849).
[5] *Ibid.*, vol. iii. p. 15 (written 1836).

assert with Mazzini that the "indisputable tendency of
our epoch is towards a reconstitution of Europe into a
certain number of homogeneous national States "as
nearly as possible equal in population and extent." [1]
Mazzini, indeed, unconsciously but enormously exagger-
ated the simplicity of the question even in his own time.
National types throughout the greater part of South-east-
ern Europe were not even then divided into homogeneous units by "the course of the great rivers and the direction of the high mountains," but were intermingled
from village to village; and events have since forced us
to admit that fact.   We no longer, for instance, can believe, as Mr. Swinburne and the other English disciples
of Mazzini and of Kossuth seem to have believed in the
eighteen sixties, that Hungary is inhabited only by a
homogeneous population of patriotic Magyars.   We can
see that Mazzini was already straining his principle to
the breaking point when he said in 1852: "It is in the
power of Greece . . . to become, by extending itself to
Constantinople, a powerful barrier against the European
encroachments of Russia." [2]   In Macedonia to-day bands
of Bulgarian and Greek patriots, both educated in the
pure tradition of Mazzinism, are attempting to extermi-
nate the rival populations in order to establish their
own claim to represent the purposes of God as indicated
by the position of the Balkan mountains.   Mazzini him-

---

[1] Mazzini, *Life and Writings* (Smith, Elder, 1891), vol. v. p. 275.
[2] *Ibid.*, vol. vi. p. 258.

self would, perhaps, were he living now, admit that, if the Bismarckian policy of artificial assimilation is to be rejected, there must continue to be some States in Europe which contain inhabitants belonging to widely different national types.

Bismarck's conception of an artificial uniformity created by "blood and iron" corresponded more closely than did Mazzini's to the facts of the nineteenth century. But its practicability depended upon the assumption that the members of the dominant nationality would always vehemently desire to impose their own type on the rest. Now that the Social-Democrats, who are a not inconsiderable proportion of the Prussian population, apparently admire their Polish or Bavarian or Danish fellow-subjects all the more because they cling to their own national characteristics, Prince Bülow's Bismarckian dictum the other day, that the strength of Germany depends on the existence and dominance of an intensely national Prussia, seemed a mere political survival. The same change of feeling has also shown itself in the United Kingdom, and both the English parties have now tacitly or explicitly abandoned the Anglicization of Ireland and Wales, which all parties once accepted as a necessary part of English policy.

A still more important difficulty in applying the principle that the area of the State should be based on homogeneity of national type, whether natural or artificial, has been created by the rapid extension during the last twenty-five years of all the larger European

States into non-European territory. Neither Mazzini, till his death in 1872, nor Bismarck, till the colonial adventure of 1884, was compelled to take into his calculations the inclusion of territories and peoples outside Europe. Neither of them, therefore, made any effective intellectual preparation for those problems which have been raised in our time by "the scramble for the world." Mazzini seems, indeed, to have vaguely expected that nationality would spread from Europe into Asia and Africa, and that the "pact of humanity" would ultimately be "signed" by homogeneous and independent "nations," who would cover the whole land surface of the globe. But he never indicated the political forces by which that result was to be brought about. The Italian invasion of Abyssinia in 1896 might have been represented either as a necessary stage in the Mazzinian policy of spreading the idea of nationality to Africa, or as a direct contradiction of that idea itself.

Bismarck, with his narrower and more practical intellect, never looked forward, as Mazzini did, to a "pact of humanity," which should include even the nations of Europe, and, indeed, always protested against the attempt to conceive of any relation whatosover, moral or political, as existing between any State and the States or populations outside its boundaries. "The only sound principle of action," he said, "for a great State is political egoism." [1]   When, therefore, after Bismarck's death German sailors and soldiers found themselves

[1] Speech, 1850, quoted by J. W. Headlam, *Bismarck*, p. 83.

in contact with the defenseless inhabitants of China or East Africa, they were, as the Social Democrats quickly pointed out, provided with no conception of the situation more highly developed than that which was acted upon in the fifth century A.D., by Attila and his Huns.

The modern English imperialists tried for some time to apply the idea of national homogeneity to the facts of the British Empire. From the publication of Seeley's "Expansion of England" in 1883 till the Peace of Veree-niging in 1902 they strove to believe in the existence of a "Blood," an "Island Race," consisting of homogeneous English-speaking individuals, among whom were to be reckoned not only the whole population of the United Kingdom, but all the reasonably white inhabitants of our colonies and dependencies; while they thought of the other inhabitants of the Empire as "the white man's burden"—the necessary material for the exercise of the white man's virtues. The idealists among them, when they were forced to realize that such a homogeneity of the whites did not yet exist, persuaded themselves that it would come peacefully and inevitably as a result of the reading of imperial poems and the summoning of an imperial council. The Bismarckian realists among them believed that it would be brought about, in South Africa and elsewhere, by "blood and iron." Lord Milner, who is perhaps the most loyal adherent of the Bismarckian tradition to be found out of Germany, contended even at Vereeniging against peace with the Boers on any terms except such an unconditional surrender as would involve the ultimate Anglicization of the South African colonies. He still dreams of a British Empire whose egoism shall be as complete as that of Bismarck's Prussia, and warns us in 1907, in the style of 1887, against those "ideas of our youth" which were "at once too insular and too cosmopolitan."[1]

But in the minds of most of our present imperialists, imperial egoism is now deprived of its only possible psychological basis. It is to be based not upon national homogeneity but upon the consciousness of national variation. The French in Canada are to remain intensely French, and the Dutch in South Africa intensely Dutch; though both are to be divided from the world outside the British Empire by an unbridgeable moral chasm. To imperialism so conceived facts lend no support. The loyal acceptance of British Imperial citizenship by Sir Wilfred Laurier or General Botha constitute something more subtle, something, to adapt Lord Milner's phrase, less insular but more cosmopolitan than imperial egoism. It does not, for instance, involve an absolute indifference to the question whether France or Holland shall be swallowed up by the sea.

At the same time the non-white races within the Empire show no signs of enthusiastic contentment at the prospect of existing, like the English "poor" during the eighteenth century, as the mere material of other men's virtues. They too have their own vague ideas of nationality; and if those ideas do not ultimately break

[1] *Times*, Dec. 19, 1907.

up our Empire, it will be because they are enlarged and held in check, not by the sentiment of imperial egoism, but by those wider religious and ethical conceptions which pay little heed to imperial or national frontiers.

It may, however, be objected by our imperial "Realpolitiker" that cosmopolitan feeling is at this moment both visionary and dangerous, not because, as Mazzini thought, it is psychologically impossible, but because of the plain facts of our military position. Our Empire, they say, will have to fight for its existence against a German or a Russian Empire or both together during the next generation, and our only chance of success is to create that kind of imperial sentiment which has fighting value. If the white inhabitants of the Empire are encouraged to think of themselves as a "dominant race," that is to say as both a homogeneous nation and a natural aristocracy, they will soon be hammered by actual fighting into a Bismarckian temper of imperial "egoism." Among the non-white inhabitants of the Empire (since either side in the next inter-imperial war will, after its first defeat, abandon the convention of only employing European troops against Europeans) we must discover and drill those races who like the Gurkhas and Soudanese, may be expected to fight for us and to hate our enemies without asking for political rights. In any case we, like Bismarck, must extirpate, as the most fatal solvent of empire, that humanitarianism which concerns itself with the interests of our future opponents as well as those of our fellow-subjects.

This sort of argument might of course be met by a
reductio ad absurdum.   If the policy of imperial egoism
is a successful one it will be adopted by all empires alike,
and whether we desire it or not, the victor in each inter-
imperial war will take over the territory of the loser.
After centuries of warfare and the steady retrogression,
in the waste of blood and treasure and loyalty, of modern
civilization, two empires, England and Germany, or
America and China, may remain.   Both will possess an
armament which represents the whole "surplus value,"
beyond mere subsistence, created by its inhabitants.
Both will contain white and yellow and brown and black
men hating each other across a wavering line on the map
of the world.   But the struggle will go on, and, as the
result of a naval Armageddon in the Pacific, only one
Empire will exist.   "Imperial egoism," having worked
itself out to its logical conclusion, will have no further
meaning, and the inhabitants of the globe, diminished
to half their number, will be compelled to consider the
problems of race and of the organized exploitation of the
globe from the point of view of mere humanitarianism.

Is the suggestion completely wanting in practicability
that we might begin that consideration before the struggle
goes any further?   Fifteen hundred years ago, in south-
eastern Europe, men who held the Homoousian opinion
of the Trinity were gathered in arms against the
Homoiousians.   The generals and other "Real-politiker"
on both sides may have feared, like Lord Milner, lest
their followers should become "too cosmopolitan," too

ready to extend their sympathies across the frontiers of theology. "This," a Homoousian may have said , "is a practical matter. Unless our side learn by training themselves in theological egoism to hate the other side, we shall be beaten in the next battle." And yet we can now see that the practical interests of Europe were very little concerned with the question whether "we" or "they" won, but very seriously concerned with the question whether the division itself into "we" or "they" could not be obliterated by the discovery either of a less clumsy metaphysic, or of a way of thinking about humanity which made the continued existence of those who disagreed with one in theology no longer intolerable. May the Germans and ourselves be now marching towards the horrors of a world-war merely because "nation" and "empire" like "Homoousia" and "Homoiousia" are the best that we can do in making entities of the mind to stand between us and an unintelligible universe, and because having made such entities our sympathies are shut up within them?

I have already urged, when considering the conditions of political reasoning, that many of the logical difficulties arising from our tendency to divide the infinite stream of our thoughts and sensations into homogeneous classes and species are now unnecessary and have been avoided in our time by the students of the natural sciences. Just as the modern artist substitutes without mental confusion his ever-varying curves and surfaces for the straight and simple lines of the savage, so the scientific imagination has learnt to deal with the varying facts of nature without thinking of them as separate groups, each composed of identical individuals and represented to us by a single type.

Can we learn so to think of the varying individuals of the whole human race? Can we do, that is to say, what Mazzini declared to be impossible? And if we can, shall we be able to love the fifteen hundred million different human beings of whom we are thus enabled to think?

To the first question the publication of the "Origin of Species" in 1859 offered an answer. Since then we have in fact been able to represent the human race to our imagination, neither as a chaos of arbitrarily varying individuals, nor as a mosaic of homogeneous nations, but as a biological group, every individual in which differs from every other not arbitrarily but according to an intelligible process of organic evolution.[1] And, since that which exists for the imagination can exist also for the emotions, it might have been hoped that the second question would also have been answered by evolution, and that the warring egoisms of nations and empires might henceforth have been dissolved by

[1] Sir Sydney Olivier, e. g. in his courageous and penetrating book *White Capital and Coloured Labour* considers (in chap. ii.) the racial distinctions between black and white from the point of view of evolution. This consideration brings him at once to "the infinite, inexhaustible distinctness of personality between individuals, so much a fundamental fact of life that one almost would say that the amalgamating race-characteristics are merely incrustations concealing his sparkling variety" (pp. 12, 13).

love for that infinitely varying multitude whom we can watch as they work their way through so much pain and confusion towards a more harmonious relation to the universe.

But it was the intellectual tragedy of the nineteenth century that the discovery of organic evolution, instead of stimulating such a general love of humanity, seemed at first to show that it was for ever impossible. Progress, it appeared, had been always due to a ruthless struggle for life, which must still continue unless progress was to cease. Pity and love would turn the edge of the struggle, and therefore would lead inevitably to the degeneration of the species.

This grim conception of an internecine conflict, inevitable and unending, in which all races must play their part, hung for a generation after 1859 over the study of world-politics as the fear of a cooling sun hung over physics, and the fear of a population to be checked only by famine and war hung over the first century of political economy. Before Darwin wrote, it had been possible for philanthropists to think of the non-white races as "men and brothers" who, after a short process of education, would become in all respects except colour identical with themselves. Darwin made it clear that the difficulty could not be so glossed over. Racial variations were shown to be unaffected by education, to have existed for millions of years, and to be tending perhaps towards divergence rather than assimilation.

The practical problem also of race relationship has,

by a coincidence, presented itself since Darwin wrote in a sterner form. During the first half of the nineteenth century the European colonists who were in daily contact with non-European races, although their impulses and their knowledge alike revolted from the optimistic ethnology of Exeter Hall, yet could escape all thought about their own position by assuming that the problem would settle itself. To the natives of Australia or Canada or the Hottentots of South Africa trade automatically brought disease, and disease cleared the land for a stronger population. But the weakest races and individuals have now died out, the surviving populations are showing unexpected powers of resisting the white man's epidemics, and we are adding every year to our knowledge of, and therefore our responsibility for, the causation of infection. We are nearing the time when the extermination of races, if it is done at all, must be done deliberately.

If the extermination is to be both inevitable and deliberate how can there exist a community either of affection or purpose between the killers and the killed? No one at this moment professes, as far as I know, to have an easy and perfect answer to this question. The point of ethics lies within the region claimed by religion. But Christianity, which at present is the religion chiefly concerned, has conspicuously failed even to produce a tolerable working compromise. The official Christian theory is, apparently, that all human souls are of equal value, and that it ought to be a matter of indifference to us whether a given territory is inhabited a thousand years hence by a million converted Central African pigmies or a million equally converted Europeans or Hindus. On the practical point, however, whether the stronger race should base its plans of extension on the extermination of the weaker race, or on an attempt, within the limits of racial possibility, to improve it, Christians have, during the nineteenth century, been infinitely more ruthless than Mohammedans, though their ruthlessness has often been disguised by more or less conscious hypocrisy.

But the most immediately dangerous result of political "Darwinism" was not its effect in justifying the extermination of African aborigines by European colonists, but the fact that the conception of the "struggle for life" could be used as a proof that that conflict among the European nations for the control of the trade-routes of the world which has been threatening for the last quarter of a century is for each of the nations concerned both a scientific necessity and a moral duty. Lord Ampthill, for instance, the athletic ex-governor of Madras, said the other day: "From an individual struggle, a struggle of families, of communities, and nations, the struggle for existence has now advanced to a struggle of empires."[1]

The exhilaration with which Lord Ampthill proclaims that one-half of the species must needs slaughter the other half in the cause of human progress is

[1] *Times*, Jan. 22, 1908.

particularly terrifying when one reflects that he may
have to conduct negotiations as a member of the next
Conservative Government with a German statesman
like Prince Bülow, who seems to combine the teaching
of Bismarck with what he understands to have been
the teaching of Darwin when he defends the Polish
policy of his master by a declaration that the rules
of private morality do not apply to national conduct.

Any such identification of the biological advantage
arising from the "struggle for life" among individuals
with that which is to be expected from a "struggle of
empires" is, of course, thoroughly unscientific. The
"struggle of empires," must either be fought out between
European troops alone, or between Europeans in combination with their non-European allies and subjects.
If it takes the first form, and if we assume, as Lord
Ampthill probably does, that the North European racial
type is "higher" than any other, then the slaughter of
half a million selected Englishmen and half a million
selected Germans will clearly be an act of biological
retrogression. Even if the non-European races are
brought in, and a corresponding number of selected
Turks and Arabs and Tartars, or of Gurkhas and Pathans
and Soudanese are slaughtered, the biological loss to
the world, as measured by the percentage of surviving
"higher" or "lower" individuals will only be slightly
diminished.

Nor is that form of the argument much better
founded which contends that the evolutionary advan-

tage to be expected from the "struggle of empires" is the "survival" not of races but of political and cultural types. Our victory over the German Empire, for instance, would mean, it is said, a victory for the idea of political liberty. This argument, which, when urged by the rulers of India, sounds somewhat temerarious, requires the assumption that types of culture are in the modern world most successfully spread by military occupation. But in the ancient world Greek culture spread most rapidly after the fall of the Greek Empire; Japan in our own time adopted Western culture more readily as an independent nation than she would have done as a dependency of Russia or France; and India is perhaps more likely today to learn from Japan than from England.

Lord Ampthill's phrase, however, represents not so much an argument, as a habit of feeling shared by many who have forgotten or never known the biological doctrine which it echoes. The first followers of Darwin believed that the human species had been raised above its prehuman ancestors because, and in so far as, it had surrendered itself to a blind instinct of conflict. It seemed, therefore, as if the old moral precept that men should control their more violent impulses by reflection had been founded upon a mistake. Unreflecting instinct was, after all, the best guide, and nations who acted instinctively towards their neighbours might justify themselves, like the Parisian ruffians of ten years ago, by claiming to be "strugforlifeurs."

If this habit of mind is to be destroyed it must be opposed, not merely by a new argument, but by a conception of man's relation to the universe which creates emotional force as well as intellectual conviction.

And the change that has already shown itself in our conception of the struggle for life among individuals indicates that, by some divine chance, a corresponding change may come in our conception of the struggle between peoples. The evolutionists of our own time tell us that the improvement of the biological inheritance of any community is to be hoped for, not from the encouragement of individual conflict, but from the stimulation of the higher social impulses under the guidance of the science of eugenics; and the emotional effect of this new conception is already seen in the almost complete disappearance from industrial politics of that unwillingly brutal "individualism" which afflicted kindly Englishmen in the eighteen sixties.

An international science of eugenics might in the same way indicate that the various races should aim, not at exterminating each other, but at encouraging the improvement by each of its own racial type. Such an idea would not appeal to those for whom the whole species arranges itself in definite and obvious grades of "higher" and "lower," from the northern Europeans downwards, and who are as certain of the ultimate necessity of a "white world," as the Sydney politicians are of the necessity of a "white Australia." But in this respect during the last few years the inhabitants of Europe have shown signs of a new humility, due partly to widespread intellectual causes and partly to the hard facts of the Russo-Japanese war and the arming of China. The "spheres of influence," into which we divided the Far East eight years ago, seem to us now a rather stupid joke, and those who read history are already bitterly ashamed that we destroyed, by the sack of the Summer Palace in 1859, the products of a thousand years of such art as we can never hope to emulate. We are coming honestly to believe that the world is richer for the existence both of other civilizations and of other racial types than our own. We have been compelled by the study of the Christian documents to think of our religion as one only among the religions of the world, and to acknowledge that it has owed much and may owe much again to the longer philosophic tradition and the subtler and more patient brains of Hindustan and Persia. Even if we look at the future of the species as a matter of pure biology, we are warned by men of science that it is not safe to depend only on one family or one variety for the whole breeding-stock of the world. For the moment we shrink from the interbreeding of races, but we do so in spite of some conspicuous examples of successful interbreeding in the past, and largely because of our complete ignorance of the conditions on which success depends.

Already, therefore, it is possible without intellectual dishonesty to look forward to a future for the race which need not be reached through a welter of blood and hatred. We can imagine the nations settling the racial allocation of the temperate or tropical breeding-grounds, or even deliberately placing the males and females of the few hopelessly backward tribes on different islands, without the necessity that the most violent passions of mankind should be stimulated in preparation for a general war. No one now expects an immediate, or prophesies with certainty an ultimate, Federation of the Globe; but the consciousness of a common purpose in mankind, or even the acknowledg-ment that such a common purpose is possible, would alter the face of world-politics at once. The discussion at The Hague of a halt in the race of armaments would no longer seem Utopian, and the strenuous profession by the colonizing powers that they have no selfish ends in view might be transformed from a sordid and use-less hypocrisy into a fact to which each nation might adjust its policy. The irrational race-hatred which breaks out from time to time on the fringes of empire would have little effect in world politics when opposed by a consistent conception of the future of human progress.

Meanwhile, it is true, the military preparations for a death-struggle of empires still go on, and the problem even of peaceful immigration becomes yearly more threatening, now that shipping companies can land tens of thousands of Chinese or Indian labourers for a pound or two a head at any port in the world.   But when we think of such things we need no longer feel ourselves in the grip of a Fate that laughs at human purpose and human kindliness. An idea of the whole existence of our species is at last a possible background to our individual experience. Its emotional effect may prove to be not less than that of the visible temples and walls of the Greek cities, although it is formed not from the testimony of our eyesight, but from the knowledge which we acquire in our childhood and confirm by the half-conscious corroboration of our daily life.

We all of us, plain folk and learned alike, now make a picture for ourselves of the globe with its hemispheres of light and shadow, from every point of which the telegraph brings us hourly news, and which may already be more real to us than the fields and houses past which we hurry in the train. We can all see it, hanging and turning in the monstrous emptiness of the skies, and obedient to forces whose action we can watch hundreds of light-years away and feel in the beating of our hearts. The sharp new evidence of the camera brings every year nearer to us its surface of ice and rock and plain, and the wondering eyes of alien peoples.

It may be that we shall long continue to differ as to the full significance of this vision. But now that we can look at it without helpless pain it may stir the deepest impulses of our being. To some of us it may bring confidence in that Love that Dante saw, "which moves the Sun and the other Stars." To each of us it may suggest a kinder pity for all the bewildered beings who hand on from generation to generation the torch of conscious life.

INDEX

309